British Social Policy

Making Contemporary Britain Series

General Editor: *Anthony Seldon*
Consultant Editor: *Peter Hennessy*

Published

Northern Ireland Since 1968[†]
Paul Arthur and Keith Jeffery

The Prime Minister Since 1945[†]
James Barber

British General Elections Since 1945[†]
David Butler

The British Economy Since 1945[†]
Alec Cairncross

Town Planning in Britain Since 1900
Gordon Cherry

The End of the British Empire[†]
John Darwin

Religion in Britain Since 1945[†]
Grace Davie

British Defence Since 1945[†]
Michael Dockrill

British Politics Since 1945[†]
Peter Dorey

Britain and European Integration
Since 1945[†]
Stephen George

British Social Policy: 1945 to the
present (third edition)
Howard Glennerster

Britain Since 1945
Jonathan Hollowell (ed.)

Sport in Britain Since 1945
Richard Holt and Tony Mason

Consensus Politics from Attlee to
Major (second edition)[†]
Dennis Kavanagh and Peter Morris

Electoral Change Since 1945[†]
Pippa Norris

The British Press and Broadcasting
Since 1945[†]
Colin Seymour-Ure

The Labour Party Since 1945[†]
Eric Shaw

The Civil Service Since 1945
Kevin Theakston

Local Government Since 1945
Nirmala Rao and Ken Young

[†] Indicates title available through print-on-demand. To order our print on demand titles: **Individuals:** please order through your favorite local or on-line bookseller. **Retailers, wholesalers, and libraries:** please place your order with Ingram Book Company. **For US customers:** 1-800-937-8000. This number has options to follow; to place an order, press #1. **Canada:** 1-800-289-0687. **All other international callers:** (+) 1-615-793-5000 ext 27501.

The series *Making Contemporary Britain* is essential reading for students, as well as providing masterly overviews for the general reader. Each book in the series puts the central themes and problems of the specific topic into clear focus. The studies are written by leading authorities in their field, who integrate the latest research into the text but at the same time present the material in a clear, ordered fashion which can be read with value by those with no prior knowledge of the subject.

Centre for Contemporary British History at the Institute of Historical Research, University of London, Senate House, Malet Street, London WC1E 7HU Telephone: 020 7862 8740 Fax: 020 7862 8812 E-Mail: icbh@icbh.ac.uk

British Social Policy
1945 to the present
Third Edition

Howard Glennerster

Blackwell
Publishing

BLACKWELL PUBLISHING
350 Main Street, Malden, MA 02148-5020, USA
9600 Garsington Road, Oxford OX4 2DQ, UK
550 Swanston Street, Carlton, Victoria 3053, Australia

First edition published 1995 by Blackwell Publishing Ltd
Second edition published 2000
Third edition published 2007

1   2007

Library of Congress Cataloging-in-Publication Data

Glennerster, Howard.
    British social policy: 1945 to the present / Howard Glennerster. – 3rd ed.
      p.   cm. – (Making contemporary Britain series)
    Includes bibliographical references and index.
    ISBN-13: 978-1-4051-5244-0 (pbk.: alk. paper)
    ISBN-10: 1-4051-5244-3 (pbk.: alk. paper)
      1. Great Britain–Social policy.   2. Great Britain–Social conditions–1945–
    I. Title.   II. Series: Making contemporary Britain.

    HN385.5.G54 2006
    361.6'10941–dc22

                                                            2006016370

A catalogue record for this title is available from the British Library.

Set in 10/12.5pt Galliard
by Graphicraft Limited, Hong Kong
Printed and bound in Singapore
by COS Printers Pte Ltd

The publisher's policy is to use permanent paper from mills that operate a sustainable
forestry policy, and which has been manufactured from pulp processed using acid-free
and elementary chlorine-free practices. Furthermore, the publisher ensures that the text
paper and cover board used have met acceptable environmental accreditation standards.

For further information on
Blackwell Publishing, visit our website:
www.blackwellpublishing.com

Contents

Figures and Tables

Figures

Tables

Acknowledgements

This book, in its various editions, would not have been possible without many people's help. It was originally Anthony Seldon's idea and his gentle pressure and advice helped me complete the first edition despite a heavy teaching and administrative load. My colleagues at the LSE Department of Social Policy and the ESRC Centre for Analysis of Social Exclusion have been generous with their expertise. That generosity of spirit is what has made them such good places in which to work. Martin Evans did much to collect the material for Chapter 2, which draws heavily on LSE Welfare State Discussion Paper WSP/86 which he jointly authored. Sophie Sarre was an enormous help in preparing material especially for Chapter 7. Jose Harris and Jane Lewis, proper historians, have sustained my interest, directed my reading and sharpened my wits over many years. I am grateful to the librarians of the LSE Library i.e. the British Library of Political and Economic Science (BP in the references) and at the Public Record Office (PRO) now the National Archives.

I am very grateful to the Michio and Yoko Morishima Fund for the help they gave me for research assistance for the first edition. Michio died in 2005 but his spirit lives, not least in STICERD, the research centre I was responsible for and still inhabit. I am grateful to Thomson Publishers for permission to reproduce Table 7.1 from page 159 of *The Year Book of Social Policy in Britain 1982*, edited by Catherine Jones and June Stevenson, Routledge and Kegan Paul, 1983. The table is taken from a chapter entitled 'Rolling back the welfare state: the rhetoric and reality of public expenditure and social policy under the Conservative Government' by Michael O'Higgins. I am also grateful to the Controller of Her

Majesty's Stationery Office for permission to reproduce Figure 1.2 from Cm. 6730, 2005 *A New Deal for Welfare: Empowering People to Work*, Department of Work and Pensions.

I had my first lesson in social policy from my father in July 1948. He took me to the last meeting of his sick club. Here was a group of men agreeing to close their organization. It had apparently looked after our family when we were ill and I was puzzled why they seemed to be celebrating the event. My father explained that though it had looked after us, everything would be better now. Something bigger and better was going to take over and we would all be safer. As I worked on the first edition, this memory, hidden for years, came back to me as I wrote. So this book is for him, now long dead. Finally, Ann has not only helped me with the successive drafts but given up summers to get them completed. We met writing a Fabian pamphlet together. We have shared much of the period covered in this book and it is for her too.

1

The British Welfare State: Origins and Myths

Origins

The very term 'Welfare State' has an uncertain paternity.

It was probably not even English! The term *Wohlfahrsstaat* was used by right-wing critics to describe the German social democratic Weimar Republic in the 1920s (Flora and Heidenheimer, 1981). It was a term of abuse. It meant a soft society over-concerned with social benefits, not with Germany's pride in itself and its military power.

Just how the term came to be translated into English and given a positive image is not entirely clear but Hennessy (1992: 121) attributes the original translation to Professor Zimmern of Oxford University, and to an economist Sir George Schuster, whom Hennessy quotes as saying, 'The best way for what I term "welfare" states to undermine the influence of dictators in "power" states is to show that they themselves produce welfare for their people.'

It was this central idea that the Archbishop of Canterbury, Archbishop Temple, picked up and popularized in his book *Citizen and Churchman*, written in 1941. It captures the feeling of the time in which whole state systems were in competition for their very survival, not just through military contest but in winning the allegiance of their peoples. The competing systems, of course, included that of the Soviet Union, not just Hitler's Germany. Russian communism was appealing to many bright young people at university and members of an older generation too, such as Sydney and Beatrice Webb, Fabian socialists and founders of the London School of Economics. The massive unemployment of the thirties caused many to question the principles on which British capitalist society was based.

In the 1930s the central government was forced to take on responsibility for the relief of the long-term unemployed and in the early years of the war the elderly poor too. The task had grown too big for local poor relief committees.

There was nothing new about the state, local and national, being involved in the relief of poverty or in financing and providing education and health care. The Tudor state had taken a close interest in containing and regulating the treatment of the poor. So had the early Victorian Parliament when it passed the Poor Law Amendment Act 1834. Mid-Victorian thinkers, dreamed of mitigating the harsh consequences of early capitalism. It was Ruskin who coined the term 'social welfare'. He hoped for a return to a pre-industrial 'citizen's economy'. 'Market relations would be totally replaced by an ethic of public service' in such a world (Harris, 1990: 10). The late-Victorian period and early years of the twentieth century saw the first major steps towards a modern welfare state. The limited and localist basis of state activity in Victorian Britain had been gradually transformed into a growing central state by the outbreak of the Second World War and was to be given a great boost by its end. Thus 1945 marks merely a staging post, not a new departure in social policy (Harris, 1992).

Michael Young, the great institutional inventor of the post-war period and author of the 1945 Labour Party Election Manifesto, was not so sure about the title 'Welfare State'. Catching future reservations he wrote in 1951:

> The very name [. . .] is against it. It must have been invented by a diabolical copywriter who knew that if the nation was not poisoned by the first word [welfare], recalling the smell of carbolic acid and the tough brown paper of ration books, it could be done to death by the second cold word [state] suggesting the Law Court, the

Sanitary Inspector and the Recruiting Officer. (Quoted in Thane, 2005: 293)

A coherent legacy

Nevertheless, the social legislation passed in the five years 1944 to 1948 does constitute one of the most coherent and long-lasting institutional legacies in modern British history. It was passed in such a short period that it sharply reflects its time. It embodies a distinctive set of political values and assumptions about the role of the state that were well understood by contemporaries, as were the compromises made between the powerful interest groups of the day. These welfare institutions had common design features, just as do the different architectural styles of Bath, Hampstead Garden Suburb, or the sixties in Britain. This was not the case in many other countries. The Second World War had more unsettling consequences in occupied Europe and in Germany itself. New welfare institutions were slower to emerge in France and Germany, for example (Ashford, 1986).

The 1944 to 1948 social reforms had eloquent advocates, like Sir William Beveridge, whose ideal blueprint was never fully implemented, but sustained the imagination of later generations. His report was also influential abroad (Hills et al., 1994).

They also had academic interpreters, the Whig historians of their age, such as Tom Marshall, Professor of Social Institutions at the London School of Economics. His writings on social policy and citizenship were to be influential all over the world (Baldwin, 1994). Richard Titmuss, also at the LSE, the official historian of social policy during the Second World War (Titmuss, 1950) reached guru status. They stamped these institutions with a moral authority and a historical legitimacy. Any attempt to reform them or attack them has produced a kind of moral outrage akin to that provoked by attacks on the monarchy.

Although many adaptations *were* made to this design in the next forty years, it was not really until the late 1980s that a similar concentration of social legislation was to occur that had a similar coherence. This time it derived from a very different kind of politics, that of Mrs Thatcher.

The Blair government adapted and extended some of those institutional changes and made its own. But it pushed social policy back to the centre of domestic politics where it looks set to remain. We discuss this further in the final chapter. What is remarkable is that the fundamentals of social policy established in the post-war period have remained.

A desire for change

The inspiration for the 1940s legislation was generated in a period of remarkable social change and danger. Common risks were widely experienced. Bombs were no respecters of class or property. Class attitudes and conflicts remained, as did fierce political disagreement during the war (Morgan, 1990). But there was an unusual readiness to contemplate fundamental institutional change. Proposals that had been bogged down in interest group squabbles for much of the previous two decades suddenly became feasible politics (Gosden, 1976; Harris, 1977).

A successful state

The emphasis on the role of the central government in these social institutions reflects the context of the time. The central state apparatus, whatever its largely obscured inefficiencies (Barnett, 1986; 1995), was *seen* as having won the war with the support of the people. Above all it had done so while securing a basic food supply, clothing, emergency medical care and jobs for the whole population in a period of extreme shortages and danger. It might have made mistakes and been crucially supported by the United States, but, in comparison with the other war machines against whom it was pitted, it had done rather well. It had, after all, emerged victorious. A popular recurrent theme of the time was 'We have won the war, now we can win the peace.'

If the agency of victory had been the state, the means had been central planning and resource allocation. Competition, even between local milkmen, had been abolished. Furniture and clothes were designed to 'utility' standards, the best designers set to produce designs that used the minimum raw material. 'Rational' planning and central state power probably reached their pinnacle in these years and with popular support.

These assumptions about the virtues of centralized state power were necessarily to colour the social policy institutions that emerged at such an unusual time. There were critics of this view, of course, notably another professor at the London School of Economics and a refugee from Hitler's totalitarian state, Professor Hayek (1944). In a brilliant attack, *The Road to Serfdom*, he forecast disaster if Britain set off down the road to planning and social provision in peacetime. He was read by a youthful Margaret – later Thatcher – at Somerville College, Oxford (Thatcher, 1993).

The world of 1945 was very different from that of the early twenty-first century. The memories of the 1930s as well as the experience of total war were strong in people's memories. The mass of the paid working population was employed in factories and manual work, mining and construction. Work in factories included women, who had been drawn into work on a much larger scale. Vast unions threw up powerful leaders. Britain was a world power. In many ways the Britain of 1945 looked like a fully employed 1930s. But it had changed. The war had changed attitudes and its economy was weak, burdened by a massive debt, which had been raised to pay for the war. Its economy had been in relative decline for decades. America had taken over world leadership. People were impatient of old ways and ready for a change.

The Basic Principles of the 1940s Welfare State

The social policies of those extraordinary years contained six central principles.

Full employment   The guarantee of a job for all those genuinely seeking work. The idea that the national budget should be used for macroeconomic purposes and not merely to balance the budget had been accepted by the Chancellor of the Exchequer for the first time in his Budget of 1941, but in 1944 the Coalition government formally accepted that post-war governments too should seek to achieve the goal of 'a high and stable level of employment'. The document itself is a dry and technical one. Nevertheless, it embodied the great shift in economic thinking that found its clearest expression in John Maynard Keynes's book, *The General Theory of Employment, Interest and Money*, published in 1936. This was arguably the most important of all the planks in post-war social policy. Sir William Beveridge had included full employment as one of the fundamental assumptions that underlay his social insurance scheme. The fact that full employment was largely achieved over the next thirty years probably did more than any other element in the 'post-war contract' to change the lives of ordinary people. But, in a caveat that was to have growing significance, the White Paper noted that if prices could not be held reasonably stable, the policy would fail (Cmd 6527, 1944, para. 49). So it was to be. For an account of disagreements within the Treasury in producing this white paper see Lowe (1999).

A national minimum   The second central element in post-war social policy was the provision of a common safety net that central government would place under all members of society, to protect them when afflicted by one of life's accidents: the loss of earnings through sickness or long-term disability, unemployment or old age, through losing income with the death of one's spouse or other exceptional reasons. There had always been ways in which individuals in extreme poverty could seek help, not only from charities but from public agencies. The old Poor Law had been such an agency. But it was local and varied in its generosity as well as being deliberately demeaning. What the provisions of the 1945 to 1948 legislation aimed to do was to remove the stigma from this experience. Linked to this goal was the intention to give reality to an idea originally advanced in the 1890s by the Webbs, the idea of a national minimum (Webbs, 1897). They saw it as the logical culmination of trade unionists' attempts to fight for a living wage. Individual trade unions would never be able to do this, they argued. The state must take on the responsibility to set a national minimum wage, hours of leisure and a standard of living for those not able to work. The labour colonies they advocated to achieve this last goal fortunately did not find support, but the idea that the state had some overall responsibility to put a floor under the living standards of its population did. As we shall see in the next chapter this was not to be achieved in the way advocated by the main architect of the changes, Sir William Beveridge, but implemented it was, largely through the agency of the National Assistance Board. The idea of setting a national minimum was not particularly revolutionary nor egalitarian. Indeed, as we shall see, Beveridge was at pains to emphasize that fact in his famous report, but it did mark Britain out from many European welfare states, which introduced quite generous pension and sickness schemes for workers but did not put in place a clear national responsibility for sustaining a basic minimum for families and non-insured workers.

Equal and free access to health and education   The third plank in these post-war reforms was the removal of the price barrier in access to two services deemed to be a basic right of citizenship: health and education. Prior to this period elementary education had been free in state schools but not secondary schooling. Access to the doctor was free to workers on lower pay but not necessarily to their families or to many other workers or the middle class. Hospitals charged for their services, though these might be remitted on a means test. Free access to health care for everyone was introduced in 1948, a principle that, interestingly, Mrs Thatcher's own reforming White Paper forty years later was to declare inviolate. Her personal foreword to the document stated, 'The National Health Service will continue to be available to all, regardless of income, and to be financed largely out of taxation' (Cm. 555, 1989). Aneurin Bevan would have recognized the language, if not the reality.

A crucial role for the centre　To make these goals a reality the central state took on clear responsibilities for the key areas of social policy: social security, health, education, and housing to a lesser extent. Local authorities in these respects became agents of a central government while retaining initiative and independence over detail.

State provision　Not only was central government given a large role in financing social services but the services themselves were to be placed in the hands of state agencies who delivered services to the voters who elected them. This was a striking change from the pre-war structure and differed sharply from the systems that were emerging in continental Europe. The 1911 national insurance legislation had built on the approved societies: trade union and occupational groups, which already existed as self-help organizations and were regulated by state rules and contributions but were self-governing. These were replaced by the central single National Insurance scheme, as we shall see in the next chapter. Much the same story held for the hospitals, very many of which were run, before the war, by voluntary self-governing trusts. These were nationalized in 1948. It is this which marks the United Kingdom out from the central European tradition in social policy. This did not happen in France, for example, where the old *mutuels* (like our approved societies), and private and voluntary hospitals, continued to exist as they had before the war. Local authorities working to strict government design standards and subsidized by central government became the main providers of new rented housing. Again this was not the pattern followed on the continent of Europe, where housing associations and other social housing agencies shared the task. Voluntary agencies, despite the intentions of Beveridge and the warnings of Archbishop Temple, were driven to the margins of social policy, tarnished with a Victorian authoritarianism and a lady bountiful image that took decades to wear off.

Continuity　Despite the clear common principles and design features of the new institutions, they were all built very firmly on previous foundations – by no means always for the good. The new secondary modern schools looked remarkably like the old senior elementary schools. The local authority old people's 'homes' *were* the old Poor Law buildings. The Health

Service retained the clear separation between GPs and hospitals and the local authority health services of pre-war years.

These new services were all initiated on the 5 July 1948, 'vesting day', just three years to the day from the election of the Labour government. This was itself a deliberately symbolic statement.

The Myths

Like any major social institution the Welfare State has produced mythologies: hostile, legitimating and just plain odd.

The classic Welfare State

The term 'classic welfare state' (Digby, 1989; Lowe, 1999) reflects a view that the welfare state had somehow reached its ideal form in 1948. Like some Greek temple it had logical, intellectually satisfying proportions. It embodied a classic compromise between the duty to work and to contribute to the community. This is reflected in the link between contributions and benefits embodied in the National Insurance scheme. It balanced the personal duty to contribute in work with the duty of the state to provide the reasonable chance of a job. Certain basic requirements of life, like health and education, were to be free and equally available in all parts of the country, hence the strong central planning powers exercised by the central government over school and hospital building and over the spread of skilled people in different parts of the country; teachers and doctors were the main examples.

Rights and obligations, central and local power, state minimum support and market production were all in balance. The whole was in harmony like the Parthenon itself. The passion and the belief that a new world was being built comes through in the second reading speeches of the ministers who introduced these bills to Parliament and justified them to Labour Party Conferences. James Griffiths and Aneurin Bevan were men capable of bringing vast crowds to their feet and making grown men cry. The National Assistance Act of 1948 begins with the phrase 'The existing Poor Law shall cease to have effect.' A 350-year-old law was destroyed at a stroke of the legislator's pen. Alas, it was not to be so simple.

Historians such as Morgan (1990) represent the 1944–8 structures as near perfect. But no social institution stands still and none is perfect even at the time of its creation. As we shall see, equality of access was not achieved merely by abolishing the price barrier and making services free at the point of use. Poverty persisted. Benefits never reached a definition of adequacy. Critiques of the structure and its results began to be voiced by those on the left and by social scientists of the post-war generation, as well as by Conservatives who had never been happy with the changes made. The aspect of the Welfare State that was most in tune with its time, the centrally planned, national monopoly element, was least perfect and has aged the most.

Economists in the 1930s on the left were fascinated by central planning that they thought was working so well in Soviet Russia. Even the young revisionist economists of the New Fabian Research Bureau in the 1930s produced outline programmes that gave a lot of weight to central planning. Yet not all those young economists agreed that this entailed centralized and nationalized industries. One in particular, Evan Durbin, and his friend Hugh Gaitskell, were convinced that this would be disastrous. Public monopoly organizations not open to competition would fall into the hands of the workers in those industries who would exploit the consumers. What was necessary, Durbin argued, was central strategic planning with smaller competing public enterprises (Durbin, 1949; 1985). He drew on psychology 'to explore what he considered to be the central problem of the public sector – personal incentive' (Brooke, 1996: 44). It was precisely this problem that was taken up and developed by Julian Le Grand (2003) and informed much of Blair's thinking sixty years later. Durbin was to die tragically in a bathing accident in 1948. He was not explicitly concerned with the social services but it could be argued that his diagnosis fitted exactly what was to happen to the National Health Service.

A consensus?

It is often argued that the period from 1945 to 1979, when Mrs Thatcher was elected, represented some era of consensus about the Welfare State. It was universally supported by both political parties. The Labour Party may have invented the Welfare State, but the Conservatives came to terms with it and extended it. Only in the age of the Iron Lady did things change.

This consensus view of the early post-war period is now under considerable attack (Harris, 1986; Pimlott, 1989). Others have suggested that if there was a consensus it only lasted for a short period. Lowe (1990) has urged that we do not abandon the idea that there was something special about the war and the post-war years. They were different from the 1930s in temper and degree of agreement and public support for social policy. At the same time there was never an absence of conflict or party battles or interest-group resistance to change. This will become evident in later chapters.

The social policy legislation of the 1940s was introduced amidst much controversy. The Conservative Party did not come to terms with it, at least in the form that it took. That party was from the outset opposed to a universalistic system of services supported out of taxation. It developed a very coherent alternative right at the beginning, in 1947–50. In many ways what Mrs Thatcher did was to implement that agenda when the economic and social structure made it opportune.

A betrayal of the working class

This myth was really a reaction to the first. The advocates of the Welfare State were claiming too much. Those on the left of politics increasingly made the case that the changes had been only superficial. The evils of a capitalist economy remained and with them the inequalities of income and power that were a necessary part of such an economy.

The most thoroughgoing expression of this view (Miliband, 1961) was that the pursuit of change and amelioration through social policy had diverted the Labour movement from its true mission: the revolutionary overthrow of the entire system. The leaders of the Labour movement had sold out, been absorbed by the trappings of power which had gained the working class nothing. No welfare state could achieve fundamental improvements in the lot of ordinary people because the state was a capitalist state:

> the state in these class societies is primarily and inevitably the guardian and protector of the economic interests which are dominant in them. Its 'real' purpose and mission is to ensure their continued predominance, not to prevent it. (Miliband, 1969: 265–6)

Other Marxists were later to challenge this view of the state as a monolithic entity and view the Welfare State more favourably (Gough, 1979) but, in the sixties and seventies, this counter to the orthodoxy of the forties was very influential amongst socially concerned young people and academics. The left began to do an effective demolition job on the Welfare State long before Mrs Thatcher began.

Yet it, too, was exaggerating and hitting at the wrong targets. It was not just Labour parliamentarians who supported the reforms of the post-war period. It is very clear from the evidence given to the Beveridge Committee by all sections of the Labour movement, trade unions, socialist societies and the women's movement that there was a wide degree of consensus about what they wanted after the war. Differences in detail there were, certainly, but on the importance of social legislation and its broad form there was really little popular dissent. The same can be seen from analysing the evidence from Mass Observation and the comments of working people to G. D. H. Cole's survey conducted for the Beveridge Committee. Unless one takes the view that the British working class were merely stupid or duped by the system, it is difficult to sustain the argument that the post-war welfare institutions did not have the widespread and very positive support of the working people of the 1940s.

The second part of the myth is also difficult to sustain: the Welfare State made no difference. It is a claim the working people of the period would have found incomprehensible. As we shall see in later chapters, slowly and gradually over the period from 1940 to 1975 there was a significant and continuous equalization in post-tax incomes and access to basic services, as well as improvements in life expectancy, health and educational attainments. In the 1980s these egalitarian trends were to be reversed again, especially in incomes and benefits. Yet this only went to show the importance of the institutions of the 1940s. It was only when they were removed or reduced in effectiveness that people began to realize just how important they had been.

Social policy had played a part in achieving these egalitarian changes but the main driving force was economic. It was the faltering of the economy in the 1970s and the changing nature of the economy in the 1980s that was to make society increasingly resemble the divisions of the 1930s. The critique of the left was unfair to the classic Welfare State but it was not entirely wrong either. What is clear is that without the institutions put in place in the 1940s the necessary economic adjustments of the 1980s would have been excruciating for large parts of the population, bad as life was in many cases.

A post-war settlement?

A more favourable interpretation of the events after the Second World War, often advanced by left-leaning historians of the period, is to see the 1944–8 legislation as a kind of temporary tacit agreement between the classes: a post-war settlement. Labour had become so powerful and had so well played its part in winning the war, that it was able to wrest concessions from Capital. In a classic compromise the ruling class was prepared to give the Labour movement significant social rights, to be embodied in the post-war Welfare State, while in return the Labour movement put off pressing for revolutionary change.

The problem with this interpretation is that it presupposes that the working class gained most from this legislation. However, the main immediate gainers from the 1944–8 legislation were the middle classes. The point was made by Brian Abel-Smith in a collection of essays by young radicals in 1958:

> Before the war, there were fairly well-developed social services, and from most of them the working classes were the main beneficiaries. With some exceptions, people with incomes under £5 per week were in the State social security system. In unemployment a single man got 20s a week, in sickness 18s a week and in old age 10s a week. Now all employed persons rich and poor can get 50s. Prices have multiplied by about two and three quarters, the earnings of the average worker have multiplied by about four. So the single working man in sickness and unemployment had a better deal pre-war than he does today. The working classes could also get free education and health services before the war. The contributor to National Health Insurance had the services of a panel doctor and anyone who was poor could go to a voluntary or local authority hospital without any payment. Secondary education was available subject to a means test . . . Middle class people who bought their own social services often paid more than the cost (to subsidise the cost of free care to the poor). The main effect of the post-war development of the social services, the 'creation of the welfare state' has been to provide free social services to the middle classes. They are now entitled to use the free health services, to send their children to grammar schools without charge, to get the same state pension as everyone else . . . Thus the major beneficiaries of the post-war changes in the social services have been the middle classes. (Abel-Smith, 1958)

This argumentative, and broadly correct, view does play down the extent to which the Labour movement objected to the stigmatic kind of provision made by the pre-war system and the extent to which working-class women gained from the National Health Service, for example. The benefit the middle class gained from the Service was to be its greatest political asset in years to come.

There is a perfectly simple interpretation of the events of the 1940s and indeed subsequent decades. It is that the institutions of the Welfare State were genuinely popular with the mass of the electorate of all classes for most of our period and it was this which both brought it into being and sustained it.

The bankrupting New Jerusalem

The Thatcher decade of the 1980s produced its own attempt to reinterpret history in tune with the dominant ideology of the day. All new political elites need to expunge the old myths and create their own. The Thatcher period was no exception. It returned to the view that had been expressed by the Conservative Party in the 1940s. The most lucid exponent was Corelli Barnett (1986; 1995). He lays the blame for Britain's relative economic decline at the door of the Welfare State. It was an attempt, as he sees it, to build a Utopia which Britain did not have the resources to achieve. This disastrous attempt was the combined work of naïve church-men, closet socialists in high places, philanthropists and believers in a new post-war order. They were able to persuade a gullible people, and the troops who were brainwashed through political education that was in the hands of socialists, while the nation's true leaders were engaged in winning the war. The central villain in this respect was Sir William Beveridge.

> It was the Beveridge Report that provided the battlefield on which the decisive struggle to win a national commitment to New Jerusalem was waged and won. (Barnett, 1986: 26)

It was the 'cunning Beveridge' who 'manoeuvred' the Cabinet into accepting the report and, as a skilful and single-minded publicist, he drove his report through and campaigned for it. He was assisted by socialists in high places who used his report to conduct propaganda with the armed forces who then went on to vote Labour in 1945.

> So it came to pass that a romantic vision a century and a half in the making had at last found incarnation in the committed programme of a British government with a crushing majority in Parliament. Yet the cost of realising this programme was to fall not on the richest country in the world, not on that Victorian and Edwardian Britain

in which that vision first had gleamed and which had made the New Jerusalemers what they were, but a country with a ruined export trade, heavily in debt to its bankers (the Sterling Area Commonwealth and the United States), and with huge and inescapable continuing burdens with regard to the war with Japan. Yet the wartime promoters of New Jerusalem had pursued their vision in the face of economic realities perfectly well known to them – on the best romantic principle that sense must bend to feeling, and facts to faith. (1986: 37)

This argument is expanded in his later book (1995). There are numerous problems with this account. Like its Marxist counterpart, it turns, in part, on the stupid gullibility of the British people, who were taken in by the New Jerusalemers. It also gives the impression that Beveridge was able to ride roughshod over His Majesty's Treasury. As we shall see, this was far from being the case. It sees the social planners as the originators of the demands for a better life after the war. The evidence from the documents of the time suggests that the government and the Treasury were very aware that there was a strong head of steam growing behind calls to improve existing benefits (Evans and Glennerster, 1993). One interpretation of the setting up of the Beveridge Committee is that it was created to head off such demands. If the people could be offered jam tomorrow in a New Jerusalem they might accept less today. Political pressures stopped the Treasury getting away with this. They insisted on higher pensions now, not in forty years' time. The problem, from the Treasury's point of view, was that all the people now had the vote, not that they were manipulated by William Beveridge.

The second problem with this kind of interpretation of history is that it assumes that the demands placed on the British economy were excessive and greater than those placed on the economies of Britain's industrial competitors (Harris, 1990). Although Britain's competitors in Europe were to outpace it economically, it was not because the Welfare State was taking more resources than theirs; it took fewer, and grew more slowly. The Health Service was the main early butt of criticism for its extravagance. Yet the total resources devoted to the new National Health Service in the 1950s fell and were modest compared to what had been the case in the 1930s (Guillebaud Committee, 1956). If the argument was that economic resources taken for health care were not available for investment in industry then the NHS did its bit by *reducing* the share of capital spending taken by health. Whether that was good for the NHS is another matter.

The centralization of financial responsibility for services led to the Treasury having more, not less, say in controlling social spending. The very diversity of the welfare systems that grew up on the continent of Europe after the Second World War have made it very difficult for them to contain their welfare spending as the British government successfully did in the 1980s.

In the companion volume to this one, *The British Economy since 1945*, Alec Cairncross says,

> The 'New Jerusalem' thesis is badly out of focus. In the context of the early post-war years the increase in the expenditure on the social services, though substantial, was not the main burden on the Exchequer. Expenditure on the social services, including education, health, housing, pensions, and unemployment benefit amounted in pre-war years to about £400–£500 million, or about £1,000 million in terms of post-war prices, and had risen to about £1,500 million by 1950. Expenditure on defence, which did not exceed £200 million until 1938 was never less than about £750 million after 1945, and rose again to over £1,400 million in 1952–3. The food subsidies cost more than any of the social services, reaching nearly £500 million in 1949. Neither of these is mentioned in Correlli Barnett's attack on the 'illusions' of the post-war years . . . If instead of the early post-war years the argument relates to the whole period since the war, then it is difficult to see why so much weight should be attached to expenditure on social welfare as a factor in industrial decline when such expenditure is known to fall short of the level in most other industrial countries. (1992: 5–6)

Where Barnett is on stronger ground is in saying that the Beveridge Report did not really add up either intellectually or financially, a subject we discuss in Chapter 2. The reality is that the reforms of the 1940s 'brought into being an austere, minimalist structure of welfare provision' (Tomlinson, 1998: 63).

The wider argument that welfare states everywhere in the world, and especially in Europe, have slowed their countries' economic growth rates has been advanced more recently by some economists, notably in the United States, and has a long history too. In a fascinating rebuttal Lindert (2004) traces the origins and consequences of public-spending growth on social programmes internationally back to the eighteenth century. Widening popular franchises, income growth and ageing are closely related to the growth and there is no evidence that higher spending has damaged particular economies. However, that conclusion depends on societies being prepared to reform their systems of welfare delivery and funding to prevent perverse economic effects. We shall explore later whether Britain has been able to do that.

Citizenship rights established

One of the most popular academic interpretations of the origins of the post-war social policy settlement was that advanced by Professor Marshall in the 1950s (Marshall, 1950; 1963). The marks of being a British citizen were the legal rights embodied in the Magna Carta, the Toleration Acts and others, won during the Middle Ages and up to the early nineteenth century. They guaranteed the negative freedoms, as philosophers call them, freedom from arbitrary state power to arrest and keep in gaol without trial, the right to free speech and worship. It was these freedoms that had been prized by the American and French revolutionaries. To these freedoms and rights had been added the right to vote, which had been won in stages during the nineteenth and early twentieth centuries. Women's right to vote had only recently been won in full. All citizens of the United Kingdom shared these rights and with them the corresponding duties to abide by the law and to exercise the vote and serve the community. These were political rights and responsibilities. Marshall argued that to these civil and political rights had been added social rights. The state undertook to maintain full employment and secure a basic standard of living in the way we have described above but in return for contributions to the society through work. This added positive freedoms to the negative civic and political freedoms that citizens had in the past. The freedom of speech was not of much value to a starving person. The guarantee of a minimum standard of life and a job rounded off the march to a fully free society. Marshall claimed that Britain, and indeed Western Europe more generally, had evolved an answer to Marxism: equality of citizenship before the law. This meant that the slide into communism that was happening all over Europe in the 1940s was not inevitable. Here was an interpretation of history designed to challenge Marxism on its own ground of historical inevitability.

Laudable as his motive might have been it was not particularly good history. Nor was it a good description of what the legislation of the 1940s actually achieved. It was true that all citizens, as of right of being a citizen, or indeed a resident in the country, could receive free health care. In that sense the National Health Service came closest to Marshall's ideal type. It was much less clear for National Insurance. People were not to receive benefits as a result of being a citizen. Such a proposal had been advanced during the Second World War by Lady Rees Williams but no one had paid it much serious attention, least of all Beveridge. Pensioners, the unemployed and the sick could only receive insurance benefits if they had contributed to the National Insurance scheme for a minimum period. They must have been full-time workers. If they were married women they did not receive a benefit as a right but only on the basis of their husbands' contributions. We discuss this more in the next chapter, but whatever the rights to benefit, they cannot be said to have attached to being a citizen alone.

José Harris (1994) has argued that the appeal to citizenship as an ideal at this time had other and more complex roots than those described by Marshall. The debates of the 1940s, she points out, laid much stress on the rights to benefit that the new insurance system gave in contrast with the means-tested benefits of the Poor Law. However, the Webbs' view of 'universality' had been of *locally* financed services, imposed on the poor.

It was the Poor Law that had for many centuries given members of the local community, as citizens, relief in times of distress. The Poor Law Commissioners and central government had indeed tried to limit those citizens' rights in the nineteenth and early twentieth centuries, not always successfully. Yet those rights to relief were grounded in citizenship, not contributions paid by male breadwinners for a defined period to a central state. The real hope of ordinary people in the 1940s was that the new system would avoid the intrusive means testing of the 1930s.

People feared the intrusiveness of the tax-financed systems of relief they had experienced in the 1930s, whether based on theoretical citizenship rights to relief or not. Harris concludes,

> Contributory insurance became the financial keystone of the post-war welfare state, not because as Beveridge claimed, interruption of earnings was the major cause of poverty, but because insurance fitted in with current evaluations of fiscal reality and with current evaluations of virtue, gender, citizenship, personal freedom and the nature of the state. It was a package that was to prove extraordinarily tenacious. (Harris, 1994: 19)

The state rolled back

Perhaps the most recent myth is that, after forty years of growing state intrusion into social affairs, Mrs Thatcher was able to reverse the tide and push back the boundaries of state power. This, too, is myth, though it suits both left and right in British politics to foster it.

Mrs Thatcher and later Conservative governments did not succeed in reducing the share of national income going to finance the Welfare State (Glennerster and Hills, 1998). Central state power grew very substantially in the 1980s. Power passed from local government to central government and from accountable central departments to hived-off appointed agencies of various kinds. The central state was deemed to be the proper agency to foster particular ways of living together and a return to 'traditional' family values. In contrast, the 1960s can be seen as a period when the role of the state in these respects was challenged. Its intrusion into partners' capacity to break a marriage contract was relaxed. Its right to make sexual acts between consenting adults a criminal offence was challenged. Its right to prevent a woman from terminating an unwanted pregnancy was decreased. In many ways it was the 1960s that rolled back the state's power to intervene in personal lives. It produced what, in retrospect, we can see as the real period of freedom, the first true revival of individualism. But it was short-lived and limited.

A Re-evaluation

In what follows I seek to tell a story not driven by any of these myths. Yet it will be, inevitably, an account of its time like any other. Its author has lived through all of the period. I failed the eleven-plus examination like four-fifths of my contemporaries. I worked in the Labour Party Research Department in the early 1960s on the programme that was implemented by the Wilson government of 1964 to 1970. I have been involved in various formal and informal advisory roles during the period of the Blair government. Inevitably any such account reflects the values of the author and the prejudices of the age. It is as balanced as I am capable of within those limits. Throughout I have suggested references that will give rather different readings of events. They are embodied in the text where the reader can note them in relation to the precise event or argument.

The United Kingdom is what the constitutional experts call a unitary state. The Westminster Parliament was the supreme law-making body when this period begins though it has ceded some of that authority to the European Union. Most social policy has applied in general terms through-out the United Kingdom until the devolution of powers to Scotland and Wales in 1999. However, social policy has always been, to some extent, differently administered in Scotland and Northern Ireland. This book does not attempt to discuss the situation in Northern Ireland but it does indicate where Scotland has gone a different route. Some of the key Acts have Scottish verisions. The Scottish Office was created in the nineteenth century based in Edinburgh. It was the Department of State responsible for education, health, social services and housing in Scotland even before devolution. The Welsh Office, created in the mid-1960s, was a much less significant outpost. Devolution opened up the possibility that each country would evolve rather different social policies in the twenty-first century. There are signs this is already happening, as we shall see in the last chapter.

Questions to Answer

1 How far would you say the basic principles on which the post-war welfare state was founded are still accepted by the general public?
2 Assess the lasting impact of possible myths advanced about social policy today and discuss how far you think those discussed in this chapter really are myths.
3 What basic human rights should citizens of any country enjoy?

2

Beveridge: Founding Father?

Beveridge: the Man
The Ambition: a New Britain
The Report: Radical, but did it add up?
The Report's Main Proposals
The Rejection of Beveridge?
Family Allowances
An Unsound Foundation

All over the world Beveridge's name is associated with British social policy. Television programmes on the latest new government statement or challenge to the Welfare State usually begin with a clip from one of the wartime newsreels showing Beveridge addressing the nation in his rather prissy 1940s style. He is often credited with founding the National Health Service, which he definitely did not do. He is more plausibly credited with founding the post-war system of social security, the subject of his great report (Cmd 6404, 1942). Yet in many ways that is also a mistake. The report undoubtedly had an enormous impact at the time. It sold in its hundreds of thousands and summaries of it were parachuted into occupied Europe and distributed to British troops. After the war the Labour government promised it would implement the report, reversing the Labour Party's pre-war hostility to insurance, rather than tax-based schemes. At the 1950 general election the party claimed that its major achievement had been to implement the report.

Yet the report, on closer study, is far less coherent than its superficial unity and grand claims suggest. Nor were some of its fundamental precepts ever implemented. Those that were, notably the flat rate or poll-tax-like system of contributions, were to damn social insurance in the long term. Unlike other European and the United States social insurance schemes, its flat rate and minimalist character meant that social insurance in Britain never won the support of the vital middle class. They never identified with it or saw it as crucial to their security in old age. If they wanted a decent pension they soon learnt they had better join their own private occupational pension scheme. That was not to be true in Europe or in the United States. Thus the failure of this crucial part of the Welfare State can be traced back to Beveridge.

Who was this man who has cast such a shadow over British social policy? Why was he so influential? What did his report say? What actually happened after it was published?

Beveridge: the Man

Beveridge was born in India, the son of one of the many Anglo-Indian civil servants who went to India with high ideals. His father became a district sessions judge in Bengal. His mother was a much more lively and ambitious person, who gave William his drive and self-confidence. The most authoritative and beautifully written account of his life and work is that by Harris (1977; 1997). His social conscience and interest in social issues were aroused at Oxford and, again like many similar young men of his generation, he went to Toynbee Hall in the East End of London. Founded in 1884, to enable young men with social concerns to find out about poverty at first hand, Toynbee Hall also gave them the opportunity do something about it in practical ways. Beveridge was no social worker, however. He wrote furiously on social issues from then on and became what we would today call a policy analyst!

He was given a fellowship at University College Oxford in 1903 and wrote for the *Morning Post* on social issues. This journalistic experience was to stand him in good stead when he came to write his report and campaign for it.

This early encounter with the poverty of the East End sparked his life-long interest in both solving the unemployment problem and giving some form of income support to workers who were unable to earn an income either through lack of a job or old age. For Beveridge, 'One of the major objectives of social policy should be to ensure that everyone shared both an adequate amount of leisure and a necessary minimum of work' (Harris, 1977: 98).

Beveridge's first major contribution to social policy, indeed, was his advocacy of labour exchanges. He had written an article on the subject for the *Economic Journal* in 1907, which gained a lot of notice, and he was asked to give evidence to the Poor Law Commission, which was considering the whole issue of poverty and its causes. It was to be influential evidence. He believed that unemployment was the result of poor information about the availability of jobs. Workers must be put in touch with the right jobs. Labour exchanges would do this. He had seen them at work in Germany and became something of an expert on the subject. He called them, at this stage, 'the final solution' to the unemployment problem.

This did not prove to be the case, of course, and over the inter-war period Beveridge struggled to understand why. He collected mountains of statistics on regional and local unemployment, believing they would reveal the answer. When Keynes's *General Theory* was published in 1936 he was shattered. Keynes had, it seemed, solved the problem in an elegant theoretical way, making Beveridge's own work redundant. Nevertheless, he became a convert. It is no surprise then that government responsibility to achieve full employment was to feature as one of the key explicit assumptions in his 1942 report. He went on to produce a popular and passionately argued book which advocated that government take responsibility for ensuring a full and stable level of employment, *Full Employment in a Free Society* (Beveridge, 1944). 'Without full employment', he wrote, 'all else is futile.' Free political institutions depended on it, as did his social insurance plans. Indeed it was knowledge that this book was on its way that prompted the Coalition government to produce its own white paper (Lowe, 1999).

Social insurance was his other life interest. He objected to the original plans for universal tax-financed old age pensions advanced by Booth and others in the late nineteenth and early twentieth centuries. They would discourage thrift and be very expensive. A visit to Germany convinced him of the virtues of the contributory principle. Workers must pay for their pensions through work. He remained steadfastly of that view. He played an important part in helping to devise the unemployment insurance legislation in 1911. He wrote a pamphlet in 1924 called *Insurance for All and Everything*, which contained most of the basic ideas that were to find their way into his 1942 report.

It is not surprising then that Beveridge saw the chance to write his report as the culmination of a lifetime's effort. Yet his appointment and the report itself was something of an accident, and certainly not what the wartime Coalition government originally had in mind.

The Ambition: a New Britain

Beveridge was 60 at the outbreak of war. His experience of academic study and of social reform gave him the conviction that he had the vision, experience and application better to advise the war effort, and he made himself available.

His thinking, often changeable, had altered in the late 1930s under the impact of unemployment, and then the advent of war. Once convinced of *laissez-faire*, Beveridge now believed that 'the so-called free market had irretrievably broken down' (Harris, 1977: 472 and 324–33).

The radicalism of the late 1930s and 1940s sat awkwardly with some of his other views on economics and social welfare. When reading Beveridge one is struck by the contradictions which occur, not only between writings, which are long periods apart, but also by the number of contradictory influences which he tried to combine in his own intellectual vision. The suggestion that he represents a coherent philosophy of 'liberal collectivism' (Cutler et al., 1986) is questionable. One of Beveridge's difficulties was that he never fully married his old ideas, for example on the insurance principle, with his new enthusiasms for a national minimum and some appreciation of the feminist case. He was, as Harris (1975) argues, not so much an originator as a fuser of disparate ideas that were in the air. Yet his ambitions were high.

Beveridge saw himself as a crusading reformer. He could put over ideas clearly and understandably to the general reader, and had a track record as a broadcaster and newspaper columnist. Social reform was written as a rhetorical pilgrimage, in which, Bunyan-like, 'five giants on the road' – 'Want, Ignorance, Disease, Squalor and Idleness' – had first to be defeated. Days after the publication of the report Beveridge led his national campaign for New Britain, based on planning, reconstruction and a new commonwealth based on service to the community and a new altruism (BP IXa 29, Notes for a speech in Oxford, December 1942 and a letter to Tawney, 16 November 1942).

Beveridge's crusade was emphasized by his view of the war as a 'revolutionary moment in history'. The opportunity was there for a new

Britain, and neither the vested interests of capital, nor the trade unions, should thwart his plans (BP IXb 28, Notes for a speech 12 October 1942). There is no doubt that Beveridge saw himself as a man with a mission; he was encouraged by Janet, whom he was to marry two weeks after its publication, to take on the chairmanship and writing of the report as a millennial task (Harris, 1977: 387).

A climate for change

External proposals for post-war planning were gaining momentum. Articles appeared in the press; *ad hoc* discussion groups formed. PEP (Political and Economic Planning) had been founded in 1931 to prepare a National Plan to rescue Britain from the depression (Pinder, 1981). Supported by the Elmhursts, it produced a series of well-researched middle ground proposals for reform. Both François Lafitte and the young Michael Young joined the staff. More to the political point the trade unions expected change. Nevertheless, within government there was both support for and considerable resistance to change (Lowe, 1990).

The Reconstruction Secretariat had already been in contact with various groups planning social reconstruction. Five months before the Beveridge committee was announced in June 1941, PEP's research into the social services was viewed by the Reconstruction Secretariat as supporting radical change:

> a clean sweep of existing legislation, but it should be possible if sufficient courage is forthcoming. At any rate further nibbling is a waste of time. (PRO CAB117/177, Davidge to Sir George Christal 27 February 1941)

Expectations were high. There were demands for increased pensions, better health insurance cover and other service improvements. A plan which emphasized the longer-term nature of reform could dampen current demands.

> There will be very strong pressure – to introduce the millennium at once. (BP VIII, 27, Hale to Chester 22 June 1942)

And, as the British Employers' Federation put it,

> We did not start this war with Germany in order to improve our social services. (PRO CAB 87/77, SIC42, 17th meeting)

Diverting pressure for change

Setting up a committee was seen as a way to meet these demands halfway and contain more radical reform. The Treasury was worried.

> The present situation is more dangerous. On the one hand, it will be claimed that our obligations are greater, on the other, the kind of proposals that are in the wind (see for example, the PEP memorandum) are much more hair raising. (BP VIII, 29 December 1941)

The committee, at the outset therefore, can be seen as an attempt to side-track social reform, not to advance it (Macnicol, 1998: 351). Yet, in the eyes of the public, it spoke increasingly in the government's name. Those who had, reluctantly, agreed to be seen to be doing something about reconstruction were on a slippery slope to planning it.

The sixteen months between the committee's formation and the publication of the report were a period in which progressive and conservative elements vied to expand or restrain the impetus for reconstruction. The committee, under Beveridge's chairmanship, was of fundamental importance, not in the development of radical ideas on social security (there were many of those already (Harris, 1975, 1977)) but because the plans that were being made by Beveridge's committee were in the government's name. The status of the committee was a typical Whitehall battleground, of little interest to outsiders but of considerable importance to insiders and to the outcome. Both the terms of reference and the interpretation of them were the subject of dispute. The establishment of the Inter-departmental Committee on Social Insurance and Allied Services was largely a response to actual and perceived trade union pressure, both for improved work-related benefits in general and to overcome the hiatus in the Royal Commission on Workmen's Compensation brought about by the employers' refusal to continue to appear during wartime. In the original discussion on the setting up of an inquiry, Greenwood, prompted by Bevin, had envisaged a small committee which would look at health insurance and workers' compensation (PRO PIN 8/85, Greenwood to Ernest Brown 10 April 1941). Once departmental representatives gathered to discuss the suggestion it became obvious that any survey of existing schemes would 'involve questions of major policy' (PRO PIN 8/85, Notes of conclusions reached at a conference 24 April 1941). The Ministry of Labour was determined not to have family allowances included; the Treasury only wanted an administrative review. Death benefits, originally included in the draft terms of reference, were excluded. The finally agreed terms of reference were: to undertake, with special reference to the inter-relation of schemes, a survey of the existing national schemes of social insurance and allied services, including workmen's compensation and to make recommendations. They could be seen as wide enough to enable radical reform or narrow enough to limit study to administrative reform only. The membership and its terms of reference were a compromise between departmental interests. It was a committee designed by committee.

Keeping a radical agenda

A civil servant or Tory backbencher as chair would have probably ensured a conservative outcome. Indeed, Sir Hector Hetherington was the civil servants' nominee. The appointment of Beveridge, kicked sideways by Bevin from any further involvement in wartime labour planning, was thus resented by conservative forces and appreciated by the radicals. Two further influences helped ensure that a radical paradigm would predominate. In Parliament, the status of the committee grew as more questions of policy were deferred because of it. The government, fending off demands for better national health insurance rates, and later family allowances, helped to increase expectations of Beveridge. In addition, the press responded to the appointment in terms which supported a radical review. Several papers had exactly the same words: 'The widest and most comprehensive investigation into social conditions has begun . . . with the object of establishing economic and social security for every one on an equitable basis' (PRO AST 7/551). These are not the words to describe a 'tidying up exercise' and the use of common copy between national and local papers points to a common briefing to that effect. Evidence also points to a covert campaign to raise the importance of the review from within government, both for propaganda purposes, but also as a mechanism by which radicals within government could maximize its opportunities. Secret instructions had gone out to 'build up Beveridge' in America. Norman Chester pressed the propaganda value of Beveridge within the War Cabinet and was later to be a strong advocate for full implementation (PRO T172/2093).

Once the committee sat, Beveridge's own ambitions were encouraged by Mary Hamilton, the Reconstruction Secretariat's representative:

> Any provision whether by the State, by local authorities or by
> voluntary effort designed to afford greater security might, at some

date, be the concern of the committee. (PRO CAB 87/76, Minutes 1st meeting)

In this way the wide-ranging and radical nature of the committee was kept open from the first, and other members sympathetic to such an approach were happy as long as they were not unduly compromised. The civil servant membership of the committee were all middle-ranking officials and most of them were social insurance specialists.

Members of the committee were not all in favour of a radical interpretation of its terms of reference. Later on instructions were given to members to react to a radical agenda by playing a straight bat, merely emphasizing points of administrative difficulty. However, those departmental representatives who were in favour of radical changes, even if cautiously so, joined in the debate with Beveridge, usually through telephone or private correspondence.

Beveridge as chairman played the decisive role in ensuring a radical review. He suggested that a wide-ranging and fundamental change was on the agenda when the committee first met in July 1941, and the first task he set the civil servants was a comprehensive review of existing provisions by each department together with its proposals for reform. Then, in late November and early December 1941, Beveridge himself drew together his long-term desire for a comprehensive insurance scheme with his new-found belief in state planning and a national subsistence minimum, to produce his own vision of post-war social security. Most of his preparation of this vision was undertaken in Oxford over a couple of weekends.

The resultant memorandum, 'Problems of Social Security and Heads of a Scheme' (SIC(41)20) was presented to the surprised officials on 17 December 1941. In Beveridge's words it

contained all the essentials of the Beveridge Report as published . . . Once this memorandum had been circulated, the Committee had their objective settled for them and discussion was reduced to consideration of means of attaining that objective. (Beveridge, 1953: 298)

Putting the genie back in the bottle

The timing of the memorandum showed forethought on Beveridge's part. It was handed out as the last item at the last meeting before Christmas 1941. To add insult to injury Beveridge also then asked Hale, the Treasury representative, to cost the family allowance assumption of the memorandum. This ensured that family allowances became part of Beveridge's remit, a position opposed by both Treasury and the Ministry of Labour, and flushed out Hale's own work for the Treasury on family allowances – a subject which the Chancellor had kept close to his chest.

Once the nature of Beveridge's intentions was clear a campaign of containment was mounted, particularly by the Treasury, for whom a commitment to such wide-ranging, and as yet uncostable, reforms was untenable. The Chancellor insisted that Greenwood altered the status of the committee to one where the civil servants who attended were only advisers. They could not be seen as party to radical reform, and would compromise government and their departmental positions on such reforms if they continued as equal partners.

Beveridge became the sole signatory of the report and the government thought that it had the opportunity to lessen its importance and retain an element of distance from the final contents. In fact, the change of status made little difference to the work of the committee; during January 1942 and throughout the year until October it continued to meet, to hear evidence and to discuss Beveridge's scheme and the problems of implementation. Later, after Beveridge had produced his first draft of the report, in the early summer of 1942, the Treasury called together all the departmental representatives and told them not to discuss points of principle with Beveridge but merely to accentuate the administrative quagmire he faced. The Treasury tried to curtail publication of the report, and when that failed, to have radical evidence, such as the proposals by the National Federation of Old Age Pensions Associations, taken from the companion volume of evidence given to the committee.

The Report: Radical, but did it add up?

Despite its single authorship the report was a compromise between Beveridge's own conflicting ideals and between his ideals and financial reality. He was not a pensions expert (Harris, 2006).

The contributory principle and citizenship

At the heart of Beveridge's thinking was a contradictory struggle between his deep desire to cover everything and everyone and his choice of method, contributory insurance through employment. He wished to give security to all but to base this security, apart from family allowances, on participation in the labour market, not on citizenship status. Why did Beveridge not choose a citizenship basis for benefits? Denmark had already introduced a citizenship element into social security. PEP was advocating finance through a universal progressive tax system, so was the left. Meade and Keynes, as we shall see, favoured a unified tax system though they came to accept insurance contributions as a temporary expedient.

Beveridge's long-standing commitment to the contributory insurance principle has already been noted. He accepted the compromise between employers, workers and the state on a contributory principle as being immutable. To have gone back on it would have lost the support of the trade unions that would be necessary if the conservatives in government were to be defeated. The historical advantage of the contributory principle was that it had given recipients moral worth through contribution. There is some evidence that the passing of the 1934 Unemployment Act, which separated the administration of insurance benefits from means-tested ones, had increased the acceptability of the contributory principle amongst working people (Harris, 1990). An extension of the contributory principle

Figure 2.1   The making of the Beveridge Report

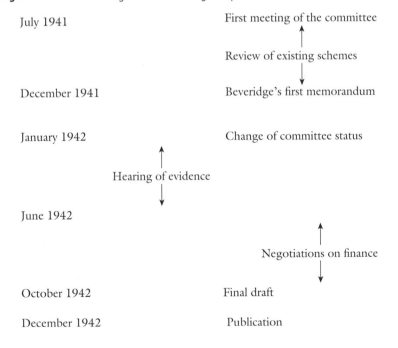

July 1941	First meeting of the committee
	↑
	Review of existing schemes
	↓
December 1941	Beveridge's first memorandum
January 1942	Change of committee status
	↑
Hearing of evidence	
	↓
June 1942	
	↑
	Negotiations on finance
	↓
October 1942	Final draft
December 1942	Publication

to cover all eventualities meant that 'We are all, so to speak, made "deserving" by Act of Parliament' (Wootton, 1943: 361).

But, as the International Labour Organization pointed out in its evidence, when it came to women and other groups not in the labour force, the contribution principle would not work (PRO CAB/79, SIC(42)39). Contributors and citizens in need were not the same thing. As the discussions advanced some groups at risk lost status either by being dropped from consideration at all or by being left to be provided for by the National Assistance scheme, because they would not fit the contributory principle. Moreover, his contributory logic lead him steadily to downgrade the generosity and acceptability of means-tested assistance. In his original heads of a scheme he makes this clear:

> An assistance scheme which does not in some way leave the person with an effective motive to avoid the need for assistance, undermines the Security scheme . . . an assistance scheme which makes those assisted unamenable to economic rewards or punishments while treating them as free citizens is inconsistent with the principles of a free community. (PRO CAB37/76, SIC(41)20)

At the first meeting Beveridge had set up a subcommittee to discuss assistance. The groups it was to provide for were defined as

> Cripples and deformed, deaf and dumb, mentally deficient, and vagrants and moral weaklings. (PRO CAB/77, SIC(A)(42))

But also destined for assistance were those whom Beveridge was to exclude from contributing: separated or single women bringing up children and those who fell out of the scheme because of administrative difficulty or cost, that is, the unemployed, self-employed and domestic spinsters. Largest in numbers would be those who would need supplementation for their insurance benefits in the supposedly transitional period and those with 'exceptional' needs, above all those with rent above a minimum level. Despite this growing residual group Beveridge stuck to his belief that insurance could cover virtually all categories of need. He was therefore led to downgrade assistance and reinforce its stigmatic nature at just the time when the Determination of Needs Act 1941 was beginning to mitigate the harshness of the pre-war means test. The abolition of the household means test and the new Assistance Board was beginning to hold out the possibility of a more humane system of means testing. Beveridge himself recognized this but it did not change his basic insistence that the contribution principle was fundamental (BP VIII, 33, Typed note, Means Tests, undated).

The flat rate contributory principle resulted in low benefits. As Macnicol puts it:

> Universality legitimated the insurance principle and the insurance principle legitimated inadequate pensions. (Macnicol, 1998: 354)

Contributions or taxes?

Modern critics of social insurance cannot understand why the state should have two kinds of tax: National Insurance contributions, which are a tax by another name, and income tax. Why have a system of collecting revenue separate from the ordinary tax system? The Treasury and the Economic Section of the Cabinet made exactly that point in the wartime debates.

The Treasury's timeless view

> did not favour assigned revenues and felt it was objectionable to give a first charge on any source of revenue. Experience indicated that if such a fund showed a balance, there was a demand for increased benefits; but if it showed a deficit, the Treasury was asked to provide a subsidy. (PRO CAB87/76, SIC(41))

The Economic Section's view of contributions was ambivalent. In the main they considered contributions were an outdated, illogical, regressive tax. James Meade was right on target here, as in most of his comments on Beveridge's draft:

> The continuation of the principle of social security financed by compulsory *insurance* premiums is probably due to conservatism rather than to any logically more cogent reason . . . Why is it not proposed to add the costs of family allowances to the Social Insurance Fund? Surely it is just as logical to finance these by compulsory contributions as it is to finance old-age pensions by these means? Why is not part of the cost of education borne by the Social Insurance Fund, while the greater part of a national health service is to be so borne? The answer, of course, is that we all see the dangers and inequities of compulsory contributions; we are therefore unwilling to add to them, but are not yet ready to drop those which already

exist – which in my view would be the sensible thing to do. (PRO T230/101, Note by James Meade 20 February 1942)

Keynes realized that arguing for a progressive tax basis for social security was ahead of its time. Beveridge's aims but not his methods were important to support. Keynes summed up the pragmatic approach in his response to Meade:

> I am very much in favour of something along the lines of Beveridge's proposals, as I gather you are . . . I agree in theory that employees' and employers' contributions are inferior to a charge on general taxes. On the other hand, it seems to me essential to retain them, at any rate in the first stages of the new scheme, in order that the additional charges on the Budget may not look altogether too formidable. (PRO T230/101, Keynes to Meade 8 May 1942)

Most workers did not at this point pay income tax, it should be remembered. It was not until the 1960s and 1970s that income tax took in the great majority of ordinary families. When Keynes and Meade were discussing the problem, financing social security out of income taxation would not only have hit the rich very hard but would have drawn the bulk of the working class into the income tax system for the first time.

In the end Meade and Keynes concluded that since the mechanism for collecting contributions existed and workers were used to it, while they were not used to income tax, they would go with 'contributions' as the only feasible immediate way to raise the revenue. But Keynes for one thought that after the war the two systems could be merged. For Keynes the flat rate contribution was a short-term administrative expedient. For Beveridge it was a matter of principle.

Securing a national minimum

In 1924 Beveridge had not seen a unified insurance scheme as a vehicle for achieving a national minimum. That was a new ideal and one he tried to fuse with his universal insurance scheme. He was convinced of this when he read Rowntree's new poverty study (Rowntree, 1941).

Beveridge was convinced by Rowntree's study that the causes of poverty had changed and were now amenable to solution though insurance benefits. The main reasons for economic insecurity and poverty had ceased to be low wages and were now unemployment and old age. The

Figure 2.2 Causes of poverty: Rowntree's evidence, 1899 and 1936, from his surveys of York

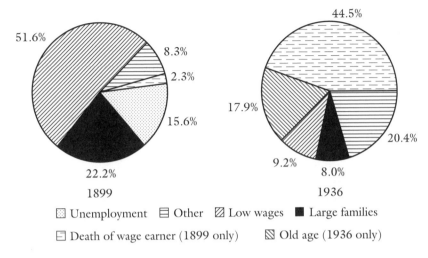

importance for Beveridge of this change, shown in Figure 2.2, is difficult to underestimate. His notes on Rowntree's book confirm that he took this causative model as his own and relied on it:

> the causes of poverty directly amenable to social insurance accounted for one quarter of the primary poverty in 1899 and for five sixths of the primary poverty in 1936. (BP VIII, 28, Draft, Scale of Benefit and Subsistence Scales)

This finding proved to Beveridge's satisfaction that a universal national insurance scheme could abolish poverty in the majority of cases if the benefits covered periods of non-earning and were set at the poverty line. This step in Beveridge's logic was suspect. He underestimated the numbers who would not be able to draw benefit because of a poor contribution record. The real problem lay in his definition of poverty.

Firstly, Beveridge took something close to Rowntree's statistical measure of primary poverty as the basis for setting his benefit levels. Yet Rowntree had always claimed that people's basic human needs required a higher regular income than that because no one could be expected to spend their income with perfect efficiency and to have no emergencies (Veit-Wilson, 1994). Secondly, the critical flaw in Beveridge's claim was that a single flat rate benefit for the whole country would be sufficient. Yet it could not take account of varying rent levels. Rent was an essential need which varied so greatly that it could not be brought within a flat rate subsistence definition. Either a common sum equal to the highest rent in the country had to be added to the flat rate benefit, which the Treasury would never wear, or benefits would not in practice be enough to live on.

Rowntree saw the problem only too clearly and said so in correspondence with Beveridge:

> I feel that if this principle is adopted it will go far to defeat the purpose that you have in view in recommending different rates of benefit, namely, to get rid of poverty. (BP VIII, 28, Rowntree to Beveridge 1 July 1942)

The problem of rent proved to be the easiest to exploit of the weaknesses in Beveridge's scheme. The matter was later discussed by the government committee, the Official Committee on the Beveridge Report (PRO PIN 8/85), which was set up to consider and if possible scupper the report. The problem of rent was seized upon to undermine the case for setting benefits at subsistence level.

The problem of pensions

It was critical to Beveridge's simple appealing plan that *all* benefits should be set at the same level: enough to meet all basic costs. That would have meant raising the basic pension from the 10 shillings a week (50p) it stood at before the war to 25 shillings for a single person and £2 for a married couple. That would have cost £3 million and Beveridge knew that was impossible to get past the Treasury. Keynes negotiated with him to reduce the cost and rescue the whole scheme. See Macnicol (1998: Chapter 15) for an account of these discussions. His report finally proposed a pension of 14 shillings for a single person and 25 shillings for a couple, which taking into account the rising prices since the war started was barely a real increase at all. He proposed that the pension rise gradually to reach the subsistence poverty level by 1965! Ernest Bevin, ex-trade union leader and long-time campaigner for better pensions, was on the Cabinet subcommittee considering the report. It was far too gradual for him. The full rate of pension had to paid immediately. Other members agreed. What that level should be remained in dispute. The Labour government finally set pension levels at 26 shillings (single) and 42 shillings a week (couple). That still left about a quarter of pensioners on means-tested additions to their pensions that were necessary mainly to cover the costs of their rent.

Women in Beveridge's scheme of things

Modern feminist writers tend to portray the social security system as containing a hidden set of assumptions about the structure of the family and gender relations. There was nothing very hidden about Beveridge's views on women's role!

The role of the family is a consistent feature of much of his writings. It was the pivotal focus of human life:

> What matters vitally to every human being, is the handful of other human beings to whom he is linked by birth or marriage, not the indifferent millions with whom he shares this changing world . . . Mating and birth, the fundamental processes by which human life is arrived at, are the same for all men and women at all times. They give rise to relations of companionship between man and woman, and mutual support between parents and children and brothers and sisters and kindred – which are at all times similar. (BP XIa, Notes for Changes in Family Life broadcast, 23 January 1932)

Society's ideal unit, he believed, was

> the household of man, wife and children maintained by the earnings of the first alone. The household should have at all times sufficient room and air according to its size – but how, if the income is too irregular to pay the rent? The children, till they themselves can work, should be supported by the parents – but how, unless the father has employment? Everywhere the same difficulty recurs. Reasonable security of employment for the bread-winner is the basis of all private duties and all social action. (Beveridge, 1924: 4)

The difficulty for Beveridge was to bring together his largely unchanged view of the family with the changes which had occurred in his assumptions about women's status. This meant an unhappy juxtaposition of his view of women as equals and their role within domestic arrangements which undermined and excluded such status.

His view of marriage was based on a companionship of different but equal partners. In this his views matched more modern 'progressive' ideas, 'the basis of what was considered an ideal marriage had changed profoundly from patriarchy to companionship' (Lewis, 1984: 120). In the 1930s he broadcast on family issues and expounded the view of modern marriage as one that was evolving into a partnership of equals. Thus, for Beveridge, the question of whether married women should work was a matter of freedom of choice, but that choice was made in an idealized partnership where the realities of power and discrimination were unrecognized:

> It is true that most married women will not wish to go on working for pay because they will have plenty of work to do as housewives and mothers. But in a free society it ought to be left to the wife herself and her husband to decide on this. (BP IXa, 80, Typed draft 'Looking ahead' undated 1945)

Equality of status for Beveridge meant that man and wife were a *team*; within this team each was performing work of the same importance. The difference was one of practice:

> More than seven out of every eight married women in peace time follow no gainful occupation; provision for married women should be framed with reference to the seven rather than the one . . .
> [Women] acquire by marriage a new economic and social status . . . On marriage a woman acquires a legal right to maintenance by her husband, as a first line of defence against risks which fall directly on the solitary woman. (PRO CAB/76, SIC(41)20, Basic Problems with Heads of a Scheme)

Women should therefore be insured through their husbands, not in their own right. The long-term legacy for British pension policy and women's rights is discussed by Thane (2006).

The Report's Main Proposals

Unification

Unemployment and sickness insurance regulated by the state had existed since 1911. It covered manual workers in certain occupations. The scope had been gradually extended so that by 1940 it covered agricultural workers and less well paid non-manual work. All people employed in these occupations had to pay contributions which would give them a defined benefit if the need arose. Widows' and orphans' benefits and pensions had been added in the 1920s. About 20 million people, or half the population, were covered in 1938. Unemployment benefits were administered by civil servants, officers of the Ministry of Labour. The national regulations on sickness benefit were administered by 800 approved societies: friendly societies, private insurance firms, trade unions and employers' provident funds. They had thousands of local branches, all separately administered.

Beveridge proposed to assimilate all this Byzantine system into one scheme administered by the national government.

> Change 1: Unification of social insurance . . . enabling each insured person to obtain all benefits by a single weekly contribution on a single document. (p. 20)

> Change 2: Unification of social insurance and assistance . . . in a Ministry of Social Security with local security offices within reach of all insured persons. (p. 22)

Pooling risks

The sickness benefit and health coverage schemes were administered by approved societies of the kind mentioned above. They collected the required contributions, the same from each worker, and paid out benefits in sickness and paid for health care. Yet some societies had members who were much more likely to be ill for longer periods – miners for example. This meant that fortunate better-off societies could give much better benefits than other workers would gain. Workers had always resented this. Hence Beveridge's insistence that everyone should pay in and receive the same benefits. Risks would be pooled across the whole of society. Health *care* should be separated from this system too and all citizens should receive treatment free on the same basis.

> Change 3: Supersession of the present system of Approved Societies giving unequal benefits for equal compulsory contributions. (p. 23)

Workers injured at work had redress from their employer under laws passed at the end of the nineteenth century and in 1906. An employer had to compensate the worker. This was again an enormously complex and cumbersome process of individuals claiming from their employers. Beveridge proposed to include industrial accidents in his scheme and remove this legally costly and time-consuming process.

> Change 4: . . . inclusion of workmen's compensation and . . . industrial accident in the unified social insurance scheme. (p. 35)

A national minimum

The remnants of the old local Poor Law remained, with local authorities administering means-tested benefits to all those who were not old or unemployed. Beveridge proposed to amalgamate all means-tested provision in one national agency, again his proposed Ministry of Social Security (Change 19).

There were many other detailed proposals but Beveridge summed up his plan thus:

> Under the scheme of social insurance, which forms the main feature of this plan, every citizen of working age will contribute in his appropriate class (self employed or employed) according to the security he needs, or as a married woman will have contributions paid by her husband. Each will be covered for all his needs by a single weekly contribution on one insurance document. All the principle cash payments – for unemployment, disability and retirement will continue so long as the need lasts, without means test, and will be paid from a Social Insurance Fund built up by contributions from the insured persons, from their employers, if any, and the state . . . benefit in return for contributions, rather than free allowances from the state, is what the people of Britain desire. (p. 11, para. 20)
>
> National Assistance is an essential subsidiary method in the whole Plan for Social Security . . . but the scope of assistance will be narrowed from the beginning and will diminish through the transition period for pensions. (p. 12, para. 23)

The flat rate principle

To base the scheme firmly in the contributory framework, everyone was to contribute the same sum and receive the same benefit. This had been the basis of British insurance schemes from the beginning but it was not the pattern followed by other countries. Better-off workers in Germany and the United States paid a percentage of their earnings into the scheme and got a pension or benefit that was a percentage of their previous earnings. For Beveridge it was crucial to keep benefits to the minimum consistent with poverty relief, to encourage people to take out voluntary and private insurance on top of the basic pension. He would probably never have got his proposals accepted by the insurance lobby if he had not made this very clear.

> The first fundamental principle of the social insurance scheme is provision of a flat rate of insurance benefit, irrespective of the amount of earnings which have been interrupted by unemployment or disability or ended by retirement . . . This principle follows from the recognition of the place and importance of voluntary insurance in social security. (p. 121, para. 304)

This was matched by the second fundamental principle of flat rate contributions.

> All insured persons, rich or poor, will pay the same contributions for the same security. (p. 121, para. 305)

The assumptions

Despite the detailed mechanics of social insurance the report may be remembered almost as much for its somewhat arrogant 'assumptions', that is, policy proposals going far beyond his remit: child allowances, cash payments to mothers for their second and subsequent children, a free national health service and full employment. As we shall see, it was the principle of a free health service explicitly stated here that galvanized the Ministry of Health into action; this, together with the full employment principle, was to be central to post-war policy.

The Rejection of Beveridge?

The Labour government claimed it had implemented the plan. Hill (1990) claims that to a remarkable extent this was indeed the case. Others, such as Hennessy (1992), seem to agree. Recent authors disagree. Lowe (1999) claims that Beveridge's most important principles were rejected immediately and the rest were abandoned later. Macnicol (1998) blames the inconsistency of the report itself. How can we explain the disagreement?

The most important structural changes *were* adopted. The old complex variety of schemes and approved societies went and were replaced by a single National Insurance scheme with local offices run by a central ministry. These elements remain to this day. The benefits and the contributions *were* flat rate. Later income-related elements were added and some abandoned again. The flat rate low floor to the scheme has also remained a persistent characteristic.

No Ministry of Social Security was created but a Ministry of National Insurance was, and a separate National Assistance Board dealing with the means-tested benefits and charged with a growing task of implementing the national minimum. But the goal of a nationally set minimum was carried through, though not in the way Beveridge intended.

Beveridge was rejected where his own scheme was a muddle or a deception. This was the case in the confusion that surrounded his claim that his benefits would be sufficient to raise everyone above the poverty line. He had never managed to define his benefit levels in a way that would have made that possible (Veit-Wilson, 1994). He rejected the idea of setting benefits exclusive of rent and having a separate housing benefit as Rowntree urged (Lowe, 1994). That was to wait another twenty-five years. The subsistence principle was to be rejected formally in the 1950s, as we shall see. He wanted benefits for the unemployed and sick to be unlimited in duration and subject to a test that the circumstances were genuine. This was rejected. He wanted pensioners to wait twenty years to draw a full subsistence pension. This was rejected because the voters would not wait. Pensioners got more than he envisaged in 1946 but were never to catch up with his implied levels of adequacy. Pensioners with only a basic pension have ever since his time been forced to apply for means-tested additions. As Beveridge's biographer puts it,

> Paradoxically, though Britain was believed to be the homeland of a Beveridge based universal insurance system, almost the opposite was really the case. It was the European countries . . . which most wholeheartedly adopted a contributory social insurance system . . . whereas Britain . . . maintained a substantial means tested tax financed welfare system directly inherited from the Poor Law . . . In other words, contrary to what most academic commentators and popular folk-law have believed, it was not contributory insurance, but 'full' services financed out of direct taxation that was the most marked

characteristic of Britain's Welfare State . . . after the Second World War. (Harris, 1990: 182–4, quoted in Lowe, 1994)

Family Allowances

The most innovative of all the cash benefits introduced at this time were family allowances. Beveridge had long favoured family allowances, introducing them for staff at the LSE in the 1920s. His biographer points out that he first became interested in them because of his concern with population questions and the steady decline in the birth-rate that was occurring especially amongst the educated middle classes and in the 'white man's world' (Harris, 1977: 341). Increasingly he became interested in the idea for reasons of labour market economics and insurance. He read Eleanor Rathbone's book, *The Disinherited Family*, in 1920 and became converted by it. Families' needs varied through a lifetime. Rathbone said that when they had several young children their needs were high but their incomes were low, driving many families below the poverty line. Yet there was no reason why employers should pay workers more money just because they had children. The worker was not worth more to an employer just because he had children to support. Rowntree's solution was to impose a statutory minimum wage sufficient to enable the average family with children to support itself above the poverty line. But, as Rathbone pointed out, this would be wildly expensive. It would force employers to pay all their employees more than the labour market required to hire them despite the fact that only some had children. The answer, Rathbone suggested, was a system of family allowances paid by the state. That would solve the problem of child poverty, a falling birth-rate and keep the labour market free. She was drawing on experience in France, Poland and Belgium.

There was another issue that was closely related and which had exercised the Unemployment Assistance Board in the 1930s and the Beveridge Committee. What should the level of benefits be? They must be below what the low-paid could earn to keep incentives to work in place. But that would mean giving benefits below the poverty line for those with children. If you gave extra benefits to take account of the number of children in a family such a worker would end up getting more out of work than in it, because though benefits took account of children wages did not. As Macnicol (1980) points out in his study of the origins of family allowances, it was *this* argument that clinched the case for having them with the Treasury and the Cabinet.

An Unsound Foundation

The appeal of the report lay in its apparent simplicity and comprehensiveness as well as its Bunyanesque prose. Yet, we have argued, that simplicity was illusory. The central flaw was the attempt to achieve a national minimum through contributory social insurance. Rights to benefit did not come as a right of citizenship. They came from a contribution record in full-time paid employment that excluded most women, the disabled and many more. The flat rate benefits that were earned were not to be set at a level sufficient to meet all financial needs, notably rent.

Paradoxically what we owe most to the reforms of this period *is* the implementation of the Webbs' old idea of a national minimum: a poverty line which the central state sustained. Beveridge claimed that that was what he was advocating. Yet he did little to advance it practically. We owe that to the much despised National Assistance Board and its successors. It was a national means-tested safety net that was to mark the UK out from many of its European neighbours and from the United States. That was what has given the UK, until recently, a good record in sustaining a low but effective safety net. Beveridge, by casting assistance as a minimalist agency, of lower moral standing, the recourse of 'cripples, the deformed . . . and moral weaklings' only made that task more difficult.

This muddling of the minimum with social insurance was also to damn the future of social insurance in the UK. As a flat rate scheme it never had a hope of securing the support of the middle class, as social security has done in the US. In 1992, after a decade of serious erosion, the decline of the state pension did not even raise a murmur in the general election. Nor was anyone taken in by the term 'contribution' any more. Politicians of all kinds simply lumped it and income tax together as a combined tax rate much as Keynes and Meade foresaw.

Beveridge's reasoning, drawn from his reading of the newly published Rowntree study, was that poverty was almost entirely caused by unemployment, which could be made a short-term phenomenon, and old age. That has proven, and is increasingly proving, ill founded. The lifetime insured population of Beveridge's world is a declining group. 'Exceptional' categories of the poor are becoming the norm. The emergence of a marginalized secondary labour force has profound implications for any notion of a universal system based on a contribution record. The assumptions Beveridge made about the relative unimportance of low wages and impermanent jobs are even less sustainable now than they were in the

1940s. So, too, are his assumptions about the family team, female responsibilities and the permanence of husband-and-wife relations.

Beveridge was caught between the Edwardian world of social policy and the post-war world he could only partially glimpse. Yet he, like us, was only a creature of his times, a mirror not a prophet. Few of his contemporaries were any more far-sighted.

Beveridge was right in arguing that people needed a basic pension platform free of means testing on which they could build their own pension requirements. The Pensions Commission (2005) has returned to the same position. He was misguided in how he planned to fund such an objective. That is why we are still discussing the issue. Beveridge was also surely right in seeing that a national minimum depended fundamentally on the broader social policy framework. This would, he explicitly assumed, consist of: a universal child benefit at a level that removed wage-earning families from the poverty line, a national health service free at the point of use and an active employment policy. What we cannot deny Beveridge is his sense of vision and his attempt to think on a large scale, despite opposition. It seems as necessary at the beginning of a new century as in his own time.

Questions to Answer

1 Draw up a balance sheet of the positive and less positive legacies of the Beveridge Report.
2 Discuss Beveridge's treatment of women in his plan and the longer-term weakness of women's position in the pension market.
3 Why was Beveridge's plan never fully implemented?

3

The Right to Health, Knowledge, Food, Shelter and Work, 1945–51

Citizenship Rights?
A National Health Service Created
The New National Health Service
Education For All
The 1944 Education Act
Labour's Policy
Children
Food Rationing
Shelter
Jobs for All
Services for Citizens?

Citizenship Rights?

The post-war social security scheme began with a Utopian plan, widespread public support and a relatively smooth political passage. The National Health Service did not. The wartime Coalition government merely edged its way cautiously towards expanding the pre-war system of national health insurance to cover most, but by no means all, of the population. Its proposals would have left the hospital system in a fragmented and financially precarious situation. The post-war Labour government wanted something much more radical. This provoked considerable controversy and the opposition of the British Medical Association. It is true that there was widespread agreement that the old system needed reform. The notion that there was some kind of broad consensus about the *kind* of health service that should be created after the war is another comfortable myth made up after the event.

In contrast the post-war social security scheme, which apparently generated such consensus, soon began to lose public support because its promises were never realized. The National Health Service soon established itself as the most popular of the institutions created at this time.

The service did, alone amongst these new agencies, embody the principles of citizenship that Marshall had claimed for the Welfare State as a whole. It sought to give equal rights of access to care, free at the point of use, to all people who needed it. Rights of access were not dependent on some contributory work record that mainly men could earn. As we shall see, it would come to fall short of these citizenship goals in many instances, but it came nearer to achieving them than the schemes that had preceded it or than the other services created at this time.

'Ignorance' was another of Beveridge's giants to be slain, though it did not feature further in his report than this phrase. As in the case of health, the principle sought in education was that of equal access, a service free at the point of use, for all those capable of benefiting from it. England adopted that principle, which we now take for granted, later than any other advanced economy. The American colonies, Prussia and France had begun to provide education by the mid-nineteenth century, or before in places such as Massachusetts. So had Scotland. England dragged its reluctant feet, fearing the challenge to established authority that an educated population would bring. When public elementary education had been introduced in 1870 it was still on a fee-paying basis. Fees for elementary education had only been removed in the 1890s. They remained for secondary, that is to say academic, grammar school education, at the beginning of the Second World War. Scholarships were available for bright poorer children to go to grammar schools free but their availability varied widely between different local authorities and different types of grammar school. The fact that some could buy their way into grammar school, while others could not, was a deep source of resentment for working families. Only very limited access to universities and other post-school education was available. Of those born between 1913 and 1922 less than 2 per cent went on to university and less than 1 per cent of children of the manual working class (Halsey et al., 1980). Yet they constituted the overwhelming proportion of the population; two-thirds of all jobs in the 1940s were manual jobs.

In no sense, therefore, were health care and education universally available to the population in 1945. The right to both had been firmly on the political agenda since the First World War but progress to both had been uneven. What the mass of the public expected was that after this second great war these goals would be reached once and for all.

The system of care for the elderly and disabled was still essentially part of the Poor Law and the care of children in danger or without parents was in administrative chaos.

Top of the politicians' immediate agenda in 1945, however, was housing. Many homes had been destroyed or damaged by enemy action. Millions of servicemen would be returning home in the next year from around the world and from army barracks. Virtually no house-building had taken place during the war. Something rapid had to be done or terrible disillusion would set in as soldiers, airmen and sailors came back to find themselves living in overcrowded slums with mum and dad and a family on its way. In the same way food, the most basic of all human requirements, was in short supply and was firmly under state control, both rationed and subsidized. Politicians were haunted by the fear of mass unemployment as war production ceased and service men and women were 'demobbed'.

A National Health Service Created

The roots of the NHS

Although the National Health Service is sometimes portrayed as if it sprang fully armed from the forehead of Aneurin Bevan, its form owed a great deal to the nature of health care before 1939. But there was nothing pre-determined about the form it took. Many possible models were under discussion in the pre-war period. (The detailed history of this period has been chronicled by Harry Eckstein (1958), Frank Honnigsbaum (1979; 1989), Charles Webster (1988) and others. Klein's (1995) history of the health politics from 1945 is the best brief account. Carrier and Kendall (1998) put the changes in a longer historical context.

The story really has many strands to it. The state had played an active role in health promotion since the middle of the nineteenth century. It was better diet, the laying of sewers, the piping of clean water, the invention of the water closet and, much later, immunization campaigns that were decisive in extending the British people's expectation of life, long before the Health Service was legislated (McKeown, 1979). The local authorities and their Medical Officers of Health led this advance and in the 1920s and 1930s took control of the Poor Law hospitals for the long-term sick and began to run general hospitals too. They were also expanding maternity and health visiting services, which inspected the health of young children under school age and set out to teach working-class mothers how to look after their children (Lewis, 1980).

One possible future direction the health services could have taken was to expand the responsibilities of the local health authorities. This had been the route favoured by the Webbs and the Minority Report of the Poor Law Commission in 1909. Another way forward would have been simply to expand the coverage of the existing national health insurance system. The hundreds of approved societies based on men's places of work could have collected the insurance contributions of their members and paid for their care. This scheme had been expanded steadily in the inter-war period and could have been expanded more to cover all but the really well off. This was the route favoured by the BMA.

The voluntary hospitals were an old-established and central part of the health provision of the country. They ranged from the great old foundations of St Bartholemew's and St Thomas's in London to the small local hospital supported by flag days. Patients paid to go to these hospitals unless they could convince the hospital almoner that they were too poor to pay. Charitable donations had proved incapable of covering these hospitals' costs and they had begun charging at the end of the nineteenth century. They were in deep financial trouble by the beginning of the Second World War (Abel-Smith, 1964; Gorsky et al., 2002). The fewer were the people who could pay their fees in the recession the higher were the fees that the middle class had to pay to cross-subsidize the costs of the poor.

A possible way out lay in the expansion of voluntary hospital insurance alongside the National Insurance scheme that covered the costs of the GP. During the war, however, the finances of the voluntary hospitals had been transformed by the infusion of large sums of public money to pay them for the care of war casualties. A steady supply of public money seemed less frightening to many working in these hospitals than it had before the war.

Yet one of the main difficulties, much discussed in the 1930s, had been the confusion and rivalry between the voluntary hospitals and the local authority hospitals. It took the war to get the Ministry of Health to collect some kind of inventory of what facilities and specialities existed where.

In the ordinary way of incremental politics the gradual growth of these various health-care systems would have probably gone on side by side. The Ministry of Health, created with such optimism after the First World War, had begun with ambitious aims to create a unified health service but sectional interests had prevented anything but incremental and opportunistic growth between the wars.

At the beginning of the Second World War the Ministry of Health tried again. Like their colleagues in the Board of Education, the civil servants began to discuss what a comprehensive pattern of health services after the war might look like. They did so against the background of great dissatisfaction with the system of health care that most people experienced. Though working men in many occupations were covered for family doctor services, many of their wives and families were not. The generosity of cover, and whether your wife and children were covered, depended on whether you worked in a healthy occupation or not. If you did, your contributions went further and could pay for better benefits. Hospital care had to be separately insured against or would mean a means test. There was, therefore, a lot of dissatisfaction with the health services of the 1930s and a public opinion survey in 1941 suggested that 85 per cent of those surveyed supported a state-organized medical service (Webster, 1988). The ministry and the officials started in a very tentative way to discuss how the local authority and the voluntary hospitals might work together on a regional basis, building on the War Time Emergency Hospital Service. Even this limited move to integration provoked a furious response from the Labour leader of the London County Council, who said the ministry and the voluntary hospital movement were trying to 'steal the people's hospitals' (1988: 31). Just as conservative was the response of the British Medical Association to the Beveridge Report's Assumption B, that there should be a comprehensive health service replacing the old patchwork of approved societies. This sideshow to the Beveridge Report proper had galvanized the Ministry of Health into action. It had feared it might lose control of the situation if it did not come forward with some ideas of its own, so positive had been the public response to this proposal, as the Ministry of Information reported to the Cabinet (1988: 28–9).

Yet the British Medical Association was furious. In 1939 it had proposed the extension of the old National Health Insurance scheme to cover the wives and children of the existing members but not to extend the coverage from the existing low-income limits. Its position had not moved since 1930. Now it was being asked to support a service that covered the whole population. It wanted to keep the insurance basis of the scheme, which would pay doctors' fees for half the population and allow plenty of room for private practice fees from the rest of the population. It was determined not to accept a salaried public service for doctors, which it felt might well result from Beveridge's initiative. All the sectional interests were therefore at loggerheads.

The first proposals

Early in 1943 the ministry drew up an outline of possible legislation. The service would be free at the point of use though charges for the 'hotel costs' of hospitals might be necessary. It would probably be paid for out of National Insurance with Exchequer support. It preserved a place for the voluntary hospitals. The basis of organization was to be local, with the medical interest represented. The scheme owed a lot to the BMA proposals of 1939 but had moved in the direction of universality.

From then until 1945 medical interests of different kinds fought over the scheme. The BMA led outright opposition to the scheme and opposed the official plan both in principle and in detail. A universal scheme would harm doctors' private fee income. Doctors refused to be run by local authorities. So did the voluntary hospitals. The BMA wanted the service to grow incrementally and to be administered by independent bodies that would be – not to put too fine a point on it – dominated by doctors.

As the discussions dragged on and as the ministry firmed up the proposals, the opposition grew. The ministry wanted to group GPs together in health centres wherever possible. That was opposed as a restriction on professional freedom. The Labour Party members of the Cabinet were growing increasingly concerned that the scheme did not go far enough.

When the White Paper of 1944, *A National Health Service* (Cmd 6502) was published it was deliberately non-Utopian. Any mention of the Beveridge Report 'was expunged at the late proof stage upon request of the Cabinet' (Webster, 1988: 55). To a significant extent the original headings of the scheme drafted in January 1943 remained, and the pre-war insurance system to cover GPs' fees would stay, though extended. The separate occupationally based schemes would remain. The local authority hospitals would be grouped together and run by Joint Boards of local councils, a proven recipe for disaster. The voluntary hospitals would remain separate under uncertain financial support.

Public reaction

The plan was not a public success, in contrast to the education White Paper published the same year, and especially in contrast to the Beveridge Report.

The more radical reformers in the Labour Party were only mildly impressed with the compromises, while the BMA blew its top, complaining that the whole thing was going too far too fast.

The BMA was blessed with a superb communicator, Charles Hill, who was not only an officer of the BMA but was heard regularly by the mass of the population as 'the radio doctor', an avuncular-sounding purveyor of homely advice on the BBC. When he and the *Daily Express* told the public that this plan would stop people getting advice from their own doctor, the battle was joined. In the period between the publication of the White Paper and the general election the government began to backtrack and give way to the medical interests.

Bevan changes tack

When the Labour Party won the 1945 election with such a large majority the BMA feared the worst, but even so it never expected to be faced with the man who had hounded the Coalition government from the Labour backbenches through the war for its backsliding on social issues, the *enfant terrible* of the Tory press – Aneurin Bevan.

Members of the BMA were meeting when the election results were coming through. Beveridge, who had been elected as a Liberal MP during the war at a by-election, lost his seat and a cheer went up. Little did they know that they would be faced with Bevan!

In his first discussion with his new Deputy Secretary, the civil servant in charge of health matters at the ministry, Bevan put his finger on the main problem with the Coalition government's White Paper proposals: its failure to produce any basis for a comprehensive *hospital* service. That civil servant was later interviewed by Bevan's biographer, Michael Foot, and said,

> Of course he was right. They [the Coalition White Paper proposals] would never have worked. I came away that night with instructions to work out a new plan on the new basis he proposed. (Foot, 1975: 130)

That new basis involved the nationalization of all the country's hospitals, local authority and voluntary, small cottage hospitals run by GPs, the large ancient foundations, the London teaching hospitals – the lot. It was this feature that was the sharpest break with previous proposals for reform and was to make the UK's health service unique. It was on all fours with the other major nationalizations that were being contemplated at the same time: the nationalization of the huge mining industry, the railways and the largely local-authority-run gas and electricity works. The plan was bitterly opposed within the Cabinet by Herbert Morrison and others who wanted to keep the local authority hospitals as well as by the supporters of the powerful independent voluntary hospitals. They were supported by the Conservative Party, whose spokesman was the minister who had negotiated the previous government's White Paper: Willink.

Why did Bevan go down this controversial road? Partly, it was the sheer incompatibility of the end he passionately wanted to achieve – equal right of access to the best medical care regardless of residence or income – with the means available. A huge variety of different kinds and quality of hospital existed in 1945, dependent on different sources of finance, some weak and nearly bankrupt, others well staffed and equipped because they were in prosperous areas where private patients could pay the fees. Local authorities were too numerous and too poorly financed to cope with the responsibility of running the nation's hospitals. A national service required national administration, he concluded.

Other possible ways out did exist, of course. The Swedes adopted a local authority model for their health service and the education reforms did the same in the UK, but Bevan could not wait for the reform of British local government.

As important as rationalizing the hospital situation was the need Bevan had to win over key members of the medical profession; without them the plan would never have flown. Perhaps more than anything the hospital consultants feared being employed by local authorities. They were not to lose much sleep knowing that their incomes would be secured by the national government. It freed them from the necessity to drum up business from GPs and rich clients to pay for their basic income. If private fees came as *extras*, that would give consultants both security and a bonus. That was the basis of the deal Bevan struck with the consultants.

Lord Moran, one of the leaders of the Royal Colleges who represented the consultant interests saw the point very early on. Bevan also gave the teaching hospitals separate Boards of Governors to administer them. The governors would have considerable independence and direct access to the minister. Regional Hospital Boards would run the other hospitals, with local management committees looking after each hospital. Both would have medical representation. Regional Hospital Boards would hold consultants' contracts. Consultants would work for the NHS and for a part of their time could take private patients if they wished.

The nationalized hospital service was, therefore, a vehicle for giving the consultants what they wanted as well as what Bevan wanted. Moreover, it was not altogether revolutionary because the wartime Emergency Hospital Service had shared many of these characteristics. These doctors knew from first-hand experience that working in such a scheme did not make them part of a Hitler state, as the BMA and Conservative Members of Parliament were to argue.

While Bevan moved to solve the hospital problem with an apparent sharp shift to the left, he responded to the GPs by giving up what had been a central plank of Labour policy: a salaried service for family doctors, much favoured by the Socialist Medical Association. Bevan favoured patients having choice of doctor. People could go elsewhere if they were not getting treated properly. Restricted choice of GP had been one of the complaints about the old 'panel' scheme. Choice was difficult to marry with a salaried service, as he argued during the committee stage of the bill. If you were a bad doctor and lost all your patients should you go on receiving a salary? The simplest thing to do was to pay doctors a basic sum to run their practice and then pay them for each patient they took on: the basis of the old pre-war scheme, in fact.

The idea that each doctor would have responsibility for a given list of patients gave the NHS another unique feature that other countries were to look upon enviously in later decades.

In paying hospitals centrally a given budget and paying doctors a fixed capitation sum for each patient each year, Bevan unwittingly built into the NHS a powerful mechanism by which the Treasury could control the costs of health care far more effectively than in any other Western country. Yet it was for exactly the opposite failing that he was to be criticized by his opponents, i.e. the profligacy of the scheme.

The battle for the NHS

Early in 1946 the BMA was informed of Bevan's outline plans, and then they were announced. He had succeeded in his prime task, which was to split the profession in its opposition. Some on the BMA were amazed he had offered them so much. Others were determined to fight this upstart all the way. The furious opposition from the BMA and Tory press actually helped Bevan to get the Labour Party to swallow some unpleasant medicine: no salaried service for GPs and the existence of private practice for consultants.

Bevan introduced the bill to the House of Commons with a speech lasting an hour and a quarter without consulting any notes, and received a tumultuous ovation from the Labour benches (Foot, 1975). It was attacked by the Conservatives for breaking the consensus there had been over the 1944 White Paper. As the bill passed through the Commons the Opposition grew more critical and took up the claims of a more and more strident BMA. Nevertheless it passed the Commons with a large majority and the Lords did not dare to reject it. The BMA, however, decided to wreck the scheme. It had tried to do the same with the 1911 legislation and was to try again with the 1990 Act. It refused to negotiate or collaborate. The chairmen of the Royal Colleges stepped in and went to see the minister to get discussions under way. They were to go on for the next eighteen months (Webster, 1988).

The new service was planned to begin on 5 July 1948, like the other great Acts of the period. Early in 1948 the BMA held a national ballot of its members as to whether they would join the scheme. Altogether 41,000 voted against the NHS and 4,000 voted for it. Bevan simply pressed ahead. Arrangements were made for doctors to sign up with a service that would begin in July. The two sides were playing a rather dangerous game of chicken.

Again the leaders of the Royal Colleges stepped in and proposed that the 'fears of the profession' that the government would force a salaried service on them, could be allayed by amending legislation. It could be drafted in a way that would make such a step impossible. Bevan accepted. Fearing another 1911 débâcle, the BMA, after much agonizing and internal dissent, decided to put the idea to the vote of all its members. A small majority voted against taking part in the NHS but it was too small a margin for the BMA to risk carrying through a full boycott. The NHS would be born in July 1948 after all.

Whatever words may be used to describe this train of events, 'consensus' is not one of them. Churchill described the period as one of 'Party antagonism as bitter as anything I have seen in my long life of political conflict' (Hansard, vol. 416, col. 2534, quoted in Foot, 1975).

The New National Health Service

The new service carried with it features of the old pre-war arrangements but it was a decisive shift and created a health system unique in the Western world. Other systems on the continent of Europe that did come to give free access to most of their populations more closely resembled the kind of mixed insurance scheme that the Conservatives favoured: mixed ownership and control of hospitals with doctors and hospitals charging fees, and patients recovering some or all of the costs from a social insurance scheme. In Scandinavia something more like the British NHS emerged but was run by locally elected councils. The key features of the NHS, legislated in 1946 and begun in 1948, were, thus, unique and were to last for over forty years.

The National Health Service Act 1946

The following were the main features of this milestone Act.

- The service was to be run on a national basis and paid for out of general taxation with a small token element contributed from the National Insurance Fund – a relic of the pre-war system. This did not stop many people assuming that they were paying for the NHS out of 'the stamp', i.e. their National Insurance contribution.
- All citizens could register with a family doctor of their choice and receive free treatment for simple ailments and be referred on to hospitals for those conditions the GP could not treat.
- GPs remained private professional people, increasingly often grouped in a common legal entity called a partnership. They owned their own premises. They received an annual payment for each NHS patient who signed on at their surgery and had a duty to provide care for that person. What this care should amount to was ill defined at this point but was taken to mean normal primary care and diagnosis. They were overseen by appointed bodies called Executive Councils, which were also responsible for dentists and chemists. Nearly half the membership was nominated by the relevant professional body.
- Attendance at hospital was free. Virtually all hospitals in the country were owned and run by the national government. They were administered at two levels. Regional Hospital Boards, covering about 5 million people, decided how to organize the hospitals, how many there should be, what should be built, and they employed the senior doctors and allocated them to hospitals. (In the past specialist doctors, or consultants, had gone where they thought they could generate enough custom from fee-paying patients. This meant there were very few in poorer regions.) At local level hospitals or groups of hospitals were run by hospital management committees appointed by the regional boards. The exceptions were the famous teaching hospitals that had their own Boards of Governors, rather like the trust hospitals of the 1990s. They received a grant direct from the central government.

- Medicines prescribed by the GP could be picked up from the chemist free. Eye tests and spectacles were free from the optician and visits to the dentist and fillings and other treatments were free too. This was to change.

Once established the National Health Service acquired popular support. It also attracted increasing Treasury concern. The economy was expanding, faster than in the pre-war period, but it was sucking in imports of raw materials needed by industry. The country was burdened by debt and in 1949 the first of many post-war sterling crises forced a devaluation of the pound. The Treasury demanded economies not only in housing but from the NHS. Bevan fought off these attacks but when the Korean War required an increase in the defence budget something had to give. Charges on spectacles and dentures were demanded and Bevan and the young Harold Wilson resigned from the government. A new phase in the Health Service's history was about to begin.

Education For All

Controversy

The reform of education was also controversial. It, too, had been bogged down in sectional interest group politics for the inter-war period. The main resistant protagonists here were not so much the professions as the churches. From the early nineteenth century on the religious issue had dominated education debate. As late as 1861 a major Royal Commission on Popular Education was arguing that the state had no role in education except facilitating the work of the churches in bringing education to the masses. For the most part 'the churches' meant the Church of England and more recently the Roman Catholic Church. To the growing Nonconformist population, especially in the new industrial towns, this was unacceptable. The radical and working-class element in the Liberal Party was to a large extent drawn from the Nonconformist chapels of the industrial towns. They were enraged at the idea that their children should be forced to go to Anglican schools and that their taxes should pay for such schools. Catholicism was gaining ground, too, and the Nonconformists were even more adamant that there should be no 'Rome on the rates'. Here was the stuff of conflict deeper than any party politics could achieve.

The 1918 Education Act had legislated for a higher school-leaving age as soon as it could be achieved. It was still 14 at the outbreak of the

Second World War. Some local authorities had expanded places in secondary grammar schools quite rapidly between the wars. About 12 per cent of the population went to such schools by 1939, but they were required to charge pupils fees and provide scholarships for those who could not pay but could pass an examination. Some local councils chose to provide a great many scholarships, others few. Some of the best grammar schools were private schools that the state had been subsidizing since 1902 (Glennerster and Wilson, 1970). More varied still was provision for the bulk of the population who went to elementary schools. Elementary education was defined as instruction in reading, writing and arithmetic. Many were still what were called 'all-age' schools. They typically consisted of schools taking children from 5 to 14 divided into two classes of about fifty children each; the 5- to 10-year-olds would be in one class and the rest in a senior class. Leicestershire had pioneered a system of separate junior and senior schools and the Haddow Committee had recommended the general adoption of such a scheme, but by 1939 only about a quarter of elementary schools had been reorganized in such a way.

The issues

Debate centred on:

- abolishing the all-age elementary schools;
- abolishing fees for secondary education;
- raising the school-leaving age to 16. The significance of this may not be evident to people a half century later but the reasoning was clear in Tawney's famous bible for many reformers, *Secondary Education for All*, published in 1924. If ordinary children were to have opportunities comparable to those enjoyed by children who went to secondary grammar schools, he argued, they must have the same length of school life. Grammar school children went to school until they were 16. Other children should be able to stay for the same period and have the same level of resources devoted to them. He did not argue they should go to the same school, it should be noted. At that point only one in ten children going to grammar schools stayed on beyond 16, so 16 would be the end of full-time schooling for nearly the whole population.

What largely stood in the way of such changes was not simply money but the fact that the churches, who still provided a large part of the nation's schools, would have to find the money to build and equip their schools up to the standards these changes would require. They could not afford to do so. Should the state provide them with the cash? Yes, said the Anglican and Catholic churches. No, said the Nonconformist churches and the left.

Thinking about reform

In the first years of the Second World War the Board of Education was mainly concerned with evacuating children from London and the south coast to get them away from air attack. They went with their teachers and were evacuated school by school. After the immediate danger faded pressure began to mount on the government to get on with thinking about the reform of education. A committee of officials came into existence in November 1940, several months before Beveridge's committee was to meet (Gosden, 1976). Unlike the social insurance committee, its education counterpart did not have an outside chairman. It was a purely internal group of senior civil servants. Indeed, it had no formal existence. It was a set of informal discussions between the five principle assistant secretaries responsible for the main areas of the Board's work. In the inter-war period the Board had drifted and lost direction under weak political leadership. Now it determined to pull its collective socks up. In an early memorandum the deputy secretary said,

> The prospect of educational reconstruction that lies ahead offers an admirable opportunity to re-establish the position of the Board as the body competent to lead and direct the educational system of the country. (Gosden, 1976: 240)

The civil servants struggled with the issues that had not been resolved in the twenties and thirties. The debates are fascinating to a modern reader who lived through the debates on education in the fifties and sixties about comprehensive education and the eleven-plus. Virtually all the issues were prefigured and hammered out in those private discussions in Bournemouth, where the Board had been evacuated. The main protagonists were the head of the secondary schools branch, responsible for the grammar schools, and the head of the elementary schools branch.

Separate systems?

Getting the churches on board was going to be the main task but the civil servants agreed that was a political problem. Where they differed was on the system they would try to sell the churches and the local authorities. The Deputy Secretary was very concerned at the early age at which scholarship exams were taking place and at the effect that preparation for these competitive exams was having on the junior schools' work. Very few of the children would after all win a scholarship but the exams were dominating the curriculum. He favoured exams at 13, which would coincide with the age at which pupils in the private sector took entrance to the 'public' schools. The head of the grammar schools branch felt this would denude these schools of their pupils and their capacity to get pupils up to standard by 16 and the school-leaving certificate exams.

The head of the elementary schools branch had much more fundamental concerns. He felt that if the senior elementary schools were merely to extend their age range to 16, this would not remove the divisions between the two systems, senior elementary and secondary grammar schools. This division would prove unsustainable in the more democratic post-war era. The war was emphasizing the essential unity of the nation. All secondary schools must have the same levels of resources and age range but even so, so long as some secondary schools remained places that prepared children for careers in the professions and other schools did not they would remain distinct and resented. He concluded,

> The obvious and perhaps the only satisfactory answer is the multilateral post-primary school attended by all children over the age of eleven. (Gosden, 1976: 247)

This view did not carry support. It was decided that the age of transfer had to be 11 and that selection for the academic schools would have to take place. However, the interchange almost perfectly reflected the debates that were to occupy the politicians and the education world for nearly thirty years after the eventual Act was passed, and that are not dead today.

Getting the churches on board

Very early on the civil servants agreed that the only way to break the log jam with the churches was to offer them enough money to build and staff the new secondary schools that would be needed for the children of their congregations. In return they would have to be more directly regulated by the local authorities. Carrying this off would be a major political task.

An outline of the group's proposals was included in a confidential discussion paper that was sent to the churches, the teachers' organizations and a few other educational bodies in 1941. The 'Green Paper', as it was called, could not have been launched in a way more different from the Beveridge Report a year later. The education press naturally knew about the document and complained at the inexplicable secrecy. More to the point it did not satisfy the churches. Fortunately, at this stage a master craftsman politician was drafted to take charge as the President of the Board of Education: R. A. Butler.

Butler was anxious to make progress and wrote to the Prime Minister seeking some reaction to his list of priorities. Mr Churchill was not impressed. He could do without a row with the churches and said, 'I certainly could not contemplate a new Education Bill' (Gosden, 1976: 269). Butler decided to ignore this and get on with the task his civil servants had begun, especially negotiations with the churches. In his autobiography he describes the interminable round of visits to bishops and archbishops, while his Labour deputy Chuter Ede saw the Nonconformists (Butler, 1971). Chuter Ede was a Nonconformist and an ex-teacher. Each made an almost perfect foil for the other.

The churchmen had something they badly wanted to achieve and would cost the government little money. In 1941 the Archbishops of Canterbury, York and Wales had issued a statement pressing the case for the Christian religion to be taught in all schools, state as well as church, for there to be religious instruction on the syllabus and for all schools to start the day with an act of worship. Over 240 MPs signed a motion supporting this. Butler, on the advice of Ede and the civil servants, tied his response to progress on the wider issues of reform: 'We will give you religion in the classroom if you support the reform of education.' In the end, part of the price that was paid for getting the churches to accept the plans for postwar education was acceptance of these measures: religious instruction and worship in state schools. They still puzzle many observers from abroad.

The details of the arrangements that Butler worked out to accommodate the churches need not detain us but anyone looking up the 1944 Education Act will be surprised to see, if not knowing this history, that the majority of the sections of the Act have to do with the relationship of various kinds of church schools with the state, the composition of their governing bodies, their rights to teach denominational education in their schools, the duty to teach religion in school and the means of agreeing what to teach! Essentially the state was to pay not only to run the denominational schools but to contribute heavily towards their capital costs. The churches would continue to be able to teach their version of Christianity.

The master craftsman had, however, done his job. Before the 1944 Education Act religion had dominated education politics. Afterwards it was never to do so again. This must be one of the most lasting beneficial legacies any politician has bestowed on his successors!

The 1944 Education Act

With this log jam broken the Act was able to make provision for:

- an end to all-age schools and a building programme to create separate primary and secondary schools in every local authority;
- the abolition of fees in secondary schools, indeed in any state school at all;
- a statutory school-leaving age of 16 to be reached in two stages, first 15 and then 16;
- the right of young workers between leaving school and age 18 to day release from work; they would go to colleges to be taught citizenship and extend their education;
- those going to university would be able to receive scholarships to support them;
- religious instruction would be a compulsory subject unless the parent held principled objections, and there was to be a daily act of worship.

The Act said nothing about the kind of secondary education there should be, about selection, or the eleven-plus as it came to be called (rather oddly since most children took these exams at age 10). Nor did it say much about technical education, though provision was made for further education colleges. With these exceptions it was to prove a remarkably enduring piece of craftsmanship. Its main administrative features underpinned the education system for the next forty-four years.

Labour's Policy

Two schools of thought

From its very origins the Labour Party had been divided about its approach to education, especially secondary education. At one extreme was the Fabian socialist Sydney Webb, who was an active member of the London County

Council Technical Education Board. 'Virtually single handed he created a scholarship ladder for the able child' (Barker, 1972: 16). The Webbs had no faith in the intelligence of the bulk of the population. For them society was hierarchical and the key to a socialist Utopia was to ensure that able people were diagnosed early and put in senior positions in the administrative machine. Secondary grammar schools and the competitive examination scholarship system did this admirably; 'the greatest capacity catching machine the world has ever seen', Sydney Webb called it (p. 17).

At the other extreme, left-wing socialists, trade unionists and the growing ranks of elementary school teachers in Labour's ranks felt suspicious or completely hostile to the idea of creaming off able working-class children, sending them to middle-class establishments and denying the bulk of the population the same access to good education. As the Labour Party gained electoral strength in urban centres and gained control of many education authorities in the 1920s and 1930s Labour councils busied themselves creating more secondary grammar schools, and scholarships to enable poor children to go to them. By the 1940s most local Labour members of these education committees actually saw the expansion of the grammar school as the way forward, especially in the north of England. They had often made their way through just such a route. This split was to emerge very clearly in the way the Labour government approached the implementation of the 1944 Act.

The realities of bricks and mortar and resource constraints were on the side of those wanting minimal change, but the political divide and the force of the civil service were to be decisive. The party's advisory committee on education had begun meeting in 1938 with a new younger generation of reformers; they were growing increasingly concerned about a system of education that was emerging with three separate streams, that for the academically able, that for the technically able, and that for the rest. It seemed to replicate the class structure and reinforce it and they looked for alternatives. The only solution that seemed available was something called a multilateral school, encompassing these three streams on a single school site.

The official report of the Spens Committee in 1939 had rejected such a solution and debate centred on whether such a model should be *one* of the models or *the* goal of future Labour policy (see Barker, 1972 for an account of the period).

In the end the committee became convinced it should be *the* long-term goal of Labour policy. The idea was still not what we today call a comprehensive school. That seeks to include all children in one school, not separate them into different buildings or streams from the outset. The multilateral idea was carried at the Labour Party Conference in 1942.

The eleven-plus

The 1944 Act, it will be recalled, said nothing about what kind of secondary schools would be created under it. Just before the general election the Ministry of Education, as it was now called (not a mere Board), issued a document advising local authorities how to plan their schools in the post-war period: *The Nation's Schools* (Ministry of Education, 1945). It suggested there should be a tripartite system with three types of school:

- grammar schools: essentially the secondary grammar schools that existed already but with access to all the places by competitive examination;
- secondary modern schools: essentially the old senior elementary schools. Just what kind of schools these would be became a matter for much discussion amongst educationalists;
- technical schools that would take students at 13 with technical abilities and probably headed for apprenticeships.

There was no encouragement for education authorities to introduce multilateral schools. Those in the Labour Party who had supported the new policy were furious. They saw the document as a move by the ministry to pre-empt the policy of a future Labour government. Many of those who spoke out were to become leading figures in the party in the 1950s and 1960s – Margaret Herbison and Alice Bacon, for example.

The two Ministers of Education whom Attlee appointed first, Ellen Wilkinson and then George Tomlinson, however, did not share the younger reformers' views. Labour councils were divided; some, like London, were strongly committed to multilateral or – later – comprehensive schools; others were opposed.

What followed was a story to be repeated in later decades. Labour Party Conference attacked the Labour government for not implementing party policy and the government mostly stuck to its position. Both Wilkinson and Tomlinson were in the Webb tradition. As Ellen Wilkinson told the Labour Party Conference in 1946, 'I was born into a working class home and I had to fight my own way through to university.' She believed children had different capacities and these were linked to distinctive types of school. (See Barker, 1972: 81–97 for a discussion of this period.)

The ministry advice was reissued with barely any move to the critics' position but in a circular issued later that year (Circular 144, 1947) it did entertain the possibility of a common or comprehensive school. It favoured a large six- or seven-form-entry school that would be big enough to generate more than one academic stream and a sixth form large enough to give pupils choice of advanced study. This was the route followed by the London County Council, Coventry and – on a much smaller scale – a few other authorities.

The Ministry of Education had to approve all plans for the future organization of schools in every part of the country. It rejected several of the plans for comprehensive schools of different kinds put forward at this point, much to the anger of the councils concerned. In 1950 the Labour Party came into open conflict with the government over the issue at Conference and in 1951 published a policy document in direct opposition to government policy calling for the reorganization of secondary schools everywhere on comprehensive lines, eliminating the eleven-plus examination. Tomlinson protested that this was simply not possible with the existing stock of buildings. This conflict of views was to dominate education debate for the next twenty-five years.

The Labour Party was reaching the end of a period in its ideological life history. The revisionists in the party were beginning to turn their attention to social policy as the central core of its concerns. The left wanted to extend public ownership still further. This contest was to consume the party for much of the next decade. The challenge to the leadership on comprehensive education in the late 1940s was the first sign of this shift of emphasis.

Again, whatever word we use to describe this series of events, 'consensus' is not the most appropriate.

Children

The evacuation of children from the big cities to live with families in more favoured parts of the country had alerted many to the extent of poverty in which many of these children normally lived. Social questions raised longer-term issues about the way services were organized before a wider audience than in the 1930s. This is well illustrated in the case of child care.

Children at risk or without parents could be placed in the hands of a local authority, as they can be today. What part of what local authority was actually responsible, however, was unclear. In 1945 two brothers were to be placed with foster parents. The family that was to have taken them had accepted another child and could not help. A child attendance officer took them to the country anyway, where the wife suggested he try two other local farms. He found a couple who had some space and seemed nice enough people – they were 'clean and tidy'. The boys were left and later murdered. The Government Report of the inquiry gives a graphic picture of a chaotic administrative process, lack of trained or even specialist staff and unclear accountability (Monckton Enquiry, 1945). A committee was set up to look at services for children at risk: the Curtis Committee. Out of it came a clear set of proposals (Curtis Report, 1946) that were legislated in the 1948 Children Act. A separate department of the county councils and of county borough councils had to be created specifically to look after the interests of such children. A chief officer, the Children's Officer, had to be appointed who would be held statutorily responsible for all such children in the authority's care. Working under this chief officer would be trained specialist children's social workers. Their training was organized under the auspices of the Home Office, who oversaw the whole service and inspected its standards, much as it did with the probation service created before the war.

A new social work profession had been created. It was to be predominantly female and the chief officer role often went to a woman too. Women had for the first time been given a route to the top in local government and in the Home Office.

Food Rationing

Much traditional social policy writing has concentrated on traditional services such as health, which have remained state services for the whole period since 1948. In fact, the most basic commodity of all, food, was also clearly part of social policy in the 1940s. During the war grain and a large part of the country's staple diet had to be imported in conditions of extreme danger through a blockade of German submarines. Food became a very scarce commodity. Left to itself there was no reason why the market should deliver enough for the whole population to live on. The few with enough money could simply have bought up the lot. The workers in the munitions factories and mines would not have been able to keep the war effort going. The government introduced a comprehensive system of food rationing very rapidly. Every member of the population was issued with a ration book. You had to register with a grocer, as you might today with a GP, and before you bought anything little bits of paper, 'coupons', had to be cut out of the book and given to the grocer; the number of coupons related to the amount of food bought. Money, except on the black market, was not the crucial means of exchange; coupons were. This ensured, not complete equality of food intake, but a minimum standard of nutrition that actually improved the health of the nation during this period. This system lasted for all the period of the post-war Labour government and was only dismantled in the 1950s.

What this history illustrates is that there is no such thing as an absolute boundary line between the market and socially provided goods and services. Where a commodity that is essential to existence becomes so scarce that its distribution by the market may destroy the society's norms and values and undermine law and order, the market will be replaced. Rationing and coupons may be unthinkable for today's trolley-pushing supermarket masses, but it was only common sense and fair play to their grandparents.

When the dire scarcity of food retreated, so did the support for rationing as an allocative mechanism. Much the same story was to unfold in the case of housing. Terrible scarcity after the war was met with a largely rationed system of provision but as housing came within the reach of more peoples' own pockets frustration with the rationing system grew.

Shelter

The first preoccupation that ministers had when the new Labour government came to office in July 1945 was to plan for the peace. Millions of service men and women would be returning to civilian life. Basic industries, including the construction industry, would have to be turned from war production to normal peaceful activities – swords beaten into ploughshares. The great fear was of mass unemployment. Second only to this was fear of homelessness. Not only were the troops returning and wanting to start families, the birth-rate was to rise sharply in the years 1945–8; but 200,000 houses had been destroyed, a further 250,000 badly damaged in the war and one in three damaged to some degree. The number of homes without lavatories or bathrooms seems unbelievable today. Nearly half of all households lacked the sole use of a bathroom. Two in every five households lacked a bath at all. Nearly a quarter had no exclusive use of a lavatory.

The number of men employed in the construction industry had fallen from a million before the war to a third of that level. Yet, unlike the other policy fields we have discussed, there was no blueprint, no committee of inquiry setting out a considered plan of action or way forward for housing, though there was for wider urban planning and land ownership (Donnison, 1960).

It is noticeable in this period that where the wartime government had tried systematically to consider the range of issues that concerned a service – social insurance, education or child care – some relatively coherent action did follow in the 1940s. The fact that no such coherent thought was given to the future of housing was to have lasting effects. The incoherent and contradictory set of policies that was to afflict housing in the post-war period can in no small part be traced to the lack of systematic thought at this time. The government in 1945, then, struggled to put together some ground plan for housing in the post-war period and to move very rapidly. It was estimated that for every family to have a home of its own would require three-quarters of a million new homes. The only agencies that Bevan, also responsible for housing, thought could respond were local authorities (Foot, 1975). Britain did not possess a national network of housing associations or organizations providing housing for the poor. The local authorities would have to be mobilized to do this vast job and paid to do so. For every house they built they would receive a subsidy for the next sixty years, to help pay off the loan they would have to raise to build the houses. This would keep their rents within the means of ordinary families. Government economic policy was keeping interest rates at 3 per cent, a figure that would seem barely possible to the home owner at the end of the century.

Building materials were in desperately short supply. Britain had little or no foreign currency reserves to pay for imports. The rest of the world was rebuilding too. Bricks and timber were in as short supply as food. The only way out, Bevan concluded, was to put the local authorities in charge of the housing drive. House-building was rationed. You had to have a building licence to start to build a house and four-fifths of all licences were given to local councils for their own building in 1948. Building materials themselves – wood of different kinds, bricks, steel – were rationed. Price controls were also in force. They only began to be relaxed in the period after 1949. Factories that were still on a war footing were given the task of making prefabricated industrialized houses – 'prefabs'. Permanent housing standards were improved, however. Standard three-bedroomed houses were enlarged from 750 to 900 square feet. The working class was to be given decent accommodation. It still shows. In later years these standards were to be reduced. Anyone who knows the history of council house subsidies and standards can walk round a council estate and date the buildings. The 1940s houses stand out as well-constructed and comfortable dwellings, in the main.

The overwhelming emphasis on building new units at all costs was to leave its legacy. Little or no thought was given to how to manage these houses once they were built, how to ensure good maintenance and oversight. This was to become worse in later periods (Power, 1988). Little attention was paid to building commercial and social facilities or creating communities. Building extra units was the prime goal.

Private renting

Most ordinary people were still tenants of private landlords, though. Desperate shortages would have led, in the short run, to landlords charging very high rents and though this might have been the logical market response it was not one that politicians could contemplate. Rent controls had been introduced at the beginning of the Second World War, as they had been in the middle of the First. Retaining them was politically popular, but it meant that the private sector saw no point in even trying to contribute to the post-war housing effort – there was no profit in it. Home ownership was severely constrained to devote most of the available resources to council housing. That also fitted in with the Labour ministers' preconceptions about the evils of private landlords and distrust of owner occupation and small builders. Given the acute nature of the housing crisis of the time, ministers' instincts and public sympathy were not far apart. This prevented the Labour government giving any fundamental thought to housing policy in the longer term. Did it make any sense to starve the private landlord sector of resources when it housed most ordinary people? What would replace it as it withered away? Was owner occupation to be confined to the wealthy and the professional classes? In the 1930s, with low interest rates and cheap houses, it had spread into the working class. Could it be stopped? Should it be stopped? The Labour Party blocked its ears to such ideas and the issues had to be fought out in the 1950s and 1960s and 1970s before the party finally reconciled itself to a plurality of home ownership as the ultimate goal in the 1980s.

Public pressure on the Labour government was not to revive the private sector but to build more council houses faster still. The first economic crisis of the post-war period began to make the Treasury fearful that the production of nearly 300,000 a year reached in 1948 could be sustained. The target was cut and actual house-building cut back to about 200,000. The Conservative Party in opposition was pressing for more and gained much support by committing itself to build, not 200,000 but 300,000 houses a year if it was re-elected.

Jobs for All

The fears of politicians and many economists that the war would be followed by mass unemployment never materialized. High demand was sustained by higher levels of public expenditure than there had been pre-war. Some wage restraint was exercised by the trade union movement which kept inflation down. Thus unemployment rarely rose above 3 per cent of the labour force. This compared to an average of 11 per cent in the pre-war period. Its scale was well within the definitions of full employment that Keynes and Beveridge had argued about during the war. Government was now seen to be responsible for the level of employment in the economy. It was no longer an act of God or the market. Of all the changes that took place in this period this was perhaps the most important for the lives of ordinary families.

Services for Citizens?

The first and overwhelming feeling that one is left with after reading the detailed accounts of this period is simple admiration for what was achieved. Here was a society and an economy reeling from the most devastating war in its history. Government had to organize and help rebuild a neglected economic infrastructure and housing stock. People had a standard of living and incomes of about a third of the level enjoyed by households in 2005. Yet the government was able to begin to house and educate and care for the health of all its citizens and accept that this was the state's prime duty. To say, in richer times, that education and health care for all cannot be afforded is simply absurd. It may well be that people no longer care or want to achieve these goals but the 1940s show that if there is a collective desire for them they can be achieved.

There are some less encouraging lessons to be drawn from the early history of these 'citizenship' services. First, it was generally perceived in the 1940s that the main barrier to equal access to health and education was one of price: the charges people had to pay to enter hospital or go to the doctor or to secondary school. This was not surprising when these barriers existed and were resented. However, merely to remove them did not mean that all sections of the community would use the services or benefit from them to the same extent. In the next decade this realization began to dawn on academic analysts and on politicians. Why this was so and what, if anything, they could do about it raised practical and philosophical issues that moved to the centre of debate in the 1960s.

Second, what universal free health care and free secondary and university education had done was very largely to benefit those just above the cut-off point at which the old systems of welfare had ceased to operate (Abel-Smith, 1958).

Third, these new services had to be paid for. The flat rate insurance contributions and the high taxes on tobacco and drink were not progressive means of taxation. The war had been financed, in part, by a brilliant new mechanism for extracting income tax from workers – Pay As You Earn (PAYE). It extended the state's capacity to tax incomes without a huge paper trail. Before the war four million people paid income tax. By 1947/8 it was fourteen and a half million. The Treasury began to worry that tax levels were deterring work and enterprise (Daunton, 2002).

Finally, all these services were creatures of their age, the age of belief in the virtues of central planning and monopoly provision. Markets and competition stank of the failures of the 1930s to most Labour politicians. The social services they created were in the image of the other economic institutions of the time: British Rail, the Gas Board. This made it possible to allocate resources more fairly to different parts of the country, to equalize opportunities of access. But it also built in a corrosive element that was to eat away at their effectiveness and popularity over the much longer term. The Health Service was the prime example. It was a monopoly, and its employees, especially the medical profession, were given monopoly power with little democratic accountability, in return for agreeing to join the service. What Durbin (1949) had predicted for the nationalized industries was to hold for the social services. They would gradually come to fall into the hands of the providers and not the consumers.

Questions to Answer

1 Why do you think the NHS has become an accepted and popular institution despite the controversy surrounding its creation?
2 What do you see as the best and worst features of the 1944 Education Act and its legacy?
3 Do all citizens have a right to health care, knowledge, food, shelter and work? Is this practical? What duties does this imply? If it applies to British citizens does it not apply to citizens of the world?

4

The New Conservatism and Social Policy, 1951–64

It is commonly believed that, after 1945, the Conservative Party came to terms with the Welfare State and between 1945 and 1975 there was a broad consensus between the parties on social policy. This is the view expressed in a companion volume to this, *Consensus Politics from Attlee to Thatcher* (Kavanagh and Morris, 1989). It is the view expressed in Marwick's standard Penguin social history of the period (Marwick, 1990). It is the basis of Morgan's history of the period (Morgan, 1990: Ch. 4) and follows on from Addison's argument in *The Road to 1945* (1975). Mrs Thatcher's own account of her decisive leadership reinforces the view. She claims she changed the spineless post-war consensus (Thatcher, 1993).

Neither view is sustainable in the light of the most recent work on the archives (Ramsden, 1980; Harris, 1986; Jones, 1992; Jones and Kandiah, 1996; Bridgen and Lowe, 1998; Whiteside, 1996; Lowe, 1999; Pimlott, 1989; Webster, 1990). We have already seen evidence in the last two chapters that there was both a wide degree of public support for many of the post-war measures and a severe limit to that support on particular issues and from particular groups like the medical profession.

The Conservative Party never did accept the universalist principles that were key to much of the 1940s legislation and between 1947 and 1950 it did manage to forge a new social policy agenda based on principles different from those of the 1945 Labour government. It is true that political reality tempered its advocacy in the succeeding decades, but a distinctive set of ideas about targeting benefits and encouraging home ownership, for example, can be traced through the policies of all post-war Conservative governments. These ideas have their origins in the important work done by the party in opposition in the 1940s.

Back to the Drawing Board

Contested ideals

The Conservative Party has always embodied within it very different strands of thought about the appropriate role for the state on social issues. There had always been those who saw the state as an organic entity, more than the sum of its individual subjects. Social policy became the handmaiden to that vision. The state should foster a sense of national unity, of belonging and allegiance; it should support traditional forms of family life and the established Christian religion.

Education policy encapsulates this last view most clearly. We have already seen it reflected in the discussions on the 1944 Education Act. It is not surprising that this organic view of the state should have been at its strongest in Tory policy during the Second World War. Butler, who was responsible for Conservative Party home policy in this period, was initially attracted to this position. He called on Karl Mannheim, an Austrian refugee at the LSE, and others, to work on Conservative reconstruction policy (Harris, 1986). Reading the reports of their work on education, even at this distance, sends a certain shudder down the spine.

They envisaged a powerful moral order that the state, through its educational institutions, would foster. The Christian religion would be firmly at the centre of school activity. This would continue into early adult life as young workers were given compulsory day release, not to train in vocational skills, but to acquire proper attitudes to citizenship. The echoes of the Hitler Youth Movement are clear. In addition, it was argued, the public schools should be taken over by the Board of Education to reduce the class divisions in society (Harris, 1986).

When these documents were circulated more widely on a confidential basis within the party, the proposals were dismissed, with some contempt, by the rank and file (Harris, 1986: 245). Nevertheless, the view that the state education system was there to instil a proper respect for authority and the British way of life is a thread that can be traced from the discussions on the 1944 Education Act to Conservative education policies of the 1990s and in ministers' views on the content of the National Curriculum. It is also reflected in the family values theme that re-emerges in the 1980s and 1990s. In contrast to this strand of Conservative thought is the very opposite: liberal and deeply suspicious of any organic concept of the state. The state is seen as a regulator of individual action that may harm others and as the rule-maker within which free markets can work. The outstanding exponent was Professor Hayek, another Austrian *émigré* at the LSE (Hayek, 1944). He was, later, to become Mrs Thatcher's philosophical mentor, but he was influential at the end of the war too.

Less radical and more pragmatically concerned with the nuts and bolts of policy were a group of young Conservative MPs – the Tory Reform Group – who saw a role for social policy, but not the extensive one that the Mannheim group did. Then there were the foot soldiers, Conservative backbenchers and rank and file, who were deeply suspicious of the direction Beveridge was dragging the country.

Forging a new policy framework

This fundamental division of ideas about social policy, and how to react to the Beveridge bandwagon, was only made worse by the fact that the Conservative leadership was preoccupied with the war effort in the early 1940s. The Conservative Research Department did not operate during the Second World War. Little coherent work came out of the study groups Butler set up to chart a post-war Conservative approach to social policy (Jones, 1992). The party's study group on the Beveridge Report was critical: it said that it was excessively costly and did not concentrate spending on the really poor. 'The Conservatives advising Churchill objected to the Beveridge Plan on financial, moral and distributive grounds' (Jones, 1992: 79).

Yet nothing coherent could be set against Beveridge and to oppose his report in 1945 would have been political suicide. The consequence was that the Conservatives lost the 1945 social policy debate as well as the election.

For a period after the Second World War there was a policy vacuum that tended to be filled by backbenchers taking hostile stands against Labour government policy, notably on the health service. Butler and those in Conservative Central Office were deeply worried by this as they thought it would be electorally disastrous. Moreover, there was division within the Party. The opponents of Beveridge's welfare state were increasingly challenged by a group of young new MPs – the One Nation Group. They explicitly accepted the basic Beveridge social security scheme but they were very critical of Labour's housing and health policy (One Nation Group, 1950; Gilmour and Garnett, 1998). Several were to become ministers in later governments – Ian Macleod, Angus Maude and Enoch Powell, and one would become Prime Minister – Edward Heath. The need for a worked-out social policy position was clear.

What emerged from this rethinking was not, however, a meek acceptance of the Welfare State as it was being created by Bevan and Griffiths. The cost, the way it was being financed, and the form it was taking were all offensive to the liberal view of the state that became the basis of Conservative philosophy. There should be some welfare provision, to be sure, but it should have a Conservative face.

Housing   The first opportunity to make a distinctive stand came with housing policy. Labour was insisting, as we saw, on local councils doing nearly all the building. Despite the rapid expansion in house-building that had taken place there was enormous impatience and popular desire to go faster. Small builders urged that they could do better if given their head. Freeing them to build, including for owner occupation, became the first distinctive challenge to the Labour government's social policy. The party was very worried that coming out firmly in favour of owner occupation would restrict its appeal as overly middle class. It decided it would favour owner occupation but cautiously. Above all it would seek to trump Labour by going for a higher house-building target. Henry Brooke was cautious about giving a number but a policy committee and then Conservative Party Conference bounced the party into committing itself to a target of 300,000 houses a year. This was the pre-war rate of house-building, but it was now unlikely to be reached without reducing the higher standards that had been set for building after the war and Conservative Central Office knew that (Jones, 1992).

A clearly distinct Conservative housing policy was hammered out that gave a much larger role to the private sector, to private landlords and to owner occupation. It remained the basis of Conservative policy through to Mrs Thatcher's period and beyond. It increasingly came into its own as more families became able to afford to buy their own homes. The party carefully tended its policy presentation to meet the needs of electoral convenience, but to suggest that it had no distinctive policy is simply incorrect. The same is true of Social Security.

Social security   From the start the Conservative Party was unhappy with the Beveridge scheme and its promise of universal flat rate pensions that were not means tested. The work that went on within Central Office was based on a fundamentally different philosophy. Social services were becoming a way to redistribute wealth and not merely a means to relieve destitution and misfortune, it was argued. To relieve poverty was legitimate. To go further was not.

When they emerged as MPs from their backroom jobs in Central Office Macleod and Powell published a pamphlet that summed up the principles that underpinned their and the party's thinking (Macleod and Powell, 1952). High taxes meant disincentives to work while the expansion of social services had produced a decline in individual initiative and family responsibility. Social policy had moved too far from the insurance principle. The Beveridge scheme involved too great a subsidy from the taxpayer and the NHS was based on large expenditure from general taxation. The NHS should return to being financed on an insurance basis. In addition, policy had moved from charging as a basis for finance. Benefits were given regardless of need. This, they argued, was a principle that should have no place in social policy.

> The question which therefore poses itself is not should a means test be applied to a social service, but why should any service be provided without a test of need. (Macleod and Powell, 1952: 5)

Conservatives, throughout the post-war period, would return to this question.

Education   In education, too, there was a distinctive line. As we saw, the Labour Party was moving steadily to a position that favoured comprehensive schools and the abolition of the eleven-plus; the Conservative Party moved firmly to support the principle of grammar school education. The 1951 Conservative Manifesto, *Britain Strong and Free*, said, 'We must safeguard the independence, the high standards and the traditions of the grammar schools.'

Health   Health was more difficult. The NHS was rapidly proving to be *the* real success of the Attlee government. The party could not attack it outright but again it was deeply unhappy with the Bevan construction. It had favoured the retention of the voluntary hospitals. It wanted to see the private sector encouraged. It considered policies to charge for services, ways of encouraging the private sector, going back to an insurance basis. It wanted to cut grants to the regional hospital boards, which were considered extravagant, and to charge for board and lodging in hospitals (Jones, 1992). Anyone familiar with the proposals trawled in 1988 for Mrs Thatcher's review of the NHS will find a very similar agenda.

The Conservative vision

The Conservative Party in 1951 therefore came to power with a distinctively Conservative liberal agenda on social policy. It had not accepted the 1945 Labour institutions or indeed those of the Second World War 'consensus'. It had its own coherent, and arguably far-sighted, set of policies. It was to prove difficult to implement them, however. The social and economic climate were not to prove fully compatible with these ideas for another thirty years. (For a guide to the official documents of the period of Conservative governments 1951–64 see Bridgen and Lowe, 1998).

Trying to Contain the Welfare State

The new Conservative government, under Churchill, came to power in 1951, when the Labour government had effectively run out of steam and was deeply divided about social expenditure. The new government was both fortunate and successful in many ways in its early years (Seldon, 1981). After the economic impact of the Korean War had receded, world trade prices worked in Britain's favour. The government could dismantle the irksome restrictions and rationing that were a hangover of the war period. Income tax reductions were made in the 1952, 1953 and 1954 Budgets in line with the philosophy the party had worked on in opposition. That required a firm grip on public expenditure despite the growing economy.

Containing the Welfare State

Butler, the new Chancellor, immediately considered ways of reducing the scale of public expenditure on social policy. The previous Labour government had begun the process. It was that which had caused the resignations of Bevan and Wilson when health service charges were imposed. More radical ways of cutting the budget were considered by the new government: the reintroduction of fees in secondary schools, a reduction in the school-leaving age, changing the school meals service and the way local education authorities were financed, health service charges. At this stage all the more fundamental changes were rejected. The government only had a small majority. Even so, it made some unpopular cuts.

A circular was issued in December 1951 telling local education authorities they must reduce their estimated education spending for the coming year by 5 per cent, concentrating in particular on school transport, playgrounds and the youth service (Circular 242). At that time there was still a specific education grant. Central government met a share of local councils' education budgets that it approved. The new Conservative government was saying: we shall not match your spending unless you reduce it in given ways. In February 1952 councils were told to reduce their school-building programmes substantially. No proposals would be approved that were designed to relieve overcrowding, replace unsatisfactory schools or enable the old all-age schools to be reorganized (Circular 245). These priorities were to remain in force for many years. 'Roofs over heads' to accommodate the new births of the post-war years dominated the Ministry of Education's concerns. The result of this circular was to reduce the value of school building projects approved from £53 million in 1951 to £39 million in 1952.

The government was pledged to increase the house-building rate to 300,000 houses a year. There was no prospect that this could be achieved by the private sector in the short run. This meant *more* public expenditure on council houses. Macmillan fought effectively to sustain that commitment. The effect was to reduce the expenditure on each house. Very early on the government took steps to get local authorities to reduce the standard of the houses they were building. The Labour government had already set a review in train. Macmillan made a virtue of the changes. There was to be a new 'people's house', good, cheap and plentiful. In fact, the controls and the design limits were very tight and precise. The overall floor space for a three-bedroomed house was to be 847 square feet, the staircase was to come off the living room, there was to be no separate access from hall to kitchen, no external storage (Circular 70/51). Approvals for three-bedroomed houses were also reduced sharply. Under the previous government four-fifths of all council houses built had three or more bedrooms. That figure was reduced over the 1950s to two-fifths.

In June 1952 the first prescription charge was imposed. The Labour government had created the legislative power to do so but had held back from implementing the change. It was a charge of one shilling (5p) on each prescription form. Other charges followed – on false teeth and spectacles. They were driven by economic considerations, not health priorities (Daunton, 2002).

Hospital capital expenditure was kept within tight limits despite growing concern in the Ministry of Health which pointed out that the level of new building had been higher in the days before the war when the voluntary hospitals and local authorities had been doing all the building. The Treasury returned to its demand that health service 'manpower' be reduced. In December a freeze was placed on administrative and clerical staffing numbers. The Treasury demanded a reduction of 5 per cent in non-medical and nursing staff. In December 1952 a circular was issued freezing establishments. Additions had to be approved by the administrative layer above. The aim was a reduction in staffing of 5 per cent in a year for certain categories of staff. Since senior medical staff establishments were held at regional level this meant ministerial approval for any increase (Webster, 1988: 302). The circular did not succeed in reducing staffing levels but it did secure a virtual freeze in numbers employed. No really fundamental reduction in the cost of the Welfare State had come out of these measures nor the reviews of spending that were initiated in this period. However, two committees were set up to consider the longer-term financing of pensions and the National Health Service (see below).

All in all, Butler, with the help of an able Treasury civil servant, Sir Richard (Otto) Clarke, was able to keep a fairly tight grip on social service expenditure during this period. From 1951 to 1956, the share of the GDP going on social security, health and education barely increased and was held at just over 11 per cent. Part of the reason for this success lay in the substantial improvement that took place in the world economy and in Britain's place within it. The economy enjoyed one of its temporary post-war booms and this put off the need for more fundamental ways of cutting public expenditure. But not for long.

Stop–go begins

In 1955 the first of what was to become a recurrent cycle of events began. The economy began to overheat, to suck in more imports than exports were earning. The bank rate was raised first to 3.5 per cent and then to 4.5 per cent. After the election in May 1955 other measures followed, including a credit squeeze on the banks, and the capital programmes of local authorities were cut. With growth slowing down it was going to be more difficult to contain spending and prevent a rise in taxes. The Treasury needed to have another go at getting the government to think radically about social spending.

Immediately after the election the Treasury put a paper to Cabinet that reviewed the spending prospects for social services over the next five years. The sharply rising school population, the result of the post-war bulge in the birth-rate, was in its more expensive secondary phase. Pensioners would begin to earn rights to a pension under the post-war scheme. All this was coming on top of a weak economic position. The share of the GNP going on social policy would rise. The Cabinet was sufficiently worried to appoint a special Social Services Committee, chaired by Butler, to consider what to do.

Lowe gives a fascinating account of the work of this committee and the way in which the spending departments essentially defeated the Treasury and hence, in the longer run, provoked the resignation of the Chancellor of the Exchequer and a new way of controlling public expenditure.

> To the social policy historian, the contrast between this committee and both the Geddes Axe and the May Report of the inter-war period is irresistible. Neither Geddes nor May in the long term staunched the relentless . . . increase in social expenditure; but they did consolidate a widespread demand for retrenchment and enable the Treasury to make significant short term cuts . . . [however this] Committee identified no acceptable economies and social expenditure continued to rise. It was, indeed, so counter-productive that Treasury officials had to seek its early demise for fear that it would rebound against them. (Lowe, 1989: 507)

The spending departments showed themselves very well briefed about the fundamental case the Treasury was making, but above all were able to gain support from the majority of those on the committee, who were spending ministers. The Treasury learned its lesson and later pressed for a fundamental change to the way public spending was controlled, to reduce the power of the natural majority spending ministers possessed in Cabinet (Heclo and Wildavsky, 1981). On this occasion the spending ministers were able to see off proposals to remove the dental service and ophthalmology from the NHS, to raise the entry age to school to 6 and reduce the leaving age to 14, and other measures.

The spending departments began to counter-attack, suggesting that areas of social spending were advantageous economically and had been neglected for too long. The publication of the Guillebaud Committee Report arguing this in relation to health was a help (see below). The Treasury wound up the committee. It is wrong to suggest that the spending departments' victory was complete, however.

Various measures were taken to reduce net government expenditure, net after discounting the income from charges. The doubling of the prescription charge was rejected but the shilling (5p) originally applied to each prescription form now applied to each item on it. Outside the work of this committee, housing subsidies to local councils were substantially reduced. Subsidies on bread and milk were abolished and local government finance was reformed.

Ever since the 1920s the Treasury had objected to the way local authorities were financed, especially the way local education was paid for (Glennerster, 1997). Local councils received a matching grant for this purpose; a percentage grant, it was called. The local authorities proposed to spend so much and, if the ministry approved, the government paid out an equivalent amount. This was a very good way to encourage an expanding education service but did not encourage economy. The Treasury had returned to its old objections several times in the early 1950s and this time got its way. The government agreed to move to a new system of local government finance under which local councils would get a block grant based on their population and other factors, which would subsidize all their activities. Service by service percentage grants would go (Local Government Finance Act, 1958). That principle remains the basis of local funding to the present day. The education world, in particular, was furious. It lost. But, in fact, such was the pressure to spend more on education, that this change in the grant structure did not halt the rise in education spending.

Lowe argues that the Social Services Committee not only failed to achieve major cuts or changes in social policy but that it sharpened the capacity of the spending departments to resist the pressure for more spending cuts, which the new Chancellor Peter Thorneycroft demanded in 1957, in the wake of yet another economic crisis. It was this failure and defeat in Cabinet that lead Thorneycroft and the rest of his Treasury team to resign in January 1958. That, in its turn, along with a critical report from the House of Commons Select Committee on Estimates (HC 294, 1958), led to the appointment of the Plowden Committee. This was, in effect, a Treasury committee with an outside chairman. It was appointed to look at the way public expenditure was being controlled. It was that committee's report (Cmnd 1432, 1961) which recommended setting up the annual reviews of public spending, the Public Expenditure Survey, that has been with us, in one form or another, ever since (Lowe, 1997a, b). Blair's government was to make them bi-annual, and finally tri-annual.

The hard politics of the time were, however, that the Prime Minister, Harold Macmillan, was not prepared to support major attacks on the Welfare State or cuts that would be damaging electorally. Cutting taxes as a central plank of Conservative policy was abandoned. The Labour Party was beginning to take the initiative on the poverty of old people. The launch by the Russians of the first space vehicle, the Sputnik, had really worried politicians in the West. It suggested that the West was lagging behind the Russians scientifically. In the USA and in the UK and elsewhere, science budgets and higher education began to be looked on more favourably. Eccles, at the Ministry of Education, reaped the reward and was a powerful figure who gave that ministry its expansionist head. He was backed by the demographics of the period. The baby boom of the post-war years was going through the schools at this point. Indeed, the official papers at the time show that demography was a key factor that helped change attitudes to public spending within government. It had been assumed that the population would remain fairly stable after the immediate post-war boom. The sustained rise in births was seen to have important implications not only for education but also for housing (O'Hara, 2004).

As Macmillan's premiership continued so the pace of public spending grew. In the race to recover credibility in the run-up to the 1964 general election the budget was increased faster still, much as it was in the early 1990s. If there was a period of consensus or at least electoral competition on the basis of social spending, this was it.

Inflation and Full Employment – an Early Warning

The overheating of the economy in 1955 and the 'bonfire of controls' in the 1950s brought the first danger signal, a cloud on the horizon that was to become the major concern of the 1970s. Robert Hall, Economic Adviser to the government from 1947 until 1961, had become increasingly concerned with the growing wage pressures that were resulting from full employment (Jones, 1994). He saw that unless some way could be found to contain such pressure full employment would not be sustainable. That was the basis of the brief wage restraint policy agreed with the trade unions and the Labour government in 1948 and 1949. A White Paper on the subject was in train before the Labour government left office but the incoming Conservative government preferred to rely on monetary policy alone to tackle inflation.

By 1955 all the signs of economic overheating, which were to become so familiar, were evident. The Treasury persuaded ministers to produce a warning shot. The result was a White Paper entitled *The Economic Implications of Full Employment* (Cmd 9725, 1956). To emphasize its importance it was presented to Parliament by the Prime Minister, not the Chancellor. It pointed out that prices had increased by 50 per cent since the war. Though some of the rise had been the result of higher import prices and removing subsidies, most was internally generated.

> there has been in this country – to a greater extent than in many other countries – a continuing tendency for prices to rise as incomes increase faster than output. (para. 11)

In an extremely lucid and non-technical way the White Paper put the stark choice: if the country wanted to maintain the commitment to full employment in the 1944 White Paper it would have to find some way of stopping this inflationary process. To sustain full employment meant sustaining a strong demand for labour and goods.

> If the prosperous economic conditions necessary to maintain full employment are exploited by trade unions and business men, price stability and full employment become incompatible. (para. 26)

In the absence of such restraint the goal of full employment would have to be relaxed. It was a warning that was not heeded. The White Paper was so much exhortation and Hall considered it a useless and poorly timed exercise not accompanied by action (Jones, 1994: 146). But it had put its finger on the fundamental problem: full employment, without some form of pay restraint, would in the end fail. (See Cairncross, 1995 for an account of the experiments with pay restraint and economic planning in the 1960s.)

Social Services: Wasted Years?

In terms of individual social services the record of the period 1951 to 1964 was mixed. The Labour Party was to accuse the government of 'thirteen wasted years'. In retrospect, this is not an entirely fair judgement. Indeed, it now looks like a period of enviable organizational tranquillity. It is true that policy did not develop greatly in any field except housing, where some very important changes took place.

Housing success and failure

300,000 houses a year   The government began with a promise to raise house building to the 300,000 a year target. Macmillan and his junior minister, Ernest Marples later of Transport Ministry fame, approached the task with great enthusiasm, fighting off the Chancellor's attempt to freeze the house-building total (Jones, 1992 and Seldon, 1981). We have already seen that to achieve the target the size and standards of houses were reduced and few if any social amenities accompanied this building. The whole thing was approached like a wartime campaign driven from the centre, using local authorities to do the building. In January 1954 the total was reached a year ahead of target. It was a great electoral success, rather akin to the Conservatives' sale of council houses in the 1980s.

After the boost in council building had delivered the target the government turned to its promised relaxation in controls on private building. Building licences still existed but instead of private builders getting only a quarter of the total they were to get half in England and Wales, less in Scotland. There were plans to encourage the sale of council houses but they were dropped and not taken up again until 1960.

The clearest break with the policies of the 1945–50 period came with the publication of the White Paper on the future of housing policy and its subsequent implementation over the next four years (Ministry of Housing and Local Government, 1953). A Memorandum from Lord Woolton the Party Chairman in 1952 had complained that the government was relying too much on public-sector housing to reach its objectives. That was inconsistent with Conservative principles (Bridgen and Lowe, 1998). The White Paper argued that local authorities' true role, once the shortages caused by the war were over, should be a residual one. They should clear and replace unfit or slum property. Private landlords should be the normal suppliers of rented property and hence rents would have to rise. Controlled rents would have to be revised, council rents raised and a free market introduced in stages.

The first step in that direction was taken in the Repairs and Rents Act of 1954, which enabled landlords to charge more rent if they kept their houses in good repair and had recently spent a given sum on repairs. This only tested the water, however, and after the 1955 election was safely won the government embarked on what it knew would be probably its most unpopular social policy: phasing out rent control altogether. It went hand in hand with the phasing out of the general subsidy to local councils to build accommodation to rent. Private landlords would have no reason to continue in the market if local councils were renting property at subsidized rents.

Rent Act 1957 This was to be the most contentious and bitterly fought legislation of the period. The government's logic was sound. If a free market in housing was desirable and its long-term aim, private landlords had to be able to charge rents that would give them an adequate return. Rents had been controlled at the outbreak of war and not increased again. Landlords had to be able to charge a free market rent. There had to be a free contract between buyer and seller. Landlords should have the right to let to whom they wished for what period they wished, otherwise they would be afraid to put their property on the market for fear that the tenant would become a permanent fixture. That was precisely the position many landlords were in. The number of privately rented properties was already declining and this would continue unless controls were ended. The main provisions of the Act were:

- Property valued at over £30 rateable value (£40 in London) was decontrolled; landlords could charge what they could get.
- All new tenancies would also be decontrolled, i.e. when someone moved.
- Where tenants' rent remained controlled it would still rise to twice the then rateable value. Rates had been revalued in 1956.
- The minister was given power to decontrol property at any time with the consent of Parliament.

The bill and the eventual Act provoked an enormous outcry. At this time there were about 6 million private landlord dwellings, mostly let to poor people. Controlled rents rose in London from 14*s*. (70p) a week to 22*s*. 4*d*. between 1957 and 1959. Outside London they rose from 9*s*. 4*d*. to 13*s*. 1*d*. (Cmnd 1246, 1960). This was not people's only or main criticism. The potential loss of security of tenure was the most worrying for many. That threat was all the greater because of the reserve power the government had taken to decontrol more property without further legislation.

So great was the outcry and the perceived electoral effect that the government backed down on two occasions. The full effects of decontrol above the valuation limits was delayed for three years by the Landlord and

Tenant (Temporary Provisions) Act 1958. Eviction powers were weakened. Then in their 1959 election manifesto the Conservative Party promised not to use the powers to decontrol further in the next Parliament.

In many parts of the country without a grave housing shortage the issue subsided somewhat. But in London, especially, it would not go away. There had been a flaw in the legislation. Landlords could charge much higher rents for decontrolled property in an area like London. Property became decontrolled when a tenant, or tenant family, moved. If they could be induced to move the owner would reap a large capital gain as the property rose in value to reflect its new rental income. There was a very substantial incentive for landlords to get rid of old tenants. The most unscrupulous did so by terrorizing their tenants. The most notable cases were in London. For some time this aroused little press attention. Then towards the end of the period when Macmillan was Prime Minister a scandal broke involving the Minister of War and a call-girl racket, which also implicated the most notorious of the landlord evictors, Rachman. He was to introduce a new word into the English language, 'Rachmanism'. This finally did attract press attention. A committee of inquiry – the Milner Holland Enquiry – was appointed to investigate and was sitting when the 1964 election took place. (For a discussion of the racial conflicts in the Notting Hill area which were an important and neglected part of this story see Davis, 2001.)

Decontrol: did it work?   One way to see rent policy in this period is a government courageously applying a painful but necessary cure. There is a good deal of truth in this view. If a private rented market was necessary there had to be some break with unprofitable rents that were at pre-war levels. The Labour Party rejected the need for private landlords and argued for the almost complete take-over of all rented property by local councils. In retrospect one can see how disastrous that monopoly landlordism would have been. The idea of expanding housing associations as alternative social landlords does not seem to have been seriously discussed. The Conservative Party favoured a completely free housing market, the Labour Party a nationalized or 'municipalized' one. Little consensus here!

The difficulty was that the Rent Act did not succeed in reviving the private landlord and it failed politically. In 1953 there had been nearly 6 million private landlord dwellings in England and Wales. By 1961 the figure was 4.5 million and by 1971 the figure was 3.3 million.

There were several difficulties with the government's logic, not least that it did not go far enough. The private landlord was not only disadvantaged because of rent control, he was also disadvantaged by the tax laws compared to other forms of investment (Nevitt, 1966). This was to be made worse during this period. Owner occupiers had originally been fairly unimportant in tax affairs. They were treated as if they were landlords of their own property and hence drawing a rent on it. They benefited by not paying rent to a landlord. Low as the tax was, owner occupiers thought the whole thing crazy.

In 1963 the Chancellor gave in. The tax on owner occupiers was abolished but they continued to get tax relief on the money they borrowed. When tax relief on other kinds of interest payments was abolished they continued to get tax relief on their mortgages. As a party seeking to encourage owner occupation all this made sense. As a party in favour of encouraging the private landlord it did not. The capital gains to be made by a landlord selling his property to an owner occupier became irresistible. In the 1950s and 1960s alone, something like 2 million private landlord properties were sold to owner occupiers (Holmans, 1987).

The government also miscalculated the degree of resistance there would be to the loss of security of tenure, an ancient right in British law. It also made eviction attractive in areas of housing shortage such as London. Thus, in the run-up to the 1964 election, rent policy, and especially security of tenure, were still lively political issues.

Health service reform 1950s style

The Conservative government approached the service with great circumspection. It had acquired great popularity. (For an account of the period see Webster, 1988; 1996 and Rivett, 1998). Crookshank, the new minister, was however not particularly interested in the Health Service. He was more concerned with broad economic matters. In the autumn came the normal discussions on next year's estimates and Butler wanted to hold the line on more public expenditure. As we have already seen, a series of proposals were discussed between officials and the Treasury: imposing a charge of a shilling (5p) on each prescription, a boarding charge for being in hospital, a £1 charge for dental treatment and the complete abolition of the ophthalmic service. The ministry officials managed to get the Treasury to drop the boarding charge but the rest went to Cabinet. The proposals were too much for them, with the exception of prescription charges, where the Labour Party was on weak ground having approved them in principle before it left office. However, backbench Conservatives were furious that a tougher and more strategic approach was not being taken against health service spending.

The revenue from the charges was soon to be eaten up. The Labour government had agreed to the external adjudication of the doctors' claim for a pay increase and Judge Danckwert's award came after the Conservatives had been elected. It essentially accepted the BMA case and cost nearly £10 million. Coming on top of the prescription charges this was not a good start for the Conservative government.

Crookshank left, not missed as a minister, and Iain Macleod, the backroom boy of the 1940s, and goad from the backbenches in his first year as an MP, took over as Minister of Health in 1952. He presided over what Webster has called 'a new stability' (1988: 200), which lasted far beyond his period in office. Webster puts this down to Macleod's 'One Nation' views. Jones (1992) has another emphasis. She argues that Macleod did want change – his work in opposition suggested that – but he was cautious because he knew he was dealing with political dynamite. The Conservative backbenchers were calling for a Royal Commission on the NHS. His battle with the Chancellor over more cuts in the hospital building programme, which he lost, together with the cost of the Danckwert award probably convinced him that something had to be done about the finance of the Health Service.

The Treasury pressed for an independent inquiry into the cost of the NHS. Macleod wanted it to cover the whole of social service spending. Butler resisted, arguing that this would look as if the Conservatives were attacking the whole Welfare State. The outcome was the Guillebaud Committee, an independent inquiry into the cost and finance of the NHS. Guillebaud was a Cambridge economist. He was chosen, over safer political nominees, because he could be claimed to be genuinely impartial. So it turned out.

The decision to appoint the committee proved a strategic blunder for those who wanted radical change in the NHS. (Perhaps this is why Mrs Thatcher firmly rejected such an independent committee in 1987.) The Ministry of Health warned at the outset that it might backfire: 'Treasury are here playing with fire and are liable to get very badly burned' (Ministry internal note quoted by Webster, 1988: 204). Indeed, the ministry was aware that needs were outrunning the supply of services and that the service was very tightly resourced compared with 1948 or even the pre-war years. Impartial observers would be convinced of this.

The committee asked the National Institute for Economic and Social Research to undertake the technical work for it. It was very dependent on the institute's findings for its own view of the economic problem.

This investigation was undertaken by Brian Abel-Smith, a young Cambridge economist, using Professor R. M. Titmuss as a consultant. Their contact with the Guillebaud Committee was minimal, but their memorandum first read by Guillebaud in January 1955, was fundamental to setting the tone of the Guillebaud Report, and in its separately published form the elegant work of Abel-Smith and Titmuss overshadowed the pedestrian Report, and achieved stature as a minor classic of modern social analysis. (Webster, 1988: 207)

What Abel-Smith and Titmuss showed was that the cost of the NHS to public funds as a percentage of the GNP had *fallen* since its inception in 1948 (from 3.75 per cent to 3.25 per cent). Capital expenditure on new and improved hospitals had fared worst. It had been *three times as high* in the pre-war period before the NHS existed. Capital spending had declined compared to current spending and even to keep up with depreciation and maintain the capital stock would require higher spending. The committee recommended a capital programme of £20–30 million. The ministry had been proved right. Not only did the report endorse the view that there was no evidence of waste and extravagance, the repeated claim of backbench Conservatives, but it also argued that charges might be acting as a deterrent to use.

The government was deeply depressed by the report. It had put off doing anything fundamental about the NHS while waiting for it. Now the report said, do not do anything; the NHS is cheap and good value for money. It does not need structural change. What it does need is more money spent on it, especially on its outdated hospitals. Conservative backbenchers were furious ('Now our hands are very largely tied' (Jones, 1992: 328)) and the Conservative Party Research Department was critical. The government was stuck with the NHS, for the time being. This did not stop further economies being demanded in the new economic crisis of 1956.

In 1957 the Chancellor Thorneycroft pressed the idea of funding the NHS entirely out of distinct health-insurance contributions (Webster, 1996). The debate on this issue was very much like that which was to be repeated regularly thereafter. They would merely be another tax and a rather regressive source of revenue that fell on employees and employers, some maintained. The Cabinet kept coming back to this idea. What resulted was not a health-insurance tax but a series of increases in the originally small allocation to NHS funds that was made out of existing National Insurance contributions. These were increased in 1957, 1958 and in 1961. Though it initially passed without too much opposition, anger grew with each successive recourse to this 'way out' (Webster, 1996: 44–89). In 1961, with the next economic crisis, prescription charges went up significantly too. However, this was to be the end of the Health Service's long period of containment.

The ministry, with the backing of this independent review, and a campaign by the Opposition for the 1959 election – 'no new hospital built since the war' – was able to convince the Cabinet to begin to institute a major hospital-building programme. It was announced by Enoch Powell, the Minister of Health, in 1961. The district general hospitals that we now see all over the country mostly date from plans begun at this time (Webster, 1996: 92–109).

The chance fundamentally to change the NHS had gone for a generation. The NHS was about to begin a new period of expansion. The Service was fortunate not only to have a forceful ex-Treasury minister as its political head but it also had two senior civil servants from a new post-war generation. Sir Bruce Fraser was Permanent Secretary and Sir George Godber was Chief Medical Officer.

It was a triumvirate of some note who took the NHS into the 1960s. (Timmins, 1995: 208)

Beveridge abandoned

The Conservatives had been as critical of Beveridge as they had been of Bevan's National Health Service and wanted to make changes that would target benefits on the poor and move away from the universality they deplored in Beveridge's plan. That universalism was really a myth, and was basically flawed (Lowe, 1993; 1994), but the aspiration to move to adequate flat rate benefits for all remained both in the popular consciousness and in Labour's pantheon of ideals. National Assistance, on this model, was only a temporary necessity for all but those on the fringe of society. The Labour Party did not know how it was ever going to implement this ideal and struggled through the 1950s to find a way of achieving it. It was important for the new government to distance itself from the ideal altogether. The problem was, how to do it without rejecting Beveridge, whose report still had the status of a biblical text?

It adopted a similar strategy to that used in the case of Guillebaud: appoint a committee to give external legitimacy to the rethinking. This time, however, the government did not make the mistake of appointing someone whose views it could not predict. Phillips, who had undertaken the critical official review of the Beveridge Report in the war, was asked to chair the committee. His report said what the government hoped it would. The attempt to provide all pensioners with a basic pension that was adequate to live on, regardless of their means, was 'an extravagant use of the community's resources' (Cmd 9333, 1954, para. 212). At the end of 1954 the government officially accepted this view and with it rejected the Beveridge Report, even as an ultimate goal. National Assistance was destined to become not a gradually declining bureaucracy, but a growing one. In the years between 1951 and 1963 the numbers on National Assistance were to rise from 1 million to 1.5 million.

In the big review of public spending we discussed earlier social security came under considerable scrutiny. The Treasury was determined to stop a growing contribution to the National Insurance Fund coming from general taxation. This was necessary if the finance of the scheme was to be sustained. Without it higher burdens would be put on the low-paid if the flat rate contribution was raised. So benefits could be frozen, but that was then thought unacceptable; alternatively ways could be found of raising contributions that would not fall on the low-paid. Other countries, notably Germany and Sweden, were developing wage-related schemes, with the higher-paid paying higher contributions for higher benefits. The Labour Party was conveniently exploring the same idea.

Macmillan, newly installed as Prime Minister, asked for a review of pensions policy in 1957 to respond to the Labour Party's emerging plans, which we discuss in the next chapter (Bridgen and Lowe, 1998). The pensions minister (Boyd-Carpenter) argued for an extension of private occupational pensions, making them a requirement for employers. This did not solve the immediate financial issue, however. It did not look very attractive compared to the Labour scheme of national wage-related pensions. The Treasury put forward an alternative. There should be an add-on to the basic Beveridge scheme. It would take the form of an additional income-related contribution. This would earn pensioners, eventually, a higher pension – though in practice a very small one. The scheme had the great virtue that the revenue came in long before any pensions had to be paid. The whole was more a form of revenue-raising than a pension scheme. People could opt out of it if they had an occupational pension scheme, much against the wishes of the Treasury (Lowe, 1993: 143)! Nevertheless, what had been agreed was a way of increasing the funding of the scheme.

As the 1959 and then the 1964 elections approached the Conservative government felt obliged to counter Labour accusations – that the old were slipping further into poverty – by increasing basic pensions. The result was that by 1963 the retirement pension and other benefits for a married couple stood at a higher percentage of average earnings than they had in 1948 (33.7 per cent compared with 30.5 per cent), though sickness, unemployment and National Assistance benefits were still lower in relation to average earnings than in 1938!

Even so, the Conservatives had essentially maintained and slightly improved on the social security benefits of 1948, funding them more from contributions than had been planned. This trend was to continue. They also officially abandoned any pretence that the social security scheme was designed to meet a person's needs without supplementation by a means-tested addition, if all that individual had to live on was the state pension or other benefit. In terms of their 1940s agenda this was not bad going. But the Conservative Party did not approach the 1964 election with any more radical proposals for the 1960s. It was not prepared to means test all benefits or to propose anything radical. The Labour Party seemed, now, to have all the good ideas.

Educational expansion comes

More kids The sheer demography of the rising child population drove much of education policy during this period. Those born in the 'bulge' years after the war began to enter primary school in the early 1950s, the secondary schools in the late 1950s and to knock on the doors of colleges in the 1960s. Class sizes were already well above what most educationalists and parents considered acceptable. Classes of more than forty in primary school were common. Winning extra resources to accommodate these numbers became a major preoccupation. On top of that, however, the 1944 Education Act had required the separation of primary and secondary schools, the abolition of all-age schools. That had not yet been accomplished. Nor had a school-leaving age of 16.

New kinds of job The social and economic structure of the country was changing and young people's expectations were rising. Job opportunities for graduates were beginning to expand, and many servicemen had been given university places on leaving the armed forces after the war. Staying on at school and going to university was no longer an outlandish ambition. If the rhetoric of equal opportunity meant anything, it meant that if you could pass your exams you should be able to go to college.

The structure of secondary education also reflected a job market that was passing. Once, a small select group in the population would go into the professions and into a few clerking jobs. The rest would go into manual occupations, and the lucky ones would get apprenticeships at 16. That kind of labour market was changing, if slowly at first. It became more and more obvious as the sixties began that that was the world of the past.

These social and economic changes explain why education gained increasing political attention as the 1950s advanced but the new Conservative government began by needing economy, and as we saw earlier, education bore a large part of these cuts. They went down very badly in political terms. The feeling was that Florence Horsborough, the Minister of Education, had not handled the situation as well as she could have done, but there was probably as much male chauvinism in this as substance. It is an indication of the low priority given to education that Horsborough was not in the Cabinet, though personal dislike by Churchill played its part. The housing programme had been given top priority and there was little left for schools, despite the 250,000 extra pupils and the new housing estates being built where no schools existed.

Pressure for change The first really politically damaging attack came from a House of Commons committee on which the Conservatives had a majority, the Select Committee on Estimates. The committee, in collecting evidence on the way public money for school-building was being used, had 'confronted overcrowding, lack of schools, heavy transport costs, a shortage of teachers and often rapidly deteriorating and even dangerous school buildings' (Eighth Report of the Select Committee on Estimates, 1952/3, para. 8).

The limits on school-building were eased slightly in 1954 and this was the first wedge in what was to become strong external leverage to raise education spending, supported by a new and strong education minister, Sir David Eccles. Buildings were only a small part of the story. The regulations passed after the 1944 Education Act had set what were meant to be maximum sizes for classes in primary and secondary schools. These limits were forty for primary classes and thirty for secondary ones. In the early 1950s over 40 per cent of primary pupils and nearly 60 per cent of secondary pupils were in oversized classes. These became the main focus of opposition, teacher and local authority attack and advice by the minister's own Advisory Committee on the Training and Supply of Teachers. Gradually more teachers were trained and oversized classes in primary schools began to fall. The proportion of secondary classes over thirty, however, remained little changed up until the early 1960s. By the mid-1950s the scientific threat from Russia and general fears about Britain's poor technological performance began to make technical education an issue, largely ignored as it had been in the 1940s.

Technical education   A study purported to show that while Britain was producing 57 engineering graduates per million population, Russia was producing 280. Russia was also producing three times as many technicians per head of population. This greatly exercised Churchill, for the first time interested in education, and Eccles was able to turn it to his advantage. A White Paper on technical education followed in 1956, with the following results:

- A building programme for technical colleges began.
- Sandwich courses were introduced so that students could spend part of their time during their courses in industry.
- A 75 per cent grant was given to colleges to put on advanced technical courses.
- Eight of these colleges became Colleges of Advanced Technology in 1957, financed directly from central government.
- The National Council for Technological Awards was created.

A creative promotional ministry   The Ministry of Education learned that by mobilizing influential outsiders in criticizing the service for which you were responsible you could gather public and political support in Cabinet and win battles with the Treasury. The 1944 Act laid a duty on the minister to appoint an advisory committee to watch over the service. Through the 1950s and early 1960s the Ministry of Education made brilliant use of this machinery to focus attention on different parts of the service one by one. The reports by educationalists and interested lay people could be relied on to see deficiencies and call for more to be spent. A sequence of such reports, backed by increasingly sophisticated social science research thumped on ministers' and journalists' desks in the 1950s and 1960s and made the case for a better education system. They included:

- *Early Leaving* (Ministry of Education, 1954), which drew attention to the high proportion of able children leaving school at 15 and recommended a more generous system of grants;
- the Crowther Report, *15–18* (Ministry of Education, 1959), which recommended an expansion of post-school education and the raising of the school-leaving age to 16;

- the Newsom Report, *Half Our Future* (Ministry of Education, 1963), which called for improvements in secondary modern schools, especially in the poorest areas of cities;
- the Plowden Report, *Children and their Primary Schools* (Department of Education and Science, 1967), which favoured the more relaxed teaching methods in primary schools, called for extra resources for schools in poor areas and an expansion in pre-school provision for all who wanted it.

Alongside these advisory committee reports was a one-off report, the most influential of them all, on higher education: the Robbins Report (1963).

Although it is difficult to remember at this distance there was considerable opposition to the expansion of universities by those who taught in them, as well as by the Treasury who directly financed universities at this point through an intermediary body called the University Grants Committee. Yet increasing numbers of young people were gaining the qualifications necessary to gain a place in university and higher education more broadly. More were staying on into sixth forms and soon, as the sixties approached, the birth-rate-bulge boomers would come to be of student age. The Treasury increased grants to universities a little but by nothing like enough to meet the increasing demand. Increasing numbers of qualified school-leavers, mostly from middle-class Conservative-voting homes, were failing to get places. Both the Treasury and the academics had to be convinced there were indeed enough able young people to justify expansion without reducing standards and that the whole thing was economically viable. A committee under the then Professor Robbins, a Conservative of considerable standing, made the case with a wealth of social statistics that became a classic of its time.

The education years   The mid-fifties to the end of the sixties was the time when education came into its own, much to many traditional politicians' surprise. This was a period in which the rising expectations of a much larger population of young people and the demands of a changing and expanding economy for their services combined to force education on to the political agenda as never before. In 1950 education had taken only just over 3 per cent of the GNP. By 1964 it was taking about 5 per cent, a figure not very different from its share today. The big push came in the 1950s and early 1960s.

Rumbling through the period was a growing issue about the eleven-plus and comprehensive education, which we shall cover in the next chapter, but it, too, reflected the deep social changes that were going on in the 1950s.

Conservative Achievements

These were far from thirteen wasted years. Controls and food rationing were gone and all but forgotten. It had been a period of unprecedented low unemployment. It had fallen to 1.5 per cent of the labour force at the end of the 1950s. It had hovered around the 2 per cent figure through the period as a whole. A property-owning democracy was beginning to take shape. The destructive rent controls were partially eroded. Education had been expanded. The system of social security had been to a certain extent targeted and means tested. The new Conservative agenda worked out in the late 1940s had begun to be delivered. But the Welfare State was not costing less. In fact, it was all costing a lot more than it had in 1951. The Treasury had been seriously defeated more than once. Attempts to cut back, or fundamentally change, the services had run into much stronger opposition than Conservatives had foreseen. That is the true lesson of the 1950s. People wanted lower taxes but they did not want their services reduced. But doubts were beginning to creep in. The One Nation Group had risen to leadership positions in this period. But another generation was beginning to ask whether the scale of welfare-state activity it had presided over was really something the Conservative Party should be ready to accept. In 1957 the Institute of Economic Affairs was founded, dedicated to the principle that free markets were central to political freedom as well as economic efficiency. That applied as much to housing, education and health as to any other part of the economy.

In 1961 a young lawyer, Geoffrey Howe, editor of *Crossbow*, the journal of moderate Conservative opinion, was voicing his concern. Had the Conservative governments of the period accepted too readily the inevitability of a large role for the state. Had they been too scared of public opinion?

> Conservatives surely must strive for a large reduction, in the long run, of the public social services . . . Over the whole field of social policy our firm aim should be a reduction in the role of the state. (Howe, 1961: 61 quoted in Timmins, 1995.)

Howe was to be Mrs Thatcher's Chancellor.

Questions to Answer

1 In what way did the Conservatives' attitudes towards the welfare state differ from those of the post-war Labour government?
2 What important changes did the Conservatives make to the post-war welfare institutions?
3 Why did spending on social policy continue to rise despite early attempts to constrain it?

5

Completing the Post-war Agenda 1964–76, Part One: the Poor and the Poorest

An Old Agenda
What is New?
Social Policy Moves Centre Stage
Reforming Beveridge
Labour Comes to Power
Conservatives Reverse Engines, 1970
Labour Tries Again
Child Poverty Again
Balance Sheet So Far

An Old Agenda

The new Labour government that was elected in October 1964 came to power with a manifesto packed with social policy commitments, yet they were mostly extensions of the agenda the old 1945 government had left unfinished. The framework of ideas that was driving the 1964 government's social policies can be traced back in a fairly unbroken line to the 1920s and 1930s. Tawney would have recognized the debates about equal access to secondary education, the public schools and higher education. Beveridge would have recognized the issues in the social security debate even if he did not agree with the proposals.

Secondary education for all, achieving an adequate universal insurance benefit system, using local authorities as mass providers of housing – all this would have been familiar to the Labour politicians of the 1940s. Indeed, most of the leading figures in Wilson's administration had been young MPs in the Attlee period. Wilson himself had been a minister.

The legislative agenda of the 1964 government was interrupted by the Labour Party losing office in 1970. When the Labour Party returned to power again, early in 1974, it picked up almost where it had left off in 1970 for its first two years. Earnings-related pensions and child benefit finished off legislation that was in the pipeline in 1970.

The intervening Conservative government – 1970–4 under Mr Heath – was in power too short a time to reverse the tide. Indeed many of the Labour government's policies were merely taken forward by the Heath administration. Where they were reversed, as in the case of pensions, the legislation was repealed in 1974.

The really decisive break in the history of traditional social policy comes in 1976. Economic crisis forced new priorities on the Labour government and changed its thinking. Mrs Thatcher's election to the leadership of the Conservative Party in opposition in 1975 produced a sea change in the Conservative approach to policy.

These next two chapters therefore take the story up to 1976, the high tide of post-war welfare ideology. Some history books on the post-war period date the 'retreat from collectivism' much earlier, from 1948 or 1961 (Morgan, 1990). In social policy this will not do. Not only was the legislative agenda of the 1960s an intellectual extension of the 1940s but the expansion of social spending as a share of the national income continued to rise in a steadily steeper curve until 1976.

What is New?

Nevertheless, it would be wrong to portray the 1960s and early 1970s merely as a sequel to the 1940s, for the following reasons:

• First, social policy was even more central to the Labour Party's ideology in the 1960s than it had been in the 1940s. The Labour Party in the 1930s and 1940s put public ownership, full employment and anti-colonialism high on its list of concerns. By the 1960s economic prosperity and social policy were central for both parties. The politics of the 1960s *was* social politics.

- Second, the emphasis of Labour policy began to shift to a greater concern with equality in society rather than merely equality of access to state services.
- Third, a new social policy agenda was emerging, outside the normal range of party politics. It questioned the state's right to interfere in matters of personal concern: sexual relations between consenting couples of whatever sexual persuasion, the state's regulation of marriage and divorce, of women's right to abort a birth, the state's right to take life and its right to censor what people read. All these were challenges to paternalist and authoritarian state power. The fact that these ideas were associated with the left in politics and not the right tells us something about the peculiar mix of ideology that goes to make up Britain's political parties.
- Cross-party, single-issue groups emerged as powerful change agents. The Child Poverty Action Group was one. The most successful was the campaign to abolish capital punishment, which attracted large, growing and emotional audiences in the early 1960s. Homosexual law reform, abortion law reform and changes to the divorce laws were much debated in the run-up to the 1964 election. Though the Labour Party had shied away from committing itself, many individual MPs in the new Parliament felt strongly on these issues, especially the younger ones.
- Finally, immigration and race relations pushed themselves into political debate in the aftermath of the rapid rise, from a very low base, in West Indian and then Asian immigration, which had begun in the late 1950s.

Thus the old politics of social policy began to give way to the new in the 1960s. We discuss this important period in the next three chapters. We begin with the battle of ideas that gripped the Labour Party in the 1950s and laid the foundation for its policy in this period.

Social Policy Moves Centre Stage

There had been a battle fought out over the Labour Party's soul in the 1950s, during its period in opposition. Social policy had been an important part of that battle.

The Labour Party has always been a broad coalition. The Labour government of 1945 to 1951 had forged a compromise between those in the party who saw socialism as being primarily about the extension of public ownership to most of the economy and those who saw its role as primarily concerned with social issues.

The 1945 government had taken forward both agendas. Were they to be equally pursued in the 1950s? Many in the party saw the social policy reforms of the 1940s as a distraction to its main purpose. The key changes brought about by the Attlee government had been the public ownership of the basic industries and they were only a beginning. As Barker puts it,

> However, it is not inappropriate that the post-war Labour adminis-
> trations should be seen in the first place as the creators of massive
> public ownership. Nationalisation was the most characteristic single
> feature of Labour policy and it provided the fold within which, under
> MacDonald and his successors, the socialist lion, the trade union
> sheep, and the starry eyed child of liberal idealism had lain down
> together . . . By 1951 it was clear that a wholly new debate was
> beginning within the party, and a wholly new statement of its
> character was needed. (Barker, 1972: 82)

The central question was to become: was the Labour Party mainly concerned with extending public ownership or with attacking inequality through social policy? The debate was reflected in *The New Fabian Essays*, edited by Richard Crossman in 1952, and in the columns of *Tribune* and later the *New Left Review*. G. D. H. Cole (1957) in his last years was to argue, without much success, that the Labour Party should concentrate on democratizing industry, giving workers a greater say in the workplace. The old and the new left insisted that the Labour Party return to its fundamental battle with capitalism. The Welfare State had changed nothing. The alternative view was that the economy had been fundamentally changed by the capacity of government to regulate the macro-economy and by the creation of a Welfare State. Improving the quality and variety of people's lives should now be Labour's goal. In that pursuit social policy would play a central role.

The contribution of social science

Concern with social policy issues had already been growing in the later part of the 1940s, as we saw in Chapter 3. Some thinking politicians' interest was aroused by the first fruits and then a growing harvest of social science research which began to show that the supposedly perfect Welfare

State institutions the party had been so proud of creating, were flawed. Jean Floud and Chelly Halsey, young sociologists working at the London School of Economics, were able to show continuing and substantial class differences in access to the new grammar schools. The examination taken at the age of 10 to determine which schoolchildren should attend was proving increasingly unpopular. A day's examination could decide a child's future. I can still vividly remember setting off, clutching a pencil and ruler for that day's exams in early 1946, and failing. The process seemed brutal and unfair to many parents, especially middle-class and aspiring working-class ones. Social scientists put flesh on this disgruntlement.

Hertfordshire tried to mollify parents by introducing a system of teachers' reports on a child's work and interviews spread over a longer period as a basis for the eleven-plus. This only worsened working-class children's prospects of entering grammar school. In 1954, in south-west Hertfordshire, 64 per cent of professional and managerial parents' children were going on to grammar school but only 12 per cent of manual working-class children (Floud and Halsey, 1957).

Yet the 36 per cent of middle-class parents whose children failed were also unhappy. They could not pay for a place in a grammar school any more and were deeply unhappy about sending their children to secondary modern schools. Expensive private school places were the only alternative. Equal secondary education for all was turning out to be a myth and the predictions made by some of those civil servants in the Board of Education during the war were turning out to be true.

Other social scientists were uncovering extensive poverty amongst the elderly, questioning established measures of poverty and the adequacy of the levels of social support the new benefits system was providing (Abel-Smith and Townsend, 1955; Townsend, 1954a, 1954b, 1957). Titmuss was the first Professor of Social Administration at the LSE and an inspiration to this group. He had been the official war historian of social policy, working in the Cabinet Office during the Second World War and he wrote what is still the definitive account of social policy during the war (Titmuss, 1950). The experience convinced Titmuss that universal social institutions that met the needs of the whole population were the only way in which a modern nation-state could be held together as an organic whole (Titmuss, 1958). The forces of a modern market economy would tear apart any allegiance individuals might have to some larger identity, be it family, neighbourhood or the state itself. In war a common external threat might awaken a sense of altruism and allegiance (Titmuss, 1950); in peace only institutions that fostered such altruism and solidarity could achieve this sense of shared identity (Titmuss, 1972). Without it the institutions of the market-place would collapse too because they depended on some acceptance of the rules of social order. Without a sense of social solidarity the free political institutions would lose their legitimacy.

One unusual Labour politician, formerly an Oxford don, was Anthony Crosland, who read not only this material but the new sociology coming out of the United States and the new economics of industry. It was uncommon for a politician to read social science so avidly. He was to produce a seminal book, *The Future of Socialism* (1956), which influenced a generation of young people just entering politics, journalism and the academic profession (Lipsey and Leonard, 1981). He was very close to the new Leader of the Labour Party who succeeded Attlee, Hugh Gaitskell. What Crosland did in this closely argued book was to reject the claims of the Marxist left that economic prosperity and social change depended on transforming the ownership structure of industry. Macro-economic planning could ensure full employment and the new large private corporations were capable of delivering economic growth. Further public ownership was pointless. What socialists *ought* to be worried about was the quality of life individuals could lead, the respect that was accorded to them and the opportunities they had to develop their potential. Education played an important part in achieving these goals.

A bitter battle followed Gaitskell's leadership and his attempt to get the Labour Party to abandon that part of its constitution that proclaimed its belief in public or common ownership. He failed, but to a very large extent the main thrust of Crosland's case was accepted. Social policy became the main element in the new Labour Party's detailed agenda. How far his ideas were a bridge to and different from 'New Labour' is discussed by Nuttall (2004).

Rethinking policy

Working parties and policy subgroups of the party's National Executive Committee were set up with sympathetic academics on them. Detailed policy proposals were produced on education, pensions and social security, housing and social and youth services. Social policy was now moving centre stage. It was given another push by another influential book, this time written by an American, John Kenneth Galbraith, called *The Affluent Society*. In it Galbraith coined the phrase 'private affluence and public squalor'. It had the attraction of offering a structuralist critique of modern capitalism which Crosland had not and it appealed to the non-Marxist left.

In a vivid passage Galbraith describes an American family setting out for a picnic:

> The family which takes its mauve and cerise, air conditioned, power-steered, and power-braked car out for a tour passes through cities that are badly paved, made hideous by litter, blighted buildings, billboards, and posts for wires that should long since have been put underground. They pass into a countryside that has been made largely invisible by commercial art . . . They picnic on exquisitely packaged food from a portable icebox by a polluted stream and go on to spend the night at a park which is a menace to public health and morals. Before dozing off on an air mattress beneath a nylon tent amid the stench of decaying refuse, they may reflect vaguely on the unevenness of their blessings. (1958: 207–8)

This passage appears in a chapter introduced with a quotation from Tawney.

The message was that public expenditure on the environment and social goods was being neglected while private consumption was running to excess. While that vision of the United States may have carried credence, the latter stages of the Macmillan administration had seen a rapid growth in public spending to which Galbraith's admonitions scarcely applied, at least not to the same extent as in America. Nevertheless, it struck a chord with both left and right in the party and provided a binding theme that underpinned the new Labour Party programme entitled *Signposts for the Sixties* (Labour Party, 1961).

The contribution of demography

Ideas do not germinate in a vacuum. Demography was providing a fertile ground for this new concern with education and pensions (O'Hara, 2004). The number of families with young and teenage children in school, coming up to the age at which they might wish to go to university, was rising fast. The number of elderly was rising too. In 1941 the number of young people under school age plus the number over retirement age had been smaller than 50 per cent of the total working population. By the mid-1960s the percentage had risen well beyond 60 per cent and was continuing to rise. The United Kingdom was to experience the impact of a more dependent population, young and old, earlier and on a larger scale than other advanced economies. The political constituency for social policy was thereby created.

The weak link

Despite the growing interest in social policy the economy remained *the* focus of much everyday political debate and Harold Wilson's point of attack. He criticized the stop–go cycles of the 1950s and the country's poor growth record. Though, to the reader, an underlying growth of 2.5 per cent, low inflation and unemployment in the 1–2 per cent range looks rather good, other countries' growth rates in Europe had been more than double that and Britain's standard of living was being rapidly overtaken by that of its neighbours. Wilson, the Labour leader who took over when Gaitskell died in 1963, was an economist and particularly effective in criticizing this *relatively* poor performance. He, unlike his predecessor, believed in a strong state role in industry and the economy, encouraging new technology and planning for growth. He managed to capture popular and technocrats' support for this emphasis (Pimlott, 1992). Yet it was a rhetoric based on little or no policy substance.

The result was that the new Labour government came to power in 1964 with a detailed social programme and a presumption that the country's growth rate could be boosted to levels nearer our continental rivals to pay for this programme. It was to be done through the mechanism of something called 'economic planning'. No one could adequately articulate what that meant, except by producing paper plans that would try to convince companies that faster growth was possible. None of the real underlying constraints on growth, notably Britain's poor export performance, was addressed. Therein lay the reason for the disappointments of the next six years.

Reforming Beveridge

Ground work in opposition 1955–64

The most detailed policy work done by the Labour Party in its period in opposition had been on reforming Beveridge's flat rate social insurance plan. It had begun with two new lecturers in Titmuss's social policy department at the LSE, Brian Abel-Smith and Peter Townsend, who were convinced that Beveridge had made a major blunder in basing his plan on a flat rate principle. They worked on their ideas and lectured to Fabian groups in London and finally produced a Fabian pamphlet arguing a new basis for social insurance (Abel-Smith and Townsend, 1955).

The case for a change

Abel-Smith and Townsend were drawing on ideas about national pensions schemes that were developing in Germany and Sweden. They accepted that insurance-based contributions should remain as the basis for entitlement to benefit. Where Beveridge had gone wrong, they argued, was in seeking to finance the scheme out of flat rate contributions. Since these imposed a heavy burden on the lowest-paid there was a limit to how far they could be raised. This had set an effective ceiling on the levels of pension that could be afforded since the Treasury was reluctant to see the insurance fund further subsidized from general taxation. Higher contributions would have to come from higher earners. If higher contributions were to be acceptable they would have to be seen to earn higher pensions. But *part* of those higher contributions could go to raising the pension floor for those on low earnings.

In principle, moreover, flat rate poverty line benefits were not a good basis for setting pensions. The relative drop in the standard of living suffered by a moderately good earner forced to retire on a low basic pension was that much greater than for a low earner. Occupational pension schemes took this relative deprivation principle into account. What was emerging therefore were 'two nations in retirement', as Titmuss (1958: 74) put it. Occupational pensions were still not within the reach of most people. They tended to tie people to existing jobs. Most ordinary workers in occupational pension schemes were paid very low pensions because private schemes could not guarantee future pensions against rising prices. Most workers who were covered were tied into their firms' pension scheme and they lost pension rights when they moved, often only taking with them their own payments into the scheme.

Beveridge, too, had been deeply suspicious of the irresponsibility of the large private insurance companies that he saw exploiting poor families. However, Beveridge was a strong believer in voluntaristic, trade union or friendly-society-based pension schemes. That is precisely why he had wanted only a low basic state pension.

What Townsend and Abel-Smith and Titmuss wanted was a single national superannuation scheme that would provide for most people what the top company pension schemes offered for their managers. The British pension scheme should move much closer to the continental ones being developed at the time, especially the German and Swedish models. This meant two things: first, linking benefit entitlements to previous earnings and second, not using actual past earnings as the basis for entitlement but

increasing future pensions in line with the general improvement in earnings in the economy. In this way pensioners' living standards would keep
pace with the rest of the society.

The 1955 Labour Party Conference debated pensions, and a motion
called for an increase in the basic pension as usual. Richard Crossman
was called on to answer the debate. He knew from Peter Shore, who
was working in the Labour Party Research Department and was later its
head, that some interesting work was going on at the LSE on these issues
(Ellison, 1988). He called on the Conference to approve the creation of
a special study group to consider the future of pensions. A committee on
social security and old age was set up and the LSE group of Titmuss,
Townsend and Abel-Smith was co-opted. The group went on working
for many years.

Right from the outset the idea of wage-related benefits was opposed
by representatives of the Trades Union Congress. To them flat rate benefits
embodied an egalitarian principle that should not be abandoned. Flat rate
pensions should simply be raised. The Titmuss group's response was that
raising flat rate contributions to pay for this increase would fall heavily on
the poorest and was hardly egalitarian. The Treasury would effectively block
any massive subsidy from the Exchequer, so the revenue had to come from
higher contributions from the higher paid. If the state scheme went on
being such a low benefit one there would be growing inequality between
those on state pension and those on occupational pensions. Here was the
real inequality.

The new plan

In the end a detailed scheme was agreed that added a wage-related
benefit on to Beveridge's old flat rate pension. It would give a combined
pension equal to about half the average worker's pay over his lifetime and
rather more, proportionately, for the lower-paid. Borrowing ideas from
Germany, these lifetime earnings would be 'dynamized', that is, increased
in line with earnings in the economy at large. Thus a worker who had
been on average earnings through his life would retire on a pension equal
to half average earnings at the time he retired and the pension would be
inflation proofed after he retired.

Richard Crossman, chairman of the subcommittee, drove this plan
through with great enthusiasm. A technical appendix setting out how the
scheme would all be financed was written by members of the social policy
staff at the LSE, 'the skiffle group', as civil servants were to call it (Labour

Party, 1957). The problem for the Labour Party was that it would take many years to come to fruition, even when implemented. What were they to offer to existing pensioners?

The Labour Party's scheme was, however, enough to worry the Conservative government. It legislated a very watered-down version of the scheme in 1959, as we saw in Chapter 4.

An alternative route?

Logically the Labour Party or the Conservative government might have taken a different route to pension reform at this time. They could have responded to the 'two nations' problem of workers excluded from occupational pension rights by legislating that all workers should be members of occupational pension schemes and that their pensions should be transferable between employers. It says something about the climate of ideas at the time that this option was not developed. It was to be, by the Heath Conservative government in 1971.

Extending the wage-related principle

Having settled on a new pensions policy the Labour Party committee went on to extend the principle of wage-related benefits to cover sickness and unemployment benefit too. Here the arguments took on a more economic focus. If unemployment benefit were set much closer to a worker's past pay he or she would be much less resistant to moving jobs and this would increase labour mobility and hence the technological revolution Wilson was so keen to see.

Labour Comes to Power

As we have suggested, the problem with selling these ideas for long-term pension reform to an electorate was that it would take a generation for the new pensions to be payable. The Labour Party executive was under much internal pressure to promise a large immediate increase in the flat rate pension if it won the 1964 election, despite the fact that the Conservatives had already increased pensions in 1963 as part of their attempt to stay in power. The Labour Party did promise a further immediate increase in the flat rate universal pension and honoured the pledge in March 1965 by raising the flat rate pension by 12*s*. 6*d*. The government had been elected with a tiny majority and Wilson knew he would have to go to the electorate again soon. He wanted quick results and immediately popular policies.

Between 1948 and 1962 the level of the basic single pension had roughly kept pace with rising male industrial earnings. It had been equivalent to about 19 per cent of average earnings in 1948 and a little less in 1962. By May 1965 the pension had been increased to just over 21 per cent of average male industrial earnings. Though this may seem a far from revolutionary step it cost a great deal of money in a budget already swollen by the commitments of the previous government and during a period of gathering economic crisis. It effectively put the more fundamental reform of pensions on to a back burner until the very end of the Wilson government.

However, the government did press ahead with introducing wage-related unemployment benefits for the reasons outlined above; the rationale fitted into the government's broader economic strategy. If unemployment benefit had to be wage-related for economic labour mobility reasons, so too did sickness benefit. It would be difficult to defend paying workers a higher benefit if they were unemployed than if they were sick. One is struck, rereading the discussions of the day, how completely topsy-turvy and transitory are the arguments used to justify social policies. Twenty years afterwards Mrs Thatcher's government was to abolish these benefits on the grounds that people would only return to work if their benefits were so low that they would have no incentive to remain on benefit. The objective was the same, the means opposite.

Means tests and a supplementary pension

There had been a different subplot to the social security discussions while Labour was in opposition. It was clear to some, as it was clear to me while working in the Labour Party Research Department at the time, that it would never be possible to raise the basic pension far enough to lift great numbers off National Assistance. The new pension scheme would take many years to come to fruition. Much more attention should be paid to making the National Assistance scheme more humane and less stigmatic. This might be done by making the system of income testing a more or less automatic process 'very much like income tax in reverse' (Glennerster, 1962: 33). A system of means-tested supplementary pensions could be created, leaving the National Assistance Board to concentrate on the really difficult cases. It was not a message many in the party wanted to hear but the need to do something for existing pensioner voters forced its serious consideration (see below and Hall et al., 1975).

Child poverty

Largely ignored at this time was the whole question of child poverty. Most families were evidently better off. Millions of new council houses had been occupied by families who were able to buy new furniture, televisions and even refrigerators from steadily rising real wages. The Conservative Party was proud of the prosperity the free enterprise economy was producing and the Labour Party was reluctant to concentrate on poor families' plight. They were to a large extent hidden from view. The family allowance, one of the first and most radical innovations of the 1945 government, had been allowed to decay and decline in real value, never having been increased since 1952. The Labour Party ignored the issue. There was not a single mention of family allowances in the speakers' guide for Labour candidates at the 1964 election (Labour Party, 1963a). Its only mention in the 1961 policy document of the party had been in relation to using the allowances to encourage staying on at school. Politicians argued privately that family allowances were deeply unpopular with ordinary Labour voters, who saw them as handouts to the feckless large family.

The best-laid plans

The politician who had most to do with the revised Beveridge plan in opposition, Richard Crossman, was a close colleague of Wilson, the new Prime Minister. He was also an immensely energetic and forceful person who was to be an unusually effective minister. He had been Wilson's campaign manager in his leadership bid. Prime Ministers tend to put such people in what they see to be their key Cabinet posts. Crossman did not end up in social security but in housing.

Social security policy, partly as a result, fell into a quagmire for the next four years. Wilson appointed separate Ministers of Health and Social Security, neither of whom were in the Cabinet, a situation that is barely conceivable today. Instead, acting as a kind of overlord for these ministries was Douglas Houghton, a sceptic about Crossman's social security plans while in opposition. Like many after him he believed, as an ex-tax inspector, that taxes and benefits could be integrated. The tax system could be used to determine and deliver a basic income guarantee for old people. But most old people were not covered by the PAYE tax system. Definitions of household income used in the social security system and taxable income were different. As many were later to find, this apparently simple idea was difficult to turn into practical policy. It delayed action on pension reform for a long period. The only tangible result was a unified pension book for those on means-tested additions to the basic pension. That meant when you went to the Post Office to collect your pension you were not easily identifiable as someone drawing a means-tested benefit.

The big gesture was made. A large increase in the basic pension was approved as part of the first Queen's speech, pre-empting resources that might have been devoted to a deeper review. Crossman looked on appalled as he saw what was happening in his old policy territory. At the first annual review of public spending in the Labour period that took place in July 1965, Crossman recorded in his diary a set of comments that were to capture the essence of that early strategic mistake:

> And then we came to Pensions . . . under cross examination they [Herbison and Houghton] got into a horrible mess and confirmed my fear that the whole strategy of our pensioneering, worked out for years before the election, had been jettisoned, almost without noticing it by the Minister under the *diktat* of Douglas Houghton. The basic idea had been that we should switch as soon as possible from flat rate to earnings related contributions and in this way pile up enormous funds in the pensions fund which we could use to dynamise the existing flat rate pension. That was cardinal. However, Douglas and Peggy had turned things upside down, by first of all conceding an enormously increased flat rate pension financed by increased flat rate contributions. The net result is the worst of all worlds as we can't raise the flat rate contributions any higher without imposing an intolerable burden on the lower-paid worker. Even worse, the income guarantee we had pledged ourselves to introduce would now be at an absurdly low level as a result of the money we had wasted on the huge initial increase of the flat rate pension. (1975, Diary entry for 17 July 1965)

Shades of 1946. These factors help explain the relatively meagre legislative outcomes of the 1964–70 government on the social security front. The rumbling economic crisis of the time explains the rest.

Social security legislation 1964–70

The 1965 and 1966 changes included the following elements:

- The flat rate pension and other benefits were increased in March 1965.
- Earnings-related benefits were added to the basic benefits for sickness, unemployment and widow's benefit. They amounted to a third of

previous wages in a band of earnings that took in people well above the average wage. The benefits were only to be paid for six months.

The total benefit was never to rise above 85 per cent of previous earnings. In return all workers paid an additional 0.5 per cent of their earnings in social security contributions. The earnings bands were extended and employers contributed more too after 1969.

- The old Ministry of Pensions and National Insurance was abolished and replaced by the Ministry of Social Security.
- The old National Assistance Board was abolished and replaced by the Supplementary Benefits Commission; it came within the scope of the ministry but was to administer a supplementary pensions scheme and supplementary allowances in a supposedly more humane way.

A new national pension scheme?

All in all this was a modest legislative achievement after the years of work that had gone on in opposition. It might just have been different. In 1968 Wilson had a change of heart. He gave Crossman the job of running a combined super-department taking in both the old Ministries of Health and Social Security: the Department of Health and Social Security (DHSS).

Crossman called back into service the old LSE skiffle group, or most of it, and work that had been under way in the civil service on the National Superannuation scheme moved into top gear. It was a very bad time to be coming up with an expensive scheme, in the aftermath of a massive economic crisis and devaluation. The line Crossman took was reminiscent of that taken by Beveridge. The scheme would come in gradually over twenty years. By phasing in a gradual rise in pensions in line with earnings on a formula basis, the Treasury would be less likely to be faced with recurrent demands to increase pensions. That would not, however, be a line of argument that would appeal to the backbenches on his own side: 'My pension plan is not in fact wildly extravagant but unfortunately we dare not say so' (Crossman, 1977: 137).

Crossman made sure he consulted the CBI and the TUC every inch of the highly complex way and managed to carry them with him. A White Paper incorporating the basic principles, worked out ten years previously in opposition, was produced in January 1969. It had been steered through the Cabinet Social Services Committee with little opposition:

This afternoon the Social Services Committee met under my Chairmanship and my complete pensions plan went through without any serious questioning except from James Callaghan, who after being Chancellor knew a great deal about it. The rest of the Ministers spent nearly all of their time asking about the effect of the scheme on the pensions of the civil service. It's mainly because Ministers get so ministerial that we have such appallingly ineffective discussion of great social issues. No one looked at the main economic impact of the scheme, its social impact or its effect on women or its effect on trade unions. (Crossman, 1977: 217)

This White Paper came out in the aftermath of a sterling crisis, a devaluation and a massive split in the government over a White Paper on trade union legislation, *In Place of Strife*. The complex legislation went ahead and was passing through Parliament when Wilson decided to call an election, mistakenly convinced by public opinion polls that he could win a snap election. He did not and the bill fell.

Conservatives Reverse Engines, 1970

Detailed tax plans had been worked out in opposition. They involved a shift from direct to indirect taxation. As the first part of this strategy Value Added Taxation was introduced on the back of entry to Europe. The second stage, a big reduction in direct tax, was to have to wait until Howe's budget in Mrs Thatcher's first term (Daunton, 2002).

During their period in opposition the Conservatives had also begun to take stock and revise their social policies. They were very worried by the new scheme the Labour Party had nearly got on to the statute book. It would have been a continuing and growing drain on the Exchequer in a period the Conservatives were pledged to roll back taxation. It had the potential to build up huge accumulations of funds from workers and use these to invest in private companies. It would offer more generous pensions than the private pension schemes could, especially inflation-proofed pensions, and might threaten the existence of private pension schemes and hence the source of much private capital for industry. The party, therefore, gave high priority to developing an alternative.

When it came to power it asked those civil servants who had spent six years working on Labour's complex scheme to devise another based on almost the opposite principles. Private occupational pension schemes, provided by the workers' own employers, should be the basis for future pensions. If this were simply left to employers there was no reason they would provide such pensions. Why should they not just 'free ride' on the state and expect it to provide means-tested pensions for their workers? If the state wanted to give up, eventually, the basic responsibility to provide adequate pensions for all, the thinking went, it would be necessary to *require* employers to provide adequate company pension schemes. The government would also have to find a way of meeting the objections that critics such as Titmuss had made of occupational pension schemes, notably that they inhibited free movement of labour and gave poor pensions that lost value when inflation occurred. The Conservative government did very quickly legislate part of the previous government's White Paper, i.e. the proposals that had been a response to the new campaign for the disabled and their carers.

The National Insurance (Old Person's and Widow's Pensions and Attendance Allowance) Act 1970 introduced a new benefit, the Attendance Allowance, from December 1971, for people being cared for at home by relatives and who needed 'frequent attention throughout the day and prolonged and repeated attention during the night'. The government also followed the previous one in increasing the level of contributions paid by employers towards the costs of social security.

A harbinger of the future was the new government's pensions White Paper of 1971, *Strategy for Pensions*, and the subsequent Social Security Act 1973. The White Paper saw the employer, not the state, as the main pension provider.

Flat rate contributions, the principle that had underpinned British pensions from the beginning and had been made into the central plank of Beveridge's scheme, were to go. There was to be a basic pension scheme provided by the state whose level was to be reviewed from year to year. It was fairly clear that this would be gradually eroded in significance. It was to be financed out of *earnings*-related 'contributions'. This was a further departure from the notion that what you paid in contributions was somehow related to your benefit. This was a simple graduated social security tax levied to pay for basic pensions. Employees would pay 5.25 per cent of their earnings up to one and a half times average earnings and employers would pay 7.25 per cent of their employees' earnings over the same income range. Everyone would receive the same benefit.

All employees, over 21 and up to retirement age, would have to be either a member of an occupational scheme approved by a government agency, or a member of the government's Reserve Scheme. This was based on essentially the same principles as private schemes, though not threatening them, and it was available if an employee could not join a scheme run by his or her employer. Steps were taken to ensure a degree of transferability between these schemes when a worker changed jobs.

The Act was passed into law but like its Labour predecessor was never to be enacted. The miners' strike and Mr Heath's defeat intervened and one of the first things the new Labour government in 1974 did was to repeal that legislation. Pensions were back on the drawing board.

Labour Tries Again

The same group of civil servants, or some of them, dusted down their 1960s files and began work again. Richard Crossman was by this time dead, but in his place was a close friend – Barbara Castle – advised by one of the architects of the original Labour plans, Brian Abel-Smith. They began to reinstate the old scheme but recognized that it was crucial to try to get broader agreement. Simply reintroducing the Crossman scheme would not carry the Opposition and it might simply get repealed after the next election. It also had to carry the occupational pensions lobby, which included many trade unions; membership of these schemes now covered over half the population.

The resulting White Paper, *Better Pensions*, and the eventual Act, the Social Security Pensions Act 1975, went a long way towards incorporating some of the principles of the previous Conservative legislation and won Conservative support when it was passed. It introduced the State Earnings-Related Pension Scheme (SERPS), which began to take effect in April 1978.

Social Security Pensions Act 1975

The main provisions were:

- The pensions paid under the scheme were to build up over the next twenty years, with the full pensions being paid in 1998.
- There were to be earnings-related pensions and contributions. Up to a 'basic amount' of weekly earnings a person was entitled to a pension of the same amount – a 100 per cent replacement rate. This basic amount was equal to the then basic pension and would be increased year on year in line with earnings.
- For the next band of earnings, up to an upper limit, the individual would earn a pension equal to 25p for each additional pound. For those around average earnings this in total meant about half pay.

- Lifetime earnings would be dynamized as in the old plan but the period chosen for this calculation would be the 'twenty best years' of a person's working life. This was done to enable women who were often not in the labour force as long as men to receive pensions related to their shorter paid working lives.
- In another element designed to give more equal treatment, a person who stayed at home to bring up children was to be counted as a contributor to the scheme. The same was true if he or she were in receipt of Attendance Allowance and therefore caring for a elderly relation or a partner, for example.

These elements made the scheme, at this point, the most 'advanced' in the world in terms of equal rights for women and carers. At the same time occupational schemes that could provide equivalent rights could qualify a person to 'contract out' and employees and employers concerned would pay a lower contribution to the state as a result. Guaranteed minimum pensions would have to be transferred to the new job or maintained in some way, and inflation proofed, or the employee would have to be bought back into the state scheme. Thus occupational pension schemes were to be preserved but subject to strict quality control and transferability rules.

The end of the story?

At last, in 1978, just over twenty years since the Labour Party had first published its original *National Superannuation* proposals, legislation implementing something like it took effect. Too late. If implemented in 1965 the scheme might have gathered support from those who were drawing its pensions by the time Mrs Thatcher came to power and the political climate changed. But the delay had been so great that it was barely in operation and the scale of the pension benefits built up so small, that the new Conservative government felt able to propose the whole scheme be scrapped. But that is for the next chapter in the story.

Child Poverty Again

In 1951 Rowntree, whose famous survey of poverty in York at the turn of the century had been so influential, and whose second survey had had so much influence on Beveridge, published his third survey of poverty in York (Rowntree and Lavers, 1951). He used the same standard for poverty as in his previous study and concluded that there had been a remarkable improvement as a result of the coming of the Welfare State and full employment. Almost no one in York was now living below his tough basic primary poverty line and less than 2 per cent of households were living below his rather more generous secondary poverty line. Those who were still poor were almost exclusively old people. Child poverty in working families had essentially disappeared. This view was to colour public perceptions for the next fifteen years.

Rowntree's definitions of poverty were later to be criticized by Townsend and others but they did not come out with dramatically different conclusions for the years of 1953–4 (Abel-Smith and Townsend, 1965). There had indeed been a real improvement in the living standards of poorer families.

Rowntree showed that without the impact of the Labour government's welfare measures, including the introduction of family allowances, a fifth of the working-class households in York would have fallen below the poverty line. That would have made sense to my parents' generation. People carry around with them two very different but equally valid notions of poverty. One is absolute. People in 1950 remembered life in the 1930s and recognized that it *was* better in 1950. Another view is that poverty is a measure of relative disadvantage. Young families might be better off than in the 1930s, but less well off relative to others. The Rowntree study fixed in politicians' heads the idea that poor *young* families were a thing of the past.

Though politicians' and public perceptions were that most families 'had never had it so good', in a phrase that was attributed to the Conservative Prime Minister Harold Macmillan, evidence was beginning to accumulate that many young families with children were not sharing in the general improvements in living standards.

There had been no study of household income levels since 1950, in contrast to the many there had been in the 1930s. Inland Revenue statistics had been analysed and suggested some increase in poverty but they were not a good basis. Evidence of falling standards of nutrition had emerged in a reanalysis of the British Food Survey (Lambert, 1964). Social workers in the field were becoming convinced that poverty faced by young families was growing. The Society of Friends (the Quakers) called a meeting at Toynbee Hall in the East End of London, the university settlement where Beveridge had first learned about poverty at the turn of the century. The meeting was addressed by Brian Abel-Smith, who with colleagues at the LSE was studying new material on trends in poverty since the 1950s. Those there were so distressed by the results that they decided to form an action group (Field, 1982; McCarthy, 1986).

Brian Abel-Smith and Peter Townsend had hit on the idea of using the Family Expenditure Survey to investigate what had happened to families' income over time. The survey was designed to provide the basis for calculating the government's cost of living index. Since the early 1950s it had collected information about a national sample of households, their expenditure, and as a check, their incomes too. It gave the only available source of information on trends in family income over time but it had never been exploited before.

The results were striking. Abel-Smith and Townsend took the National Assistance levels set by the government as the basis for defining a poverty line. If government set this as a basic minimum income it was legitimate to say that those who fell below it were in poverty. Over the period since 1953 the number of families falling below this line had risen and had risen particularly amongst young families with several children.

This way of calculating poverty was to cause considerable controversy. Critics argued that to use the government's own National Assistance scale to define poverty was misleading. If the government chose to increase the National Assistance scale rate it would automatically increase the level of poverty on these measures. Generosity by government would lead to *more* poverty. This was a perfectly valid criticism in theory and later studies of low incomes were to use different methods. In practice, however, the government's basic assistance levels had kept fairly close to increases in earnings in the economy. What Abel-Smith and Townsend were showing was that, compared to the average household, families with children had been falling behind in their living standards and that many families with a low-paid head of household were trying to bring up their children on an income well below that which they would get if that person was unemployed and on benefit.

The two academics played their publicity cards carefully. They arranged to have the results published just before Christmas when the newspapers were looking for human interest stories.

The report, *The Poor and the Poorest*, was to become famous. It did attract a lot of press and television coverage and forced child poverty back on to the political agenda for the first time since the 1940s. So as not to lose the political momentum the action group (see above) was urged to become a national organization. Tony Lynes, Titmuss's research assistant, was appointed to run the central office more or less single-handed. The organization was called the Child Poverty Action Group (CPAG).

This was an interesting development in its own right and was to set a precedent for other similar small pressure groups campaigning for particular social groups in the late sixties and seventies: the Disablement Income Group, Shelter and its campaign for the homeless, a revived MIND pressing the rights of the mentally ill, and many others. This constellation of groups came to be called the 'poverty lobby' and took its inspiration from CPAG.

The first fruits of their lobbying was to persuade the government to look again at the level of family allowances. It was not, however, a very propitious time. The economy was running into one of its periodic foreign exchange crises. The economy was not growing as fast as had been hoped and the public expenditure plans were going to have to be cut back before long. To add another major commitment was not going to be easy. The minister, Margaret Herbison, tried with little success to get the Treasury to give her a larger budget to meet the costs of an increase in family allowances. In October 1967 she was given a tiny sop. Family allowances were increased for *fourth* and subsequent children by a small sum equivalent to about 1 per cent of average earnings. The trade-off the Treasury demanded was an increase in the price of school meals and milk. Herbison gave up in despair and resigned. Faced with the difficulty that an across-the-board increase in family allowances cost so much money, the Treasury argued that if the government must act on child poverty it should introduce a special new means-tested benefit for working families; this was the kind of plan that was being discussed in the United States at that very time.

CPAG and its backers were convinced that the stigma and administrative problems that would surround such a scheme would lead to many, perhaps most, of those for whom it was intended never receiving it. Family allowances did reach virtually everyone entitled to them and they reached mothers. CPAG then came up with an ingenious way of targeting the money on the poorest families while keeping family allowances. Let the mothers draw the benefit and tax the extra benefit away from the average taxpayer. The Treasury and the Inland Revenue objected, defeating the idea in 1967, but in the end the Cabinet came to accept it after intense lobbying by the CPAG and, significantly, some trade union leaders. In 1968 family allowances were increased to a level higher than they had been in 1945, in relation to the average pay packet, but the standard rate taxpayer had the increase taxed away. This was the beginning of a new debate about how and whether to target support for poor families that is still very much alive in the twenty-first century, as we shall see in Chapter 10.

The CPAG became so fed up with the government's response and with the fact that it was letting the value of other benefits slip back again that it let off a broadside in the run-up to the election whose catchphrase title was to stick: 'the poor are getting poorer under Labour'. It did have an immediate impact on the Labour Chancellor, who in 1970 concentrated most of his tax cuts on the poor. The attack also endeared the group to the Conservative Party. The group's proposals to increase the level of family allowances and reduce the scale of the tax relief richer families with children got was put to the shadow Tory Chancellor Iain Macleod. Field describes the occasion (Field, 1982: 38–9). Macleod, despite suffering from advanced arthritis, displayed what Field called 'the best political probing mind I ever came across'. Macleod committed the Conservatives to do something about child poverty, and more than that, to implement the CPAG plan.

In fact, when they came to power later that year, the Conservatives did not do so. Macleod had died in July 1970. Instead they took off the stocks the new means-tested benefit for working families the Treasury had tried to persuade the Labour government to introduce. It was enacted in about six months as the Family Income Supplement Act 1970.

This was to be a 'temporary' measure, making the maximum impact from spending a small sum of money. It was targeted on those in work on very low pay and with children. As their incomes rose, however, so these families would lose their benefit. This could encourage families not to raise their incomes and trap them in poverty, critics argued (Field and Piachaud, 1971). It was an argument that was to become a major focus of debate for the rest of the century and beyond.

What is striking in retrospect, however, is that a government could be so embarrassed by an attack from a small group that was campaigning on behalf of poor families and that the Conservative Party should see this as a cause worth taking up. Far greater child poverty was to occur in the 1980s with little or no political embarrassment or outcry.

The coming of child benefit

While in opposition the Labour Party had time to reflect again on the issue of family allowances and child poverty. It was opposing the means-tested family income supplement, so what would it do instead? It pledged in its 1974 manifesto to go for what Eleanor Rathbone had advocated after the First World War, a benefit for each child. The manifesto did not say how this would be paid for. The Child Benefit Act was duly passed in 1975. By then the oil crisis was hitting the economy and the government put off implementing the scheme. Instead it introduced a benefit targeted on single parents (see Chapter 7).

Barbara Castle, who had been a strong advocate of child benefits and took the bill through the Commons, was removed from the post of Secretary of State for Social Services when Wilson resigned and James Callaghan took over as Prime Minister. He had opposed the move to increase family allowances in the previous government, if Margaret Herbison's account is to be trusted. Frank Field, who was closely involved in the events, relates that what happened immediately after Castle lost her post was that the Labour whips began a devious campaign to undermine the government's own statute (Field, 1982: 18). Backbenchers were told the trade unions were against implementing the measure. The trade unions were told the backbenchers were against it. The plan was to offset the increase in the cash child benefit by abolishing the tax relief parents got for each child. This relief was worth nothing to poor families and a great deal to rich families. However, it also had the feature that trade unionists were supposed to oppose: the loss of tax relief came off the pay packets of men and the child benefit would go to mothers.

Shortly after he became Prime Minister, Callaghan had 'ambushed' a group of TUC leaders (the 'Neddy Six') after a regular formal meeting and pointed out the aspects of the scheme he hoped they would find unacceptable, in such a way as to secure their opposition. When they returned to the TUC General Council it was pointed out that the child benefit switch had always been TUC policy. It was agreed it should continue to be so despite Callaghan's objections and should be implemented in a way that would carry members' support. (This account comes from a TUC member of staff at the time.)

Cabinet discussions on the matter were leaked. With a furious Barbara Castle operating from the backbenches (Castle, 1980) and the CPAG lobbying ceaselessly, the Cabinet was shamed into implementing its predecessor's legislation. Child benefit for each child replaced the perversely targeted child tax allowance that Titmuss had attacked thirty years or more earlier.

Balance Sheet So Far

The first Wilson Labour government had left office with the tag 'the poor are poorer under Labour' hung round its neck. Was that fair? Professor Atkinson's account remains the most balanced:

There can be little doubt that social security received much more attention from the Labour Government of 1964–70 than it did during the preceding thirteen years . . . What is more controversial is whether the Labour measures were sufficiently large – or even of the right kind – to make a significant contribution to the reduction of inequality in Britain. (1972: 12)

Notice the shift in the goal posts, here, from Beveridge's criteria. Atkinson, in tune with emphasis of the time, was asking whether overall inequality had been reduced, not whether the absolute standards of living of the poor or their basic incomes had been improved. At that time the idea that *absolute* living standards of the poor would decline was not even considered. It was to happen in the 1980s when the 'poor becoming poorer' was to take on a new meaning.

Effort

Labour had planned a faster rate of growth in public spending when it reached office than the previous government: 6.6 compared to 4.8 per cent per annum in real terms. It achieved a 6.5 per cent increase per annum in real volume terms, pretty good shooting in the economic climate of the time with a sterling crisis intervening in between. The social security budget increased from 7.2 per cent of the GDP to 9.3 per cent between 1964/5 and 1969/70. The government cannot be faulted in terms of sheer expenditure. But to some extent these figures were misleading. Unemployment was beginning to rise – a point to which we return. There were more old people and part of the increase in family allowances had been clawed back in tax increases. Adjusting for these factors, however, there was still an increase in the percentage of the GDP going to social security from 7.2 to 8.6 (Atkinson, 1972) so the additional effort was real enough.

Between May 1963 and November 1969 basic insurance benefits had risen in value by 14 per cent. Most of that increase had happened in that first March 1965 rise and beneficiaries had suffered from not having their benefits uprated in the aftermath of the sterling crisis until November 1969. Take-home pay had suffered as a result of the rise in flat rate contributions, as Crossman had noted at the time in his diary. So the low-paid worker with a family was only 7 per cent better off in 1970 than in 1964. The new earnings-related benefits were of relatively little help to the poorest-paid. Supplementary benefits had been made more generous, however. Here was the first move to targeting by a Labour government boxed in by public spending pressures and its promises to the poor.

Despite spending so much more on social security the Labour government had left office with little credit, quite unlike its 1945 predecessors. On both occasions the main beneficiaries of the government's innovations were not the very poorest but the rather less poor.

In 1974–6 the achievements, in the Labour Party's own terms, were more considerable. The final implementation of the national pensions plan and the introduction of child benefit were real achievements in a period of world economic crisis, even if child benefit had to be prised out of the government. This was to be the furthest the 1945 social policy agenda was to go. It was its high-water mark.

Questions to Answer

1 In what ways can the legislation of this era be seen as the 'high-water mark' of the 1945 agenda?
2 What was the case for the new child benefit? Why was it opposed? Does the case for it remain?
3 Why did social policy move centre stage in this period?

6

Completing the Post-war Agenda 1964–76, Part Two: From Equal Access to Equality?

Health Care
Social Work
NHS Reform Again
Education and the Pursuit of Equality
Housing
Race Relations
Equal Pay

Health Care

If social security and child poverty had become contentious in 1964–70 the Health Service experienced minimal changes to its structure but real growth in spending. The Labour Party came to power with no really new ideas. It was sufficient to restore the NHS to the glory it had once been in 1948. Then it had been completely free at the point of use. There had been no charges on prescriptions, dental or opticians' services, or spectacles and dentures. The party had fiercely opposed the prescription charge increases of 1961 and was committed to abolishing them altogether. It did so very early in its period of office, in February 1965. It was to be a short-lived nostalgic return to the 1940s.

By 1967–8 the economy was in deep trouble. The pound had to be devalued and cuts in public expenditure were called for by the Treasury. Rather than cut the hospital building programme the Ministry of Health offered the Treasury a restoration of prescription charges – at a higher rate than they had been when Labour took office: 12.5p per item. This was a blow to the party faithful and to the government's self-confidence.

More new hospitals

The big hospital building programme had been begun by the previous government in 1961. Given the lead time on hospital design this pro-gramme really got into full swing only in this Labour period. Many of today's district general hospitals, especially the really big ones, date from this period, suffering from much of the same design brutality as many of the housing estates of the same period. Yet, to its credit, the government did hold to that programme, more or less, despite the sterling crisis and devaluation. Other later governments might not have done! On reaching office Labour committed itself to increase Health Service spending in real volume terms by 4.8 per cent a year. This was cut back after the economic crisis of 1967 to a rate of increase of 3.8 per cent but it was still higher than the previous government's plans. The Labour government could claim it had given higher priority to health than its predecessors (see Table 6.1).

A GP charter

There were the normal fisticuffs with the doctors. The BMA put in a claim for a 30 per cent rise and were given 10 per cent in 1965. They talked of resigning from the service. In the course of discussions they proposed a charter for the family doctor service. Kenneth Robinson, the minister, negotiated an agreement that gave more financial support to GPs' basic practice costs and some more obligations to provide a basic service (Timmins, 1995: 217–25). More health centres were built, in which groups of GPs could work with others such as community nurses and health visitors.

Scandal

Ever since the Health Service had been created, and indeed for long before it, the long-stay services in hospitals for the elderly and mentally ill and handicapped had been a disgrace to a humane society. They were

Table 6.1 Planned and actual expenditure of Conservative and Labour governments, 1963/4 to 1976/7

(i) Planned average annual growth rates in constant prices

	Volume terms, growth in percentages per annum				
	Conservative plans	Labour government plans		Conservative plans	
Service	1963/4 to 1967/8	1964/5 to 1969/70	1968/9 to 1971/2	1970/1 to 1974/5	1972/3 to 1976/7
Housing	3.8*	7.1	3.2	−0.4	−4.4
Education	5.7	5.7	3.8	3.3	3.4
Health and Welfare	3.0	4.8	3.8	3.3	3.4
Social Security	4.8	6.6	5.1	2.1	1.3
Roads	6.9	7.2	7.5	6.1	5.15
Defence	2.7	0.0	−1.9	−0.9	1.4
All public expenditure	4.1	4.2	3.0	2.6	2.2

* includes Environment

(ii) Actual as against planned growth rates in constant prices

	Volume terms, growth in percentages per annum					
	1964/5 to 1969/70 (Cmnd 2734)		1968/9 to 1971/2 (Cmnd 4234)		1970/1 to 1973/4 (Cmnd 4578)	
Service	Actual	Planned	Actual	Planned	Actual	Planned
Housing	3.8	7.1	−1.6	3.2	5.9	0.0
Education	4.9	5.7	4.0	3.8	4.9	3.5
Health and Welfare	3.4	4.8	3.2	3.8	5.2	3.2
Social Security	6.5	6.6	9.7	5.1	4.0	2.5
Roads	5.7	7.2	5.5	7.5	3.9	6.2
Defence	−2.4	0.0	−3.1	−1.9	−0.8	−1.4
All public expenditure	4.1	4.2	1.4	3.0	5.5	2.0

Note: The figures show increases in the amount of services provided, not their cost.
Source: Glennerster, 1975

becoming worse, as the very costly staff needed to keep them bearable became more difficult to recruit. In 1961 the government had assumed, on the basis of recent reductions in admissions to mental hospitals, that many could be closed. This helped to keep down the apparent cost of the new building programme. It was to be mainly devoted to building new large district general hospitals and not to replacing these very old institutions, many a hundred years old. Conditions in them were appalling. One remarkable campaigning woman, Barbara Robb, finding out from personal experience how bad they were, put together a series of accounts in a book called *Sans Everything* and used it to launch a campaign to improve, or else close, long-stay facilities.

Shortly afterwards the brutality and poor care being meted out in Ely, a long-stay hospital for the mentally handicapped in Cardiff, were opened to public scrutiny by a nurse writing to the *News of the World*.

Kenneth Robinson had asked a young Conservative lawyer to undertake an official inquiry. He was Geoffrey Howe. His report was devastatingly critical of conditions, staff morale and management and arrived on Richard Crossman's desk to be dealt with. The civil servants were keen to give the whole thing as little publicity as possible and do nothing. Crossman saw this as a way of extracting more resources for his department and especially of improving conditions in these long-stay institutions, which he had become convinced were an outrage and would prove a political embarrassment. Instead of burying the report he decided to maximize publicity for it. He telephoned Fleet Street editors, gave 'exclusives', told them a dynamite report was on its way (Crossman, 1977: 418, 421, 425–30). As a former journalist he knew how to manipulate a scandal for his own purposes. Against his department's wishes he established an inspectorate, actually called the Hospital Advisory Service, to monitor conditions in these institutions. We see, here, the first cracks in the popular edifice of the NHS. These were institutions hidden from public view, dealing with people with no ability to complain, who were incapable of exercising any power of exit or market sanctions. The employees, many poorly paid and with little or no training, had excessive power over the patients. The fact patients were being looked after as part of the popular and politically sensitive NHS had made no difference. They were out of sight and out of mind and it was in the interests of the bureaucracy and the professionals to keep them that way. The series of scandals that came to light in this period tell us something about the decline in standards that can take place in any institution that is hidden from public gaze (Martin, 1984). Theoretical democratic control was not enough to save these patients. Press exposure and the fear that there might be more such did begin to put a tighter form of accountability in place. There were wider lessons here for the service at large. It was a cloud on the horizon for those who could see it.

At the end of Crossman's period of office a White Paper had been drafted setting out a phased plan for improving the services available for mentally handicapped people, and building up community facilities. It will seem somewhat old-fashioned in approach to today's readers. It relied on fairly large hostel accommodation but it was the first attempt to look long term at the needs of this group (Glennerster and Korman, 1983). It was adopted and published by Crossman's Conservative successor, Sir Keith Joseph, with virtually no changes (Cmnd 4683, 1971).

A new structure for the NHS?

It was during this period too that, prompted originally by the Royal Colleges, the government started to think again about the structure of the NHS. The medical profession had never been entirely happy with the local authorities continuing to have health responsibilities and had pressed for the local health services run by local councils to be brought within the ambit of the National Service and thus more effectively within the profession's sphere of influence.

In 1968 the Minister of Health published a Green, or discussion, paper setting out a possible reorganization of the NHS, the first of many in the next twenty years. It was a hurried document which was, as much as anything, a response to the big changes that were being proposed for social work. Social workers were then often part of the empire of the local authority Medical Officer of Health. This first Green Paper was really a last minute attempt by the Ministry of Health to counter the loss of social work functions which this committee – the Seebohm Committee – was proposing (Cmnd 3703, 1968). This had already happened in Scotland as a result of the Kilbrandon Report (Cmnd 2303, 1964).

Social Work

These two committees created the modern social work profession. It is therefore worth looking at their origins (Hall, 1976).

On one level these are demographic. The rapid increase in the number of births immediately after the Second World War had resulted in a much larger than normal teenage population in the late 1950s. They became the focus of commercial attention, from pop groups and record companies to scooter and motor-cycle manufacturers. They also committed crimes, as all teenage groups had done, crime being concentrated in that age group. Teenage delinquency became a matter of public concern and political interest. Part of that concern was channelled into a debate about families with difficult children and families at risk. The Ingleby Committee (Cmnd 1191, 1960) had made tentative proposals to co-ordinate preventive work between the multiple agencies concerned with family welfare. The McBoyle Report (Cmnd 1966, 1963) was more radical in its proposals for Scotland. At this time social workers were trained by numerous specialist bodies. Probation officers had one kind of training. Child-care workers had another, mental health workers another, hospital social workers another, those working mainly for welfare departments with the elderly mostly had no training at all. Social workers were employed by a variety of public and private agencies. They were fragmented and very weak as a group. Part of the agenda was to increase the professional status and power of this disparate collection of professionals.

Some reformers argued that there *was* a common thread of principle that underlay all these activities, at least at the level of basic training. New courses had been set up, like that at the LSE, which taught this generic base and gave a common qualification in social work. The children's service had done extremely well. Could this not be the forerunner of a larger social work department? The Scottish solution was to merge probation and all the other social workers in one social work department. This was done in the Social Work (Scotland) Act 1968.

In England specialist social workers were badly divided. Many wanted to retain their independence, others saw the case for merging. There was also conflict at the level of central government departments. The Home Office did not want to lose control of its child-care and probation service. The Ministry of Health did not want to lose control of its welfare officers and of the new social work assistants it was training.

The government decided to appoint a committee to review what it called 'local authority and allied personal social services'. The committee, chaired by Lord Seebohm, had only one representative on it from the medical profession: Professor Jerry Morris, an epidemiologist, joint author with, and personal friend of, Professor Titmuss. Another member of Titmuss's department, Roy Parker, was on the committee and was to play a particularly influential role.

Seebohm's logic

The unquestioned assumption was that social work would remain a predominantly public sector, local authority responsibility. If you wanted social work to acquire anything like the status of medicine it would be necessary to create a unified and large social work department with a powerful chief officer, like the Chief Education Officer or Medical Officer of Health. It would give social work not only bureaucratic power but a career structure. To do that meant putting together enough foot soldiers to justify the appointment of a general. So, to the existing responsibilities of the Children's Departments, the committee added the various social workers in the existing health and welfare departments, their home helps and the residential care of elderly and disabled people. Though many of these were *not* professional social work activities in the full sense, they added numbers and budget size to the departments and hence their power in the local authority hierarchy. It was an exercise in bureaucratic and professional power politics.

To back up the claim to professional status a single training body for social work was to be created, modelled on the General Medical Council and later professional statutory bodies; it was to be the Central Council for the Education and Training in Social Work (CCETSW).

The new social services departments

When the Ministry of Health officials woke up to the significance of these recommendations for the Medical Officer of Health's role they rushed out their own Green Paper suggesting that non-social-work services like home helps should not be taken away from the local authority Medical Officers of Health. The Home Office was also unhappy. It wanted to and did keep probation out of the new social service departments. The report was published in July 1968, almost at the same moment as the Russian invasion of Czechoslovakia, and got less than massive attention in the press. The resulting bill was introduced and passed with little debate and no opposition from the Conservative front bench. It had cross-party support and was passed not long before the Labour government lost office in 1970. Crossman, who took over responsibility for the report when he became Secretary of State, was bored with the whole thing, whereas he had had a lively interest in the pensions plan:

when I got to my room at 70 Whitehall I found an official from the Home Office with a long and official virtuous draft on the kind of speech they thought I ought to deliver. After an hour's talk with them trying to get it straight, I left these three officials to do it for me while I went across to the House to listen to the final part of the Common Market debate. (1977: 835–6; Diary entry 25 February 1970)

The new 'Seebohm' social services departments of local authorities, as they were called, came into operation in 1971 and were encouraged by the new Conservative Secretary of State, Sir Keith Joseph, to submit to him ambitious plans for expansion. Here, certainly, was a clear example of consensus between the parties. The battle had been between the professions and the central government departments with whom they were most closely associated. It is an example of what Dunleavy (1991) calls the 'bureau shaping' activities of government departments and civil servants in their own interests.

Social work had carved itself out a new empire and a hierarchical career structure. It was a similar story, but on a larger scale, to the creation of the Children's Departments in 1948. There was a difference. Those had provided a career structure and senior posts for women. The new highly paid directors of social services were to be mostly men! The idea that social work might be anything other than a primarily statutory, state-employee-based profession was not seriously debated.

There were also some genuine concerns for the groups in need. The Seebohm Report took as its guiding principle the notion that there should be one department that offered help and support for families in need at any period in their lives. The new departments should not be seen merely as a place where bad parents or sick and damaged people went. It was to be, so far as possible, a universal service providing support at periods in the life cycle when it was needed.

One single department concerned with most aspects of 'welfare' as the public generally understands the term, is an essential first step in making services more easily accessible. (Cmnd 3703, 1968, para. 146)

This report represents, perhaps, the high tide of post-war universalist ambitions. It was a bridge too far. The new social services departments would, in the tighter economic climate they would soon inhabit, inevitably spend most of their time with the poor and the frail and the ill. They would never become the general recourse for the ordinary family. It was romantic to believe it could ever have been otherwise.

NHS Reform Again

A second go

Crossman had not been satisfied with the hurried Green Paper on Health Service reform that had been produced by Kenneth Robinson as a preemptive strike against Seebohm. With Seebohm nearly on the statute book what was to become of the NHS? Crossman produced a second Green Paper (DHSS, 1970). He accepted the medical profession's pressure for the inclusion within the NHS of all medical and related professional activities. The local authorities' health departments, weakened by the loss of functions to the new social work and social services departments, should be removed and responsibility for the community health services transferred to the NHS. Area health authorities would be created that would run the local hospitals *and* the community services. To encourage collaboration with the new social services departments they would cover exactly the same geographical area.

The private hope of Crossman and his adviser Abel-Smith was that at some time these area health authorities would merge with the local authorities, bringing both the social work and the medical services under the democratic control of the same agency. That was precisely what the BMA feared. The area health authorities were to be directly responsible to the Department of Health and Social Security. The intermediate regional layer would go. It was by far the neatest and most streamlined structure to be proposed for the NHS since the Second World War. But it removed the layer that the profession had pressed Bevan to put in place and on which it had most leverage: the regions, then called regional hospital boards. The second Green Paper fell with the government.

A third go

The Conservative government accepted the BMA's objections. A regional tier was introduced into the plans set out by Crossman. Below the areas were to be district authorities charged with the operational management of the services. They were based, essentially, on the catchment areas of the large district general hospitals built in the 1960s and 1970s. Areas were to be planning units, not the driving force, of the system. The medical profession had thus removed power from those bodies with the strongest local authority links and placed it at the point where they could have most impact. The loss of direct local authority control of services was partly recompensed by local authority representation on the area authorities and partly by the creation of community health councils that were composed of lay people appointed to act as consumer watch-dogs. Again the Conservative government fell before these changes could be implemented but they were so nearly in place that the Labour government of 1974 decided not to revoke them, merely increasing the powers of the community health councils.

Byzantium

The resulting structure was the most Byzantine ever imposed on a UK public service. There were regional health authorities with a team of multi-professional officers supposedly acting in unison. There were area teams of officers doing the same and district teams below them. As Roy Griffiths, Mrs Thatcher's adviser, was to say ten years later, Florence Nightingale would have paced through this maze 'searching for the people in charge' (Griffiths Report, 1983, para. 5).

What Seebohm and the new NHS had done, however, was to separate into two statutory camps the social workers and the medical and related professions, like nursing. Social services departments would employ the one and the NHS the other. There would be a joint consultative machinery to link the two services but for those dependent on both, like the elderly, the mentally ill and the handicapped, the results were not to be good.

Planning and rationing health care

When the Conservatives returned to power in 1970 they were committed to containing public expenditure but not to reducing or cutting back services like the NHS. How could that circle be squared? The Heath government believed that the application of new planning and budgetary tools invented in the United States in the 1960s would help get more out of the given budget, just as it was hoped that the internal market would do this in the 1990s.

A pilot programme budget for health and social services was drawn up in 1971 and subsequently developed (Banks, 1979). Crossman had found that when he wanted to give more priority to services for the mentally handicapped no one knew what was already being spent on them. How would you ever know whether you were succeeding? The department wanted to make a better case to the Treasury for resources. How could it do so when it did not know what priority groups were getting what or what the implications of an ageing population were? So far from being a tool to cut health spending the DHSS was using the programme budget to sharpen its weapons in the battle for funds with the Treasury.

By the time Barbara Castle became Secretary of State this planning and budgetary tool had been well developed. She decided to use it not merely to battle with the Treasury but to give explicit planning guidelines to the lower tiers in the NHS to shift priorities towards the groups that had been the focus of the *Sans Everything* and the post-Ely policies in the last administration: the elderly, the mentally ill and the handicapped. She published a priorities document setting out budgetary and service targets for each. This was a courageous exercise in open planning that was not to be repeated. The difficulty was that the NHS was not like a large company or the armed services. The lower tiers were run by medical politics and no one was clearly charged with managing the changes (Glennerster and Korman, 1983). They frittered away as they trickled down the complex hierarchy we have described. This was the height of optimism about the capacity of rational planning to solve the problems of the NHS, what Klein calls 'paternalistic rationalism', and it was to decline steadily thereafter (Klein, 1989: 105).

The final part of this rational plan for the NHS was the attempt to allocate resources more fairly between areas of the country. We saw in Chapter 3 that health resources in the 1930s and before followed the capacity of consultants to attract private fees and benefactors to give hospitals endowments. The coming of the NHS had changed matters much less than might have been expected. Budgets in the post-war period had tended to be rolled forward in an incremental way, perpetuating the inequalities of the past. The 1964 Labour government had not helped matters by approving a lot of hospital-building in London. Research by Culyer and colleagues at York, and others, had attracted attention to this issue. Since the main losers were the northern regions where Labour was strong, equity and political advantage seemed to coincide. The government set up a working party to find a way of allocating health service budgets on a more scientific basis than last year's budget plus or minus 'x per cent'.

The Resource Allocation Working Party did so and produced a formula that came to be named after it, the RAWP formula. It allocated money on the basis of a region's population and its relative health needs – actually death rates from different conditions. Though criticized, it was probably the most sophisticated system of its kind anywhere in the world. It remained in use for more than a decade, shifting resources to the north and other deprived areas. It was replaced by more sophisticated district-based allocations in the 1990s and allocations that went down to Primary Care Trusts by 2006. It must be counted one of the real technical achievements of the period. (For a detailed account see Glennerster et al., 2000.)

Education and the Pursuit of Equality

Abolishing the eleven-plus

Education had been central to Anthony Crosland's vision of a fairer and more equal society. Class divisions stemmed, in large part, from Britain's segregated education system. He was to become Secretary of State for Education in Wilson's government in 1965 and charged with implementing the changes he had pressed on the party in his book ten years earlier.

In the 1960s education was the political talking point. Bad landlords and high private rents might worry the poorer and older voters but they were of declining electoral importance. Younger educated and middle-class parents cared about education and their numbers were growing. The labour force was changing. The numbers of pupils staying on into sixth form and applying to university was growing rapidly, as we saw in the last chapter. Secondary modern schools that provided no school-leaving qualifications were less and less relevant to this new population. These schools themselves began to build up examination courses. The pressure to obtain the restricted grammar school places intensified. Abolishing the eleven-plus had an increasing electoral appeal.

Yet many Labour councils with ex-grammar school pupils on them, who were proud of their grammar school provision built up since the 1920s, were less sure. Wilson himself seemed equivocal. He was interested in expanding technical education and higher education of a vocational kind. Where he stood on grammar schools, as an ex-grammar school boy, tended to be obscured in pipe smoke.

Pressure

That, at least, was how it seemed to two ex-employees of the Labour Party Research Department as they discussed matters after lunch on Boxing Day

1964, with their wives nursing two children of under a year. Were they going to have to sit the eleven-plus like their fathers? The grammar school defence groups were already forming. The likelihood was a Wilsonian compromise and fudge around the corner. A ginger group was called for. This was almost a year before the CPAG was to be formed on the same logic. Various people known to be interested and expert were approached. One parent who had older children at comprehensive school lived nearby and had been interviewed on the radio; she was the wife of Tony Benn. Perhaps she could be roped in. A group of interested people collected together and decided to launch something called the Comprehensive Schools Committee. An article in the *Guardian* with an address to write to elicited hundreds of letters wanting to know more about comprehensive education. Local groups were formed and Caroline Benn became the best-informed person in the country on the subject. Her regular reports on the subject sold out rapidly and were sent for on the morning of publication by the Department of Education, by taxi. She briefed her husband and later one senior civil servant remarked, not altogether happily, 'it is like having another bloody Minister of Education in the Cabinet'. The civil service persuaded ministers not to legislate on the matter, probably wisely, as it turned out. A circular, the famous Circular 10/65, was issued to local education authorities saying that it was government policy to abolish the eleven-plus examination system and selective secondary schools. The government wanted local authorities to produce plans for secondary education of a non-selective type and would they please do so within a year. LEAs were given a choice of how to do it. Schemes that had been tried by existing local authorities in the 1950s were described. Existing buildings could be used and grouped into lower and upper schools or middle and senior schools with every child moving on from one to another. 'Let us get a few of the really good authorities that everyone respects to play ball and the rest will follow', was the civil service advice. There would be no permission to build new grammar schools.

It worked. By the 1970 election nearly all local areas were well on their way to switching to comprehensive education. The circular was withdrawn by Mrs Thatcher when she became Secretary of State for Education in 1970. Indeed, she insisted on it being done on her very first day in office (Timmins, 1995: 292). But authorities of all political persuasions continued the change and more comprehensive schools were founded in her period than in the time of any other minister. Reintroducing the eleven-plus, denying most children access to grammar schools and hence access to the booming clerical and semi-professional jobs that were being created, was simply not practical politics. Nor did it make sense to the chief education officers of the day. Building one secondary school for local children was more economic in rural and small county town areas, the Conservative heartlands.

When the Labour government came back to power it did introduce legislation to require local councils to abolish selection but the battle was, by then, all but won. Whether it achieved the egalitarian results Crosland and other reformers had hoped for is more debatable and would be difficult to judge until much later. We shall return to the point in Chapter 10.

Raising the school-leaving age to 16

This had been legislated for in 1944 but no government had been able to free the resources to do so. The Conservative government had promised to in 1968. That coincided with the economic crisis of 1967–8 and one of the economy measures was to put off the change until 1971.

Educational priorities and disadvantage

The government had not come to power with any strong policy for primary or pre-school provision, except reducing class sizes. The Central Advisory Council for Education, whose reports had been so influential in the Conservative period, produced one more on primary education – the Plowden Report – in 1967. It endorsed and encouraged the child-centred, relaxed and informal approach to primary teaching that had developed in the late 1950s and 1960s and had become much admired abroad. It also began to come to terms with important changes in the social structure and accepted more explicitly than any previous report that equal access to services was not enough to ensure equal benefit. Despite all the improvements to the basic standards of schooling that had been achieved since 1945, and the excellent results achieved by the most able, differences in achievement between the highest and the lowest were greater than in most advanced economies. Similar results were found in the 1990s (Green and Steedman, 1993). However, a big international study at the turn of the century suggests that the relative gap compared to other countries may have narrowed (OECD, 2001). This is discussed further in Chapter 10.

Standards in many inner-city schools and other deprived areas were particularly disturbing. Members of the team had visited the United States as part of their investigations and were influenced by what they saw, in particular the programmes of compensatory education. It was not enough simply to provide ordinary average schooling in these deprived areas, they argued. What was necessary was distinctive and *better* education than normal to compensate children for the lack of stimulus their environment and their families could give. Schools in such areas should be given special help, their teachers paid more.

This idea did not go down well with the teachers' unions, and sociologists talked about the ecological fallacy: not all or most poor children were in schools designated as poor. But it was the first attempt by an official committee to come to terms with the problems set for schools by poverty and deprivation. (The Newsom Committee, 1963, on secondary modern schools a number of years before had recognized some similar issues but not developed a coherent response.)

Plowden urged that pre-school education was vital and especially for children in such areas. It should be made available to all families who wanted it for their children but it should come first in the poorest areas. The report was followed by the sterling crisis later in 1967 and there was little money to implement its proposals. In 1972 Mrs Thatcher produced a White Paper proposing a phased introduction of pre-school provision for all parents who wanted it. That was to be a casualty of the 1976 crisis like much else. It was a goal that was not to be reached for thirty more years (see Chapter 10).

Higher education

The big breakthrough in the expansion of higher education had been achieved in the period of the 1959–64 Conservative government with the Robbins Committee Report (1963), as we saw in the previous chapter. Most of the actual expansion fell to the Labour government to implement. What the Labour government added was the creation of a public sector of vocationally and technologically based institutions – the polytechnics – and the Open University.

The binary system created

Hugh Gaitskell had set up a study group to settle what Labour's policy towards higher education should be and to attempt to pre-empt the Robbins Report (Labour Party, 1963). We discuss later its distinctive contribution, the Open University. In other respects the committee said much the same as Robbins, stressing the case for university expansion of the traditional kind. It had supported the merger of the Colleges of Advanced

Technology into the university system. As chairman of Labour's Home Policy Committee Wilson had other ideas. A separate committee was set up to work on further and higher vocational education. It opposed the wholesale expansion of the universities. These were not capable of delivering the officer class that would lead Wilson's technological revolution. Nor would they attract working-class children. A new kind of institution was called for that linked with local industry, like the further education colleges, but doing work that would be of higher educational standard. These institutions would span the range of work from part-time vocational courses to top-rate research and teaching that would outdo the universities (Robinson, 1968). Here was a quite distinctive and opposing philosophy to that of Robbins or the Crosland wing of the Labour Party.

Though the Labour Party accepted the Robbins Report and made no public commitment to a different policy, when Wilson became Prime Minister this alternative was pressed forward. It had powerful support within the Department of Education (Timmins, 1995: 246). In 1966 Crosland published a White Paper proposing the creation of a separate but equal system of new polytechnics (Cmnd 3006), run by local authorities but drawing on a national recruitment of students. The demand for student places was thought to be growing faster than Robbins had forecast and the polytechnics were to provide the extra places. They grew rapidly, not least because government came to see them as a cheaper way to expand higher education. By the 1980s they were taking equivalent numbers of students to universities.

The polytechnics did not retain the very distinctive character their more enthusiastic proponents hoped for. They gradually moved nearer and nearer to being cheaper and more teaching-based universities. The Conservative government accepted the logic of the drift (Cm. 1541, 1991) and merged the two parts of the binary system into one. The polytechnics became 'new' universities.

King and Nash (2001) argue that the 1960s marked a decisive break in the history of British higher education. It was the end of the application of 'liberal humanist principles' – university freedom, the pursuit of knowledge for its own sake. New universities were supported and expanded because of 'the alleged contribution of university education to national growth and productivity' (p. 88). I think this is only one explanation. The pressure from parents who want to see their children set on lucrative careers is as important. After all, similar expansion has taken place in countries with and without major central government funding of their universities.

A University of the Air?

How could university education be extended to that part of the population who were past normal university age and were already in work or were at home bringing up children? As early as 1960 Professor Sir George Catlin had suggested a 'university of the air' (see Hall et al., 1975 for an account). Michael Young, that most original of ideas men, founder of *Which?* consumer magazine and much else, was experimenting with and writing about using television to educate people in their own homes. About the same time Harold Wilson had returned from the Soviet Union, much enthused by the idea of using correspondence courses on a mass scale to teach university degrees. Acting as secretary to the Labour Party study group as I was at that time, it occurred to me that these two ideas might be put together. What the eventual report said was,

> We propose that, as an experiment, the BBC sound radio and television and the ITA should be required to cooperate in organising a 'University of the Air' for serious adult education. [There would be correspondence courses and] Wherever possible students should meet regularly at area colleges for the equivalent of university tutorials. (Labour Party, 1963b: 34)

That remains the basis of what is the Open University today.

The idea became Wilson's own particular passion. He gave the job of implementing it to Aneurin Bevan's widow, Jennie Lee, when he won the 1964 election. The DES thought the whole idea barmy and resisted it throughout. It was only her direct line to Wilson that got the Open University on to the statute book and into reality (Hall et al., 1975).

More higher education

Thus, up to about 1972 higher education expanded faster than it had ever done before, not merely catering for the big increase in the number of 18-year-olds but substantially increasing the proportion of the population going to higher education. The Labour government expanded higher education as a whole faster than Robbins had recommended. More teacher training places and more advanced further education and polytechnic places were created. In the 1960s higher education doubled in size. The percentage of the age group entering full-time higher education rose from 7.7 per cent in 1958 to over 13 per cent in 1972.

It was not an achievement to be underestimated and it slowly began to change the nature of the labour force in a major way (Glennerster and Lowe, 1990). After 1972 the expansion ran out of steam for a period. The salaries that new university graduates earned fell relative to the 1960s as the supply of graduates rose. The government cut the real value of student grants in the early 1970s, so both the rewards fell and the costs rose. The percentage of the age group entering higher education was not to rise again until the late 1980s.

Private education

The public schools had long been an obsession with those on the left in British politics and for good reason. Tawney had advocated their reform. There had been a committee of inquiry on ways of integrating the public schools more closely with the state sector during the Second World War (the Fleming Report, 1944). (In the absurd ways of the English, 'public' schools mean private schools. To be more precise, they mean the very small group of elite private schools that belong to the Head Masters' Conference.)

These schools had for long been the entry gate to the class elite that ran British society. In 1964, 87 per cent of the Conservative Cabinet had gone to public schools, 76 per cent of Conservative MPs (15 per cent only of Labour MPs), 76 per cent of judges, half the positions at the top of the civil service, nearly 60 per cent of the directors of the leading firms, and so the list went on (Glennerster and Pryke, 1964). Three-quarters of all sixth formers in 1967 were in this small number of schools. All sections of the Labour Party were keen to break this class stranglehold which fitted ill with the meritocratic technological future Wilson was presenting.

There was, however, no agreement about what to do, despite much agonizing in opposition. Some wanted to make the schools illegal and take them over, as Bevan had done with the teaching hospitals. Others felt this was wrong in principle and electorally suicidal. The debate was often conducted in terms of the clash between the pursuit of equality and people's individual freedom to educate their own children in the way they wished. The reason for the indecision was therefore not pure lassitude but reflected a genuine principled dilemma of a very sixties kind. The best the party could come up with was the phrase in its manifesto that a Labour government, if elected, would, 'set up an educational trust to advise on the best way of integrating the public schools into the state system of education'. (I well remember the hours of debate that went into that wording!)

The result was the Public Schools Commission. It was a typical committee of the great and the good with representatives of the public school sector and state schools and local authority people on it. It divided its work into two phases. The first would deal with the group of schools that aroused most passion, the elite boarding schools such as Eton and Harrow. The second would consider the future of those private grammar schools that had, since 1902, received a direct grant from central government in return for offering free places to some pupils.

Neither report was unanimous. The majority First Report (DES, 1968) recommended removing the schools' tax advantages unless they collaborated with the state sector in providing places for state school pupils who needed boarding education for personal and educational reasons. The direct grant schools were to lose their grants unless they became comprehensive schools though they could opt into the local education system fully if they wished to. No action was taken by the Labour government before 1970 on the integration policy but tax advantages that parents gained in paying their children's fees were withdrawn in successive Finance Acts, from 1968. (In practice rich families found their way round these curbs too!) When that government left office there was a Green Paper on these issues in draft called *Education for a New Generation*, which never saw the light of day (Glennerster, 1972).

When Labour returned to power it did abolish the direct grants to private grammar schools; as recommended in the Second Report of the Public Schools Commission (DES, 1970). They were phased out by the 1976 Education Act. About a quarter of the grammar schools, mainly the Catholic ones, became local authority comprehensive schools and the rest became independent day schools.

More equality?

Whom did all these changes benefit? We discuss some of the longer-term trends in the last chapter of this book. Immediately, however, the new comprehensive schools did expand the range of subjects and school-leaving qualification opportunities available to the average child who would before have gone to a secondary modern school. This shows up in the much higher qualification rates and higher staying-on rates in the 1970s and 1980s. The effects are difficult to disentangle from the longer statutory school life introduced at the same time. But overall the research suggests that the averagely able and below average children definitely gained from comprehensive education. The achievements of the most able do not seem to have been affected at all significantly, though there is dispute about this (Glennerster and Hills, 1998). If this is true the long-term impact was to some degree egalitarian.

Perhaps more important was the change to the school-leaving examination system that followed. 'O' levels designed for the grammar school system were replaced by the less restrictive General Certificate for Secondary Education (GCSE) in England. Scotland had always had a less restrictive exam system. GCSE recognized achievements by those with a wider spread of ability, used less traditional exam methods and encouraged more ordinary children to stay on. In particular it seems to have sparked the rise and rise of girls' attainments (Machin and McNally, 2005).

The rapid expansion of higher education places in the 1960s did increase participation amongst all classes or social groups, though the trend had been in progress since the 1930s or earlier (Halsey et al., 1980). The 1960s expansion seems to have benefited most, not the top professional and managerial classes nor the working class, but the intermediate groups, clerical, service occupations and lower professional groups like teachers' children. These were groups growing rapidly in social significance and electoral clout.

The bastions of class privilege, the public schools, had escaped. The picture is, therefore, mixed but overall it was middle England that had gained again. In an early evaluation of this period I allocated the total increase in education expenditure between 1962/3 and 1968/9 between the social groups who could be said to have benefited (Glennerster, 1972). There had been an overall increase of 85 per cent. The professional and managerial group had benefited by an increase of 136 per cent, manual working groups by about 75 per cent. The expansion of higher education and the larger numbers from these classes staying on at school explained this.

If the middle class had gained disproportionately from the education changes of the period, did the working class gain from the housing policy?

Housing

We have already seen that Wilson chose to appoint Richard Crossman to the housing ministry and not to social security or education, which had been his previous briefs, because of the central importance the Prime

Minister placed on housing. The Labour Party had promised to increase house-building to 500,000 houses a year.

Rents and the private landlord

Top of the agenda, though, was the repeal of the 1957 Rent Act and the restoration of some kind of security of tenure to those in privately rented housing. This had been thought to be a potent electoral asset at the election and it was important to deliver on it. Whether the politicians were right is another matter (Banting, 1979).

The committee of inquiry discussing the problems in London where Rachman had operated had still not reported and swift action was needed. An emergency Act restricting landlords' eviction powers was passed. For the larger legislation Crossman called in outside experts, notably Arnold Goodman, Crossman's solicitor and general fix-it man, and David Donnison from the LSE, whom Titmuss had suggested he consult. The ministry did not take kindly to this outside interference at first. Crossman describes a typical encounter at which he was presented with a paper to approve, as he left the office for home, which was supposed to be a summary of proposals drawn up by these outsiders. Somehow, the paper included almost none of them, only the proposals the Ministry had already put to him (1975: 90).

The outside group was to be influential in shaping the legislation, since the party had come to power with no clear idea of how it was going to deal with the issue of rent control and security of tenure despite having made it a central plank in its election campaign. (See Banting, 1979 for the best brief account.) The party believed that landlords were evil people, or at least that the system was evil, and that it was enough simply to freeze rents. The advisers argued that this would make private rented property unsustainable and it would disappear, to the disadvantage of poor people. There had to be a means of enabling landlords to increase rents from time to time and the rents had to be high enough to keep landlords in business. The ministry wanted a formula. The advisers thought a flexible approach was much more workable, with a local rent officer setting rents. The rents of existing tenants, which had remained controlled at the very low 1939 level, would have to be raised. Despite having campaigned on the basis of stopping rent increases the Labour Party's new Rent Act would permit their more general increase.

The Ministry officials were both surprised and delighted: It was a bill to raise rents. It was something the civil service would never have dared to suggest. For the first time we had a Minister prepared to put some flexibility into the rent control system. It's odd that it should have been a Labour Minister of Housing. (Banting, 1979: 50)

The part of the bill that caused most difficulty was the clause that gave the minister power to remove the controls on the existing very low rents on a region-by-region basis. He faced such backbench opposition from his own side that he had to amend the bill in committee, limiting the increases that could result. In the event no minister was to use this controversial power.

This compromise between rent control and the market lasted, with modifications, until Mrs Thatcher's era. It did not succeed in halting the decline in private landlord property – which had all but disappeared by the mid-1980s – but it may have slowed it down.

The council housing drive

Wilson had instructed Crossman to launch a 'housing drive', language reminiscent of the 1940s. The party had, it will be recalled, committed itself to increase house-building to 500,000 a year. The White Paper of 1965 pledged to do that by 1970. How was this to be achieved?

Crossman began by having dinners with the leading building contracting firms (1975: 30, 81). If the government wanted to build more quickly, they told him, it would have to concentrate on the large cities and undertake comprehensive redevelopment there. It would have to use industrial building methods. This would also fit the futuristic technological image Wilson was so taken by. Crossman visited the ministry's architects and was encouraged by their enthusiasm for mass-produced housing. In Oldham 750 houses were being built by these methods. 'Why not rebuild the whole thing? [i.e. 300 acres of the city centre] Wouldn't that help Laing?', he asked (p. 81).

Wilson's support for the housing budget was crucial. Crossman describes the Cabinet discussion (1975: 153–5). The Cabinet was told by the Treasury that it could not spend more in the next four years than the previous Conservative government had planned to do in its pre-election expansion plans for higher education, hospitals and roads.

The one social service they felt it was popular to cut back was public sector housing . . . It was my contention that whereas the other Ministers could fairly be asked to be content with the amount of money in the Tory estimates that was unreasonable in the case of housing. (p. 153)

Crossman proposed raising the target to the figure Wilson had suggested, using industrialized types of building to keep the costs down and use factory capacity that existed. There then ensued a sharp debate with the Chancellor and other ministers who were being told they could have no more money. Wilson took a vote, announced it tied, argued strongly for an increase and declared that that was what the Cabinet had decided.

It was the number of units built that mattered for political purposes. The capacity to say that the number was bigger than the Tories had achieved was what really mattered, just as it had for Macmillan after 1951. What those houses were like to live in, whether they would last, what they would cost to maintain, whether fungi would grow on the walls, how the local authorities could manage such large stocks of houses effectively – these questions were not asked (Power, 1988). They were not important to the politicians.

The influence of the construction industry on the Ministry of Housing and on local councils to build high-rise accommodation in this period and before is documented by Dunleavy (1981). One is tempted to make an analogy with the American Military–Industrial complex. What had grown up in the years of vast public housing schemes was a public housing–construction industry complex, a production process that kept building housing units for the benefit of the construction industry and politicians regardless of their social worth (Timmins, 1995: 185–8).

In the event the sterling crisis put paid to Wilson's ambitions. In 1967 over 400,000 houses were built in a year in Britain for the first time and in 1968, 413,000. There it stalled, cut back by the measures that were taken to meet the sterling crisis in 1967/8. By the end of 1969 the number built had fallen to 370,000. Instead attention began to shift from the destruction of old houses to renovation, with the White Paper *Old Houses into New Homes* (Cmnd 3602, 1968).

In concentrating on nationally driven housing policies we should not ignore the way in which local politics gives local character and local stubbornness to the way policies are interpreted. Some local authorities responded to government subsidies and prompting with massive slum clearance and high-rise building. Others were more cautious. Some built as few as possible. Manchester stuck to its more traditional council housing approach and was unwilling to follow fashionable trends, its civic culture shaping its housing policy (Shapely et al., 2004).

Owner occupation

Owner occupiers had always been considered Tory voters by Labour politicians. Yet as their numbers rose steadily it began to dawn on them that this attitude was merely electoral suicide. The 1965 White Paper on housing (Cmnd 2838) explicitly recognized this. Once the current slum clearance plans were completed building for owner occupation should take over. That was 'normal'. It reflected the 'long term social advance which should gradually pervade each region' (Timmins, 1995: 234). In 1966 the Labour government produced another significant White Paper, *Help Towards Home Ownership* (Cmnd 3163). It pointed out that the tax relief owner occupiers gained was a kind of subsidy which went disproportionately to higher-income mortgage holders. Those who did not pay tax got no help in becoming owner occupiers. Though academics had been making this point for many years this was the first official recognition of the equity problem involved. The proposal that followed was designed to help low-income families who were wanting to buy. It reduced individuals' mortgage interest with a direct subsidy so long as they gave up the right to claim tax relief. Though it did not last and did not reach many people it was the first attempt to rationalize the rather perverse way owner occupation has been supported by government.

Race Relations

One of the really important and lasting changes that affected the social structure of modern Britain began in the late 1950s and became a nasty political issue in the 1960s. It was the scale of immigration from the Caribbean and then East Africa and the Indian subcontinent.

Until the late 1950s Britain was an overwhelmingly white society. Even immigration from white Europe was strictly limited. The exodus from Russia and Eastern Europe of Jews in the early part of the century had led to the 1905 and 1914 Aliens Acts, which had given the state wide powers to control entry, demand work permits and powers of deportation. Few of those who gained entry were black.

One of the consequences of the very high levels of employment in the 1950s was a shortage of labour. This led to the increasing employment of women in traditionally mixed and women's employment – teaching and clerical work – but it did not lead to the employment of women bus drivers. Instead London Transport went to the West Indies to recruit. The restrictions on entry did not cover those from the Commonwealth. They were considered British. London Transport had trail-blazed and many individuals from the Commonwealth followed, lured by the considerable job opportunities in Britain at that point.

Those who came settled in the traditional areas to which newcomers had gravitated in the past, such as Notting Hill in London, excluded by price and discrimination from living in most other places. Living along-side poor white families they rapidly became the object of sharper discrimination and prejudice as their numbers grew. Notting Hill experienced the first race riot in 1956 and a largish vote for a Fascist candidate at the 1959 election. (For a vivid brief account see Kullmann, 1960.)

Immigration became a political issue. It was not that the numbers of people entering the country at that point was large. Net immigration between 1951 and 1961 was less than 200,000 over the whole decade. The problem was that the immigrants were black. The Conservative government felt it had to respond and passed the first Commonwealth Immigrants Act in 1962. Vouchers were issued only to those who had a job to come to or who had educational qualifications or training likely to be useful to the British economy. Wide-ranging discretionary powers were extended to the authorities.

The Labour Party, initially, took the high moral ground and opposed the second reading of the bill. The Leader of the Opposition, Hugh Gaitskell, said,

> The immigrants are healthy, law-abiding, and are at work. They are helping us. Why then do the Government wish to keep them out? We all know the answer. It is because they are coloured and because in consequence of this there is a fear of racial disorder and friction. This is the real question. Why do we have so much hypocrisy about it? Why do we not face up to the matter? (Hansard, 16 November 1961)

It was not an hypocrisy confined to the Conservative Party, however. Many Labour councils were arranging their priority council house waiting lists to exclude immigrants. When the Labour Party came to power in 1964 it did not repeal the Act, after a very sharp lesson in the feelings of the electorate. In a mixed constituency a Conservative candidate was able to make very effective use of the race issue, so defeating the intended Foreign Secretary, Patrick Gordon-Walker.

What the new government did was to introduce a measure designed to make certain kinds of blatant discrimination illegal and to discourage others. (See Bindman and Carrier, 1983 for a discussion of this and later legislation. A contemporary and widely read account was Rose, 1969.)

Race Relations Act 1965

The 1965 Act made discrimination – defined as 'treating a person less favourably than another on the grounds of colour, race, or ethnic or national origins' – a civil wrong when done in relation to the facilities of 'certain places of public resort'. Effectively this covered discrimination in pubs, dance halls and hotels but little else. It failed to touch at all on the critical areas of employment and housing. Furthermore, the sanction for breach of the law was to prove so nebulous as to be actually non-existent. In the event of a failure to conciliate a dispute by the Race Relations Board, set up to administer the law, the case could be referred to the Attorney-General who had power to obtain an injunction in the County Court. But not a single case reached the court in the lifetime of the Act. (Bindman and Carrier, 1983: 126)

A pattern had been set, however, for social policy in this field. A clamour for more restrictions on immigration would be acceded to, followed by a measure to protect more fully those from ethnic minorities who were already in Britain. It was, indeed, raised to the level of a principle by James Callaghan, the Labour Home Secretary a few years later when the Labour government was faced by an upsurge in immigration from East Africa. Here Asians were being expelled by the African governments. If we want to preserve good race relations, Callaghan argued, we must stem the inflow and balance it with positive measures to help eliminate discrimination for those who are here already.

The 1968 Commonwealth Immigrants Act further restricted entry but it was balanced by the 1968 Race Relations Act, which substantially extended the 1965 Act to cover employment and housing and strengthened the enforcement procedure. This Act was based on American experience with civil rights legislation but it fell short of it in several respects. Individuals had to take action to claim discrimination had taken place against them. In the United States class action could be taken on behalf of a whole group. The courts could not insist on target quotas or affirmative action to ensure equal opportunity. Nor was there any concept of 'indirect discrimination', practices that would in general tend to discriminate against a group, such as an employer's power to require certain kind of uniform. The concept of indirect discrimination was included in the later 1976 Race

Relations Act but it has been very narrowly interpreted by the courts. The year 1968 was not only one of tougher action to stem immigration, it was also one of massive race riots in the United States. Though the problems were on a much larger scale and different, analogies were drawn and fears raised. Enoch Powell made a widely reported speech predicting 'rivers of blood' as a consequence of the growing population of ethnic minorities.

The Home Office, inspired by American experience and by an uncommon civil servant, Dereck Morrell, thought that special measures should be taken in areas where there was poverty and a high proportion of incomers. The aim was to stimulate local people in these areas to work together and create a new multicultural civil society. Their poverty made this a rather Utopian remedy and it ended in disillusion.

Equal Pay

Social policy is traditionally thought of as a redistributive device, taking the incomes earned in the market-place, taxing them and giving benefits to families and individuals. It has rarely, in Britain, been concerned with regulating wages for social purposes. Wages Councils did strengthen groups of workers in certain industries with weak bargaining power. They were abolished in the 1990s. Britain had never had a minimum wage. That had to wait until 1999.

Increasingly in the post-war years women moved into the public sphere of paid work. Yet their rewards were consistently less even when they were doing identical work, such as teaching. On top of that they tended to be employed in 'women's occupations' that were traditionally paid less. Unequal rewards for women for equal work became less and less acceptable though change was very slow.

Social policy is not just a matter of government legislation. Inaction is just as definite a policy as action. For many years governments did not accept that unequal pay for men and women was a legitimate cause for concern. A tacit or *de facto* policy of inequality existed.

There had been a Royal Commission on Equal Pay as early as 1949 and in 1951 the International Labour Organization had passed a convention calling on member states to adopt equal pay. It took twenty years before legislation was passed in the UK. Bruegel (1983) notes some of the contributory events that preceded the passing of legislation in 1970. There was a strike by women workers at Ford, Dagenham, in 1968 and trade union pressure was exerted through a National Joint Action

Committee in 1969. The Minister of Labour at this point was Barbara Castle. But probably as important, employers knew that membership of the EEC, which they favoured, would require equal pay anyway. The CBI was, thus, not too resistant to the idea. As in other areas of equal opportunity Europe has been an important lever for change.

The Equal Pay Act

The eventual legislation made a distinction between earnings that were the consequence of different *worth* and earnings that were different despite *equal* worth. It was the latter that constituted discrimination.

There are two ways of measuring worth that are embodied in the Act. The first is that the person be engaged in 'the same or broadly similar work' and the second relates to work of 'equal value'. A woman doing the same or similar work as a man who was paid more had to show that any differences between her work and that of this comparable man were of no practical importance (Bruegel, 1983). The Act only dealt with differences or injustices within a firm. If a firm paid very low wages to a primarily female staff, in a laundry for example, it could not be caught by the Act and many firms with low wages were of this kind.

Where women were doing different work it was possible to call for a job evaluation to judge whether the work was of equal value. Firms were not obliged to undertake such an evaluation though. Moreover, even where a job was deemed of equal value the tribunal could determine that different pay was justified because of 'material difference' in the circumstances. The man might have longer service or do more overtime. Both were likely to tell against women.

Redress lies with the individual or the union acting on the individual's behalf. In the past unions were male dominated and might not have been supportive, though this has been changing. In the immediate aftermath of this legislation and the demand for women in the labour market, women's hourly earnings rose quite sharply. The median average hourly pay of women relative to men rose from 63 per cent in 1972 to 73 per cent in 1976, and then rose more gradually reaching 79 per cent in 1991 (Machin and Waldfogel, 1994) and 87 per cent by 2005.

The Sex Discrimination Act 1975 gave women the theoretical right to equal access to jobs and to equal treatment within them. The legislation did not, however, deal with indirect discrimination and the consequences of a segregated labour market. Women continue to work in lower-paid and part-time employment. Assumptions about the gendered division of paid and unpaid work and the absence of child-care facilities make the remaining differences very difficult to tackle. This is where equal pay legislation on its own can do little without further social policy intervention.

In the 1940s day care provision had been rapidly run down after the war. Pre-school provision has been very slow to develop and was not designed for working mothers' convenience. This was to remain true until the early part of the next century (see Chapter 10). Most working mothers with young children have relied on family members and childminders. Women's role as carers weakens their position in the labour market and their lower earning power in the market-place justifies their position as carers. Thus the rights to equal pay and access to the labour market were important both practically and symbolically but, given the gendered division of work, these were not substantive rights.

The 1975 Employment Protection Act introduced statutory maternity provision. Subject to being employed for two years over 16 hours per week, five years for those working shorter hours, a woman had the right to stop work for 11 weeks prior to the birth and to return to work 29 weeks after it. Pay was given for 6 weeks at 90 per cent of the woman's average earnings minus the statutory maternity allowance payable under the 1975 Social Security Act, and for 12 weeks at Statutory Sick Pay. The 1975 legislation guaranteed reinstatement to similar work (not the same job). Various entitlements, e.g. to pensions, were not continued through the period of leave. Though these formal rights were an important breakthrough many women found the lack of affordable child care a barrier to their practical return to work.

As with social security legislation, women had made some progress towards equal treatment in the public world of paid work but the implications of the private world of the family and gendered roles within it remained largely unchanged or beyond the reach of social policy.

Questions to Answer

1 Why was the eleven-plus abolished and higher education expanded?
2 Why were social services departments created and social work and medical care given separate agencies to dominate? What may have been the consequences?
3 Why was race relations legislation seen to be necessary in this period? What did it try to achieve and how?

7

Morality, Family and the State: the Legacy of the Sixties

Homosexual Law Reform
Abortion
Divorce
Lone Parents
Domestic Violence
Sex Education

Economists and market liberals more generally often discuss the excessive power of the state almost exclusively in terms of its powers to tax, provide services and regulate the economy. More directly intrusive, however, is the state's power to regulate personal behaviour. The state sets the framework within which couples live in a legal relationship called marriage, it determines the age of consent to sexual intercourse, it makes certain kinds of intercourse criminal acts, it forbids or regulates the grounds on which abortions can be undertaken legally. The courts set precedents and rules which determine what happens when a marriage breaks up. All of these functions profoundly affect the quality of people's lives and are part of social policy. They interact with the more traditional forms of social policy, such as social security and social work.

Social policy, as we saw in Chapter 1, is not only concerned with pieces of social legislation. It concerns various functions performed by the state (local and national), the tax system as well as cash benefits, and also functions of the courts, the police and the penal system. One of the most difficult areas of all for governments to tread is the boundary line between the family and the state's legitimate functions. Another is between the state and the employment market. Each affects the other, as we have seen in the case of equal pay. The role women can play in the family is constrained not just by social norms (*de facto* policy if government does not seek to change them) but by the employment market and by government provision or support for child care. More care of children and frail and dependent people is undertaken by family members than the state could ever undertake, or should. Indeed, in so far as government merely assumes families will take the strain, this is a *de facto* policy. There is much that governments cannot change about family or individual behaviour. But at the basis of Anglo-Saxon social policy has been the view that the family is a private world in which the state should have no role. Like the market, the state regulates its existence, the contractual basis of marriage, and indeed supports and encourages the institution, but should not actively intervene within it. In fact, it has been drawn in to protect children within families that are harming their children. That has been the case since the late nineteenth century. Whether it should protect the woman as the weaker partner was one of the issues that came to be part of policy debate in the 1970s, both with regard to divorce and to domestic violence. The issue concerned not just provision of refuge from violent males but the whole question of policing and its role in domestic situations.

The 1960s marked an important phase. The state's right to intervene in sexual matters was questioned and modified. Initially the debate remained outside the party political contest and was taken up by private Members of Parliament.

Though it is commonplace to see the 1980s as the decade of individualism and rolling back state power, in the field of morals and personal life it was the 1960s that reduced the intrusiveness of the state and extended individual freedom, while the 1980s and 1990s did the reverse. Jane Lewis (1992a) has called the 1960s 'the permissive moment', emphasizing the fleeting nature of the trend. Yet the legislation passed in that period was 'momentous' in that it has lasted and has directly affected very large numbers of people, probably more deeply and personally than the changes to the structure of pension schemes or the National Health Service.

The younger generation of the sixties had grown up during the Second World War. The war had opened up a ferment of debate and fundamental questioning about society. More of this generation had undergone secondary and higher education. It was an era of optimism and economic growth as well as the security of knowing that jobs were available for young people. The very shortage of labour had attracted women into the labour force in growing numbers, not least in teaching, nursing and social care. This increased their economic and intellectual independence.

Contraception was not only limiting the time women spent having children but made exploratory sex more safely possible and, because less guilt ridden, more enjoyable. AIDS had never been dreamed of. A number of trends therefore combined to make this a period of moral questioning and change which fitted alongside the economic structural changes we have so far discussed.

The faith of many intellectuals, reminiscent of earlier thinkers such as Hegel, Mill and Durkheim, was that collective welfare, full employment and education would facilitate individual growth and autonomy, 'moral individualism'. In harmony with this goal the state should match its role of collective provision with a withdrawal from spheres that were not properly its province – regulating sexual behaviour, for example. What this thinking did not take on was the task of questioning the role of women in the family and the state's part in this. That was for feminist writers in the 1970s and 1980s to do. The first concrete official expression of this questioning of the state's role in relation to sexual behaviour comes with the Wolfenden Report in 1957.

Homosexual Law Reform

At the end of the Second World War a new Director of Public Prosecutions was appointed, Theobald Mathew, who with approval of the Home Secretary and support of senior officials began to take a much tougher line against homosexual practices, which were a criminal offence. Fear of prosecution made individuals a security risk. The defection of two known homosexuals – Burgess and Maclean – from the Foreign Office to Soviet Russia only heightened the pressure to do something. The number of convictions for gross indecency rose from 800 a year pre-war to 2,300 in 1953. The convictions often involved the police acting as *agents provocateurs*. The popular press broke the previous taboos in 1952 with a series of lurid accounts of the practices of 'evil men' (Weeks, 1990). There was a series of highly publicized trials. The whole criminalization process seemed, in its own right, to be creating an assault on public decency. It was probably this which led the Home Secretary, Maxwell-Fyfe, after a particularly high profile trial, to appoint the Wolfenden Committee in 1954 to look at both homosexuality and prostitution. It also followed a report from the Church of England's Moral Welfare Council in 1952 that recommended reform.

Wolfenden Report 1957

The committee's report contains what remains a classic statement of principle about the appropriate role for the state in relation to the private lives of individuals.

> Our primary duty has been to consider the extent to which homosexual behaviour and female prostitution should come under the condemnation of criminal law . . . We have therefore worked with our own formulation of the function of the criminal law so far as it concerns the subject of this enquiry. In this field, its function, as we see it, is to preserve public order and decency, to protect the citizen from what is offensive or injurious, and to provide sufficient safeguards against exploitation and corruption of others . . . (para. 13)
>
> It is not, in our view, the function of the law to intervene in the private lives of citizens, or to seek to enforce any particular pattern of behaviour, further than is necessary to carry out the purposes we have outlined. (para. 14)

The law should protect young people, those with some mental defect and any individual from abuse but should uphold 'the importance which society and the law ought to give to individual freedom of choice and actions in matters of private morality' (para. 61).

It took ten years for the recommendations on homosexual law reform to be enacted. It was discussed as a possible element in a Labour Party policy document in the early 1960s but it was considered too politically dangerous. Crossman noted in his diary a remark by Harold Wilson:

> HW   That boy [Peter Shore, head of the Labour Party Research Department] is trying to put in everything, including a passage on Wolfenden, which would cost us, at a rough estimate, 6 million votes. (Crossman, 1981: 944)

However, the law was being made to look an ass by the mid-1960s and it was this, as well as the more liberal climate, which led to legislation in 1967.

Sexual Offences Act 1967

Homosexual acts between consenting males over the age of 21 were decriminalized. Despite pressure from the Homosexual Law Reform Society, conspiracy to commit and seeking to commit or facilitate homosexual acts was still an offence. These sections have been used to prosecute magazines for publishing contact listings. No legislation was passed concerning lesbian activity. It had never been criminalized. Victorian assumptions that it did not exist, or if it did it was not harmful, persisted.

A backlash

For many years, throughout the late 1960s and 1970s, this change in the law came to be accepted. Gay rights groups campaigned to change public attitudes to sexual orientation, with some success. A number of local councils began supporting gay organizations and this became a peg on which to hang a more general attack on 'loony left' councils. One council, Haringey, was attacked for having in its library the book *Jenny Lives with Eric and Martin*.

What really began a backlash, however, was the coming of AIDS. Fear, and the popular association of AIDS with homosexuality, began to refuel anti-homosexual feelings. An editorial in *New Statesman and Society* (vol. 115, no. 2963, 1988) captured the way the issue had become a party one:

> The Conservatives have already reaped untold electoral benefit from the 'loony left' campaign. Labour are indelibly seen as the gay party. The Conservatives are now positively coming out as the anti-gay party to milk for all it is worth the growing hostility towards homosexuality felt by the majority of people in this country.

This backlash did result in one piece of legislation: Section 28(1) of the Local Government Act 1988, or 'Clause 28' as it was referred to in the campaign for its abolition. Under it,

> A local authority shall not
> (a) intentionally promote homosexuality or publish material with the intention of promoting homosexuality;
> (b) promote the teaching in any maintained school of the acceptability of homosexuality as a pretended family relationship.

In 1977 the gist of this section had been included in a bill in the House of Lords. The government of the day had rejected it on the grounds that it was not possible to legislate about the proper content of teaching on such a subject. It is a mark of how far politics had moved in the next decade that the legislation was passed in 1988.

A counter-move?

In 1994 an amendment to the Criminal Justice Bill was moved to lower the age of consent for homosexuals to 16, the same as for heterosexuals. This had been discussed by the Wolfenden Committee on the grounds that most countries have the same age and that any difference was discriminatory. Wolfenden had taken the view that young men needed a longer period of protection from the possible attentions of older men, and in which to make up their minds over such an important decision. In the end, the House of Commons compromised on the age of 18, once again bringing it into line with the age of majority; Wolfenden had used this age (21 at the time of his report) as a yardstick, but it had been reduced to 18 after his report. The House of Lords rejected an attempt to reinstate the age of 21.

Abortion

The Abortion Law Reform Association (ALRA) had been campaigning since the 1930s but had made little headway. A House of Commons debate in 1952 lasted one minute. The 1961 thalidomide tragedy raised the issue and put it into a different, public health category, a move enhanced by the growing awareness of the hazards of back street abortions.

In 1962 an opinion poll showed that 73 per cent of the public favoured abortion when a foetus was deformed (Potts et al., 1977). The ALRA stepped up its activities and lobbied private members. Kenneth Robinson in 1961 and Renée Short in 1963 both had their bills talked out, but the Lords gave serious attention to a bill introduced by Lord Silkin in 1965. Medical opinion was divided. GPs seemed to favour wider scope for abortion but the BMA and the Royal College of Obstetricians and Gynaecologists opposed it, believing they might be forced to act against their consciences, and fearing being dictated to by patients and government. They then moved to arguing that there should be a conscientious objection clause in any legislation (Simms, 1985).

In 1967 a new Liberal MP, David Steele, drew the right to introduce a private member's bill and chose abortion law reform. It was similar to the bill introduced by Lord Silkin earlier and this time it passed.

The Abortion Act 1967

The Act did not introduce abortion as a right or on demand. It extended the previously very restricted categories of women who could be given an abortion. Doctors, two of them, had to give their approval. A woman could have an abortion up to twenty-eight weeks of term if two doctors agreed that either the child would be handicapped or

> the continuance of the pregnancy would involve risk to the life of the pregnant woman or of injury to the physical or mental health of the pregnant woman or any existing children of her family, greater than if the pregnancy were terminated.

Saving the woman's life was no longer the sole criterion.

Yet the decision was still a medical one and the decision to stop a pregnancy was different in nature from one to continue:

> If a woman plumps for motherhood, no member of the medical profession will ask if she is emotionally or financially ready for such a commitment, whether she has given it enough thought, whether her relationship can stand the strain. (Suzanne Moore, *Guardian*, 8 October 1992)

This was very far from abortion on demand, therefore. The Lane Committee (1974) found that about 70 per cent of women seeking abortions had been accepted by the NHS, a further 10 per cent by private clinics and 20 per cent were not accepted. Women have also been treated later than might ideally be the case because facilities have not kept pace with demand.

This was always a measure that raised deep moral issues though it has never become *the* dominant social policy issue that it has been at times in the USA. Attempts to modify the legislation have been varied, from trying to control the charitable sector's right to perform abortions, to shortening the period in which abortion is legal. The only change to have succeeded concerns this last point. The maximum term was reduced from twenty-eight to twenty-four weeks by the 1990 Human Fertilization and Embryology Act, on the grounds that, owing to medical advances, foetuses are viable at an earlier stage of development. That has remained unchanged into the present century despite recurrent debates about reducing it further.

Divorce

Lewis (Kiernan et al., 1998: Ch. 3) traces the shifting legislative attitudes to marriage and divorce during the twentieth century. These swung from a highly patriarchal view at the beginning of the century, through the promotion of radical reforms in the 1930s, back to a period of conservative reaction between 1940 and 1960. Concern with sexual promiscuity and the dangers to marriage caused by the conditions prevalent in the Second World War produced a period in which changes to the marriage laws were largely out of bounds for politicians. Some tried, like Mrs Eirene White in 1951. The Royal Commission on Marriage and Divorce (Cmd 9678, 1956) was concerned that the growing emancipation of women would lead women to neglect the duties inherent in marriage. It rejected calls for harsher penalties for divorce but emphasized the need for better education about marriage before marriage and improved marriage guidance and conciliation after it. But attitudes to marriage were changing. The quality of the relationship now mattered more (Giddens, 1992).

The reform of the divorce laws can also be seen as part of a more general attempt to remove the state from intrusive control over individuals whose marriages had broken down. In the 1960s such individuals could not free themselves legally without going to degrading lengths. They had to be caught in an adulterous act, a prearranged one if necessary. As well as the number of 'hotel divorces', the number of couples who were cohabiting while still locked into an official marriage with someone else was growing. In 1963 Leo Abse MP reintroduced Mrs White's bill. It was defeated but it prompted the Archbishop of Canterbury to set up a group to review the law. Change was on its way. The Law Commission, a new body set up by the Labour government to review existing laws, reported on the divorce laws. It argued that to release couples from such a false situation would facilitate remarriage, help reduce extra-marital affairs and support the institution of marriage, not undermine it (1966). It is therefore wrong to see this legislation as driven by libertarian instincts to break up the family. It was driven by both respect for the traditional institution of marriage and a belief that it would be better served by honesty and mutual respect rather than by state enforcement.

The Family Law Reform Act 1969

The Act introduced 'no fault' divorce. This did not mean that fault was no longer an issue but it did mean that there were now two criteria for divorce available that did not imply fault. The sole ground for divorce was now to be 'irretrievable breakdown'. There were five proofs of such a breakdown: adultery, unreasonable behaviour, two years' desertion, two years' separation if both parties consented to divorce, or five years if the divorce was contested.

Under Section 4 of the Act a respondent could plead that she or he would be caused 'grave financial or other hardship' if the marriage were dissolved. In this instance the court could take account of the conduct of the parties and not grant a decree. This section and the five-year delay was put in to protect women who feared that after years of support they would be left high and dry for a younger woman. The bill was attacked as 'a Casanova's Charter' by Lady Summerskill, an ex-Labour minister and feminist campaigner. She said that women, although they should not be trapped in bad marriages, needed some protection for their more vulnerable position. For this reason, too, it was agreed not to enact the 1969 Act until the Matrimonial Proceedings and Property Act 1970, which gave the weaker party more rights to property on divorce, was in place.

The various new pieces of legislation of the period were consolidated into the 1973 Matrimonial Causes Act. This added a three-year bar on petitions for divorce after marriage. The 'grave financial hardship' clause was elaborated to include 'the loss of the chance of acquiring any benefit which the respondent might acquire if the marriage was not dissolved'. This would cover, for example, a stake in a husband's pension. In dividing up property, present and foreseeable needs and ability to pay were to be taken into account. So, too, were unpaid contributions to the family's welfare. The Act's aim was to

> place the parties, so far as it is practicable and, having regard to their conduct, just to do so, in the financial position in which they would have been if the marriage had not broken down and each had properly discharged his or her financial obligations and responsibilities towards each other. (Section 55(1))

While the spirit of the 1969 Act had moved away from issues of conduct, the 1973 legislation, and the way the courts interpreted it, moved conduct back in. The courts had notions of a woman's proper role in marriage. Women in cohabiting partnerships that broke up had to prove they had made greater contributions than a married counterpart (Smart, 1984). The law remained both supportive of marriage and of women's traditional role within it.

However, the rule that parties should be restored to their original financial position proved hard to implement. The maintenance requirements were very broad, and men who remarried had great difficulty in meeting them as well as supporting a new family adequately.

Rehabilitative maintenance or 'clean break' settlements had come to be introduced into case law in the early 1970s (Smart, 1984). It was introduced into public policy in the 1984 Matrimonial and Family Proceedings Act. Maintenance would be paid according to the earning capacity of the recipient as well as of the payer. The older the child the greater the expectation that the ex-wife should work.

The personal and the political

What we had, then, were some very important moves to reduce the intrusiveness of the state in sexual matters in the 1960s. It was limited and did not give free licence to abortions, or to sexual relations for young men. Marriage was still carefully constructed in a traditional mould. Lewis argues that, paradoxically,

> Deregulation of personal relationships effectively served to increase the privatisation of the family and ironically further to distance the personal from the political. (1992a: 64)

Nevertheless, in the longer run, the greater freedom to break marriage contracts had repercussions for the state and the taxpayer. If couples could negotiate 'clean breaks' that left one ex-partner dependent on social security, the state was brought back into the equation. Why should taxpayers, many of whom were couples who had not divorced, pay for those who had? In a period of rising social security spending and tax resistance the state would soon enter the arena of marriage breakdown in a very heavy-handed way, at least where one of the previous partners tried to turn to the social security system for support. Concern about the state of the family would re-emerge in the 1990s as those worried about traditional family values reacted to the social changes taking place.

Single parenthood, in particular, whether because of broken marriages or otherwise, began to become an issue of political concern in the late

1960s, though the emphasis was first on the needs of the single parent rather than the taxpayer.

Lone Parents

The issue of the state's responsibility for lone parents has always been tangled up with moral concerns. From the 1834 Poor Law onwards widows have been in a class of their own. A widow had not caused her change of status. She was not at fault. Yet her circumstances meant that she was often unable to support herself. In many cases she might have been expected to enter the labour market, and often did, but the state did tend to assume responsibility, giving outdoor relief under the Poor Law and then in the 1920s introducing widows' pensions. Other types of lone parent were deemed 'at fault' in some regard: the separated, the divorced, the deserted and the unmarried (always the smallest group). Moreover, governments have always feared collusion. Couples would not actually be living separately, but would pretend to and draw benefit. Alternatively, benefits might 'double up' maintenance payments ordered privately through the courts. They feared that giving benefit would encourage lone parenthood, making it easier. The tangles facing the government in the 1990s were not new (Lewis, 1994; Kiernan et al., 1998).

Beveridge had deliberated long and hard over how to treat lone parents. Were they deserving or undeserving? Should they be treated as mothers or workers who should be required to seek paid employment? Society's attitudes to the last question have changed over time (Lewis and Piachaud, 1987). Increasingly the expectation has grown that single mothers should be in paid employment. In the 1940s the view was that motherhood came first.

Beveridge took the view that unmarried mothers were undeserving and should be the province of the National Assistance Board. He recommended that all other lone mothers should receive an insurance-based benefit high enough to preclude the need to work. The children would attract family allowance. This never happened because of the doubling-up problem.

> Beveridge clearly acknowledged the importance of women's work as mothers, but his commitment to social insurance meant that he could only give them entitlements as wives, which in turn meant that it would inevitably be difficult to provide benefits for deserted wives whose husbands had a legal obligation to maintain. (Lewis, 1994)

Consequently widows retained their favourable status and others were obliged to rely on usually low or non-existent maintenance payments from their ex-husbands, topped up by National Assistance. But the role of mother still predominated. The National Assistance Board did not insist that lone mothers register for work in order to claim assistance.

Through the 1950s the number of lone parents had risen only slowly. Then the effects of the divorce law changes became very evident. By the late 1960s divorce and separation had become more important reasons for single parenthood than widowhood. In 1961 the number of persons divorcing for every thousand married couples was two. By 1971 it was six and by 1991 it was over twelve. In 1961, 2.5 per cent of households were lone parent families; by 1971 the figure rose to 4 per cent, by 1981 to 6 per cent, by 1991 to 10 per cent and 12 per cent by 2005.

The Labour government appointed a committee to investigate the problem in all its aspects. The Finer Report was published in 1974. It recognized discrepancies between public law (government policy) and private law (what the courts decided in individual cases). It wanted to unify the two, giving ultimate responsibility for the administration of maintenance to the state. The state would carry the prime responsibility for ensuring that the families' needs were met and would then recoup maintenance from the father. It would have made all lone parents eligible for a non-contributory guaranteed maintenance allowance. This would have had a non-means-tested children's component, and a carer's component, which would taper off to allow women to earn and receive some benefit and would disappear when the parent carer's earnings reached the level of male average earnings.

By the time the report was published political interest had waned. There was little debate in Parliament (Lewis, 1994) and virtually none of the recommendations were implemented. The economic crisis was upon the government and a new and potentially expensive benefit was not going to win favour. A few things were done. Lone parents were given an additional allowance when child benefit was introduced. A higher disregard was introduced to enable them to take some part-time work and keep in touch with the labour market. This policy was extended in 1980 with the introduction of the 'tapered earnings disregard'.

Finer's main concern was not pursued at the time; it was an attempt to fuse public and private law, and to reduce the overlap in responsibilities between the courts and the state for maintenance of the family's basic living standard, this maintenance being in the child's interest.

The next attempt to tackle that issue had to wait until the 1990s, when it was reinforced by the Treasury's need to save money. This change was also driven by concern about the rise in divorce and marriage breakdown. Divorce was too easy and those who left marriages should pay the costs, it was thought. While Finer was trying to put maintenance squarely in the public sphere, the legislation of the Major era aimed to re-privatize it (see pp. 214–17).

Domestic Violence

Though the 1960s encouraged individual freedom in sexual matters, drawing the boundary between intervention and privacy was difficult. A good example of the ambivalence of the state towards the privacy of the family has been its attitude towards domestic violence. This includes rape and sexual assault within marriage, child abuse, elder abuse and wife battering. The issue that has had most prominence is 'wife battering' or violence towards the female partner and it has led to the most policy response.

In 1972 a group of women in Chiswick, in West London, were conducting a high street campaign on prices in the shops and in the course of talking to women they discovered the importance of domestic violence. This, not inflation, was uppermost in many women's experience. One of the price campaigners was Erin Pizzey who saw the need to provide some kind of refuge or way of escape for women, together with support and advice. Chiswick Women's Refuge was a highly publicized response to this need. It was a self-help group which managed to raise enough money to keep a large house on the High Road as a hostel and place of refuge. It operated an open door policy and ran into continual battles with the authorities over public health and other regulations. This only served to increase public attention (Rose, 1985). The movement spread and made some local authorities consider providing refuges themselves. In the main, though, this has remained outside the statutory sector.

In 1975 a House of Commons Select Committee reported on violence in marriage. It reviewed existing ways of dealing with it, and found them wanting. While criminal law on assault was theoretically adequate to deal with domestic violence, it was not adequately enforced by the police because the home was not considered an appropriate place for them to intervene.

There was even more difficulty with the civil law. A woman could obtain a non-molestation order or an exclusion order but only as part of some other process such as divorce, damages or judicial separation. These were lengthy processes and fundamental ones too. For a vulnerable woman who was being regularly beaten, initiating divorce proceedings might well make the whole situation worse. Furthermore, only court bailiffs could serve or enforce injunctions and they only worked during office hours (McCann, 1985).

The Law Commission had been reviewing matrimonial law in the magistrates' courts since 1973 and recognized that existing law did not give adequate protection to women in these situations. In 1976 the Domestic Violence and Matrimonial Proceedings Act was passed. It was followed in 1978 by the Domestic Proceedings and Magistrates' Courts Act. The 1976 Act applied to both married and cohabiting couples. Non-molestation orders and injunctions could be obtained without recourse to other proceedings and without notification to the other party. Injunctions could involve the power to arrest. The 1978 Act was intended to give recourse to the magistrates' court and hence speedy justice. However, the powers of these courts was also limited. Magistrates could make personal protection orders which excluded the husband from the home, but unlike the 1976 Act, it could not bar him from the surrounding area (Kennedy, 1992).

Case law

A common tactic used by the courts is to bind *both* parties over to keep the peace. This disposes of the need for a contested case and is aimed at neutralizing hostility between the parties. The result is to brand the victim as violent and to place an equal responsibility for the disturbance on each party. It reflects a certain ingrained belief that the woman must have done something to provoke the attack. Exclusion injunctions have tended to be temporary, allowing the woman a limited period in which to find alternative accommodation and there has been a reluctance to grant exclusion orders because of the perceived conflict with the property rights of the husband (McCann, 1985). An exclusion order is deemed permissible so long as it is in the best interests of the *children*. A woman is given protection because of her status as a mother rather than as an afflicted party as such. Even so the courts have moved to give increasing protection to women; specialist Domestic Violence Courts have been created (for the current law, see <www.womensaid.org.uk> and <cps.gov.uk/publications/dos/DomesticViolencePolicy>).

Policing

Law is not enough on its own, it must be enforced. The police were initially reluctant to get involved and were not trained to do so. In 1985 the Metropolitan Police Force's Working Party into Domestic Violence was set up and reported in 1986. It concluded that most officers' responses were inappropriate and unhelpful, that police policies were inadequate and that training was virtually non-existent. Training dealt with the issue under the heading 'domestic dispute', trivializing it rather than dealing with it as a crime.

A Home Office report in 1986 also emphasized the need to keep the criminal justice system out of domestic situations and the need for education for couples, to minimize conflict. By 1989, however, the Home Office had moved to recommend that special police units be set up to deal with domestic violence. The Crown Prosecution Service is now responsible for deciding the charge in all but the most minor cases.

Provision of refuges

The 1977 Housing (Homeless Persons) Act gave local authorities powers to provide accommodation for *mothers* escaping violence. Authorities may only accommodate their own tenants. A woman wanting to move out of the area has no right to accommodation. Local authorities have since 1976 been under great pressure to spend less and few refuges have been set up by them. The main response has been by the voluntary sector. This lack of provision seriously restricts the capacity of the courts if there is nowhere for the woman to go. The whole complex area of policy illustrates the delicate balance that policy must keep when tackling the privacy of the family.

Sex Education

In the two decades after the Second World War sex education in schools was not particularly controversial. It was not controversial at all for the Ministry of Health who advocated more of it, particularly as a weapon against venereal disease. The Ministry of Education was more cautious. It was not in a position to lay down curricula of any kind at this time (see p. 198) and was certainly not going to do so on sex. But it did issue encouraging guidance. The material used changed as social norms changed. By the 1980s increasingly frank advice about contraception provoked the anger of the newly emerging 'family values lobby'. Drawing on similar campaigns in the US they pressed government to give parents the right to withdraw their children from sex education classes. Victoria Gillick took legal action to secure this against her local authority. The 1986 Education Act required local authorities to ensure that if sex education was given it should be done 'in a manner as to encourage due regard to moral considerations and respect for human life'. The 1993 Education Act required reproduction to be taught in the biology curriculum, but it left other aspects of sex education to school governors. In the most recent period the importance of sex education has been reasserted but remains controversial. (For discussion of these issues see Hampshire and Lewis, 2004, on which this section draws.)

Questions to Answer

1 Why were the 1960s said to mark the beginning of the 'permissive society'? What reasons may lie behind these changes?
2 What should be the state's role in regulating an individual's sexual behaviour and at what age? What conclusions did legislators draw?
3 What dilemmas does single parenthood pose for social policy? Has social policy made it more possible and acceptable and is this wrong?

8

The Party Over, 1976–88

It was the economic crisis of 1976 that finally broke the continuity in the social policies of the post-war era. As Anthony Crosland, who was in the Labour Cabinet in 1975, put it, 'The party is over.' He was actually talking about the finance of local government for which he was responsible, but he was summing up a much deeper sense of change in the climate of ideas about social policy, which began in this period. Like all periodization, the choice of this point to mark the break is problematic. For many years after 1976 more stayed the same than changed in social policy. Major institutional change took more than a decade to come but the climate of ideas and above all the economic and social structure did begin to change decisively at about this time.

A check to growth

One clear discontinuity was in public spending. It had been dictated by the visiting team from the International Monetary Fund, on whom the

Labour government had called for help. Such crises had happened before – in 1949, 1951, 1956, 1961, 1967, 1971. But once they had passed, the growth of public spending on social services as a share of the national income had continued. This time it did not, at least for a decade and a half. The share of the nation's resources going to social policy was to stabilize and then decline in the period from 1981 to 1990, the first time this had happened in the twentieth century except as a consequence of war.

Social policy and the economy

In the longer run the strain of trying to contain the rising demands for health and other spending prompted politicians to search for fundamental structural change in the Welfare State, as we shall see in the next chapter. More immediately important, however, was a reappraisal of the relationship between social policy and the economy. In the 1940s and 1950s both the Labour and Conservative governments, and the civil servants advising them, had been acutely aware of the economic needs of the country. Stafford Cripps and Hugh Gaitskell, Chancellors in the first post-war Labour government, had been puritanical in their determination that the Welfare State should not take resources from the export drive. Butler had been determined that it should not take away from private consumers' spending power in the early 1950s.

The philosophy that drove the Wilson government was a reaction against perceived private affluence and public squalor. The system of public expenditure planning that had been introduced in 1961 may have actually made it more difficult for the Treasury to control spending than it had been in the 1950s (Glennerster, 1975; Wright, 1980). The Cabinets of the time set targets for government spending based on what were no more than *hopes* of how far the economy would grow. It rarely grew as intended. Moreover, departmental spending was preserved in real terms even when prices rose, something no private firm or household could do.

By the mid-1970s even Labour politicians came to believe that economic growth should be given priority over social spending. The British economy had consistently performed less well than its competitors since the Second World War, indeed for much longer. Perhaps it was, after all, true that this was the fault of the Welfare State. The basis of Labour support, manufacturing industry, seemed to be in terminal decline. Some economists were arguing that the reason lay in there being 'too few producers': too many teachers, social workers and doctors and not enough people producing goods (Bacon and Eltis, 1976). Others contested this view. The structural changes taking place in the economy were a result of changing consumer preferences. People in Britain, and other economies too, actually wanted more health and education and not more manufactured goods (Glennerster, 1976). But many economists argued that the government's first claim on capital and on labour was 'crowding out' other economic activity, not least wealth creation (for a contemporary discussion of this debate see Blackaby, 1979). These views became dominant and certainly shaped the thinking of the Conservative Opposition at this time, but they also strongly influenced that of the Labour government. If the Welfare State was eating into the manufacturing base of the country it was also eroding Labour's natural base of electoral support.

There was a feeling, shared by those on the left and the right of politics, that capitalism was finally in crisis (Gamble and Walton, 1976; Gough, 1979; O'Connor, 1972) and the Welfare State was, in no small measure responsible, if rightly. The climate of economic thought in the 1960s had been favourable to social policy. Now that conventional economic wisdom was reversed. The Labour government decided not just to curb public spending but to shift the emphasis within it, supporting industry and economic growth more generally, shifting the emphasis within social programmes to policies that would foster economic efficiency.

The best example of this change of emphasis was the speech that the new Prime Minister, James Callaghan, made at the trade union college at Oxford – Ruskin College – in 1976. Education had become too concerned with giving children a good time, standards were too low and schooling was too little geared to the needs of a modern economy, he argued. 'A great debate' on the issue was needed. After a consultation period the resulting White Paper said,

> Young people need to reach maturity with a basic understanding of the economy and its activities, especially manufacturing industry, which are necessary for the creation of Britain's economic wealth. (DES, 1977)

This theme was to run through the education policy of not just that Labour government but the following Conservative governments too. Almost exactly the same sentiments can be found in the next Conservative government's White Paper on schools eight years later:

> By the time they leave school, pupils need to have acquired, far more than at present, the qualities and skills of a technological age. (DES, 1985)

Various attempts were made to link school and workplace and encourage technical and vocational training in schools and after. A series of schemes were adopted to subsidize employers to take on young people and give them a basic training, very rudimentary in the early versions.

Giving up Keynes

The impact of the crisis on established ideas about full employment was even more profound (Burk and Cairncross, 1992). This was not just any sterling crisis. The oil price shock, caused by all the oil producers raising their prices, had sparked world-wide destabilization and, in Britain, this boost to inflation, as unions and firms tried to pass on the consequences, built upon the long-term accelerating inflation rates of past decades. It pushed inflation – not unemployment – to the top of politicians' concerns and it caused a fundamental reappraisal of the Keynesian approach to economic management.

In the twelve months from July 1976 retail prices rose by 17 per cent. It looked as if inflation was simply going to explode and the economy with it. The inflation caveat, entered so long ago in the 1944 White Paper on full employment (see p. 5), now assumed central importance. Full employment could only be sustained if inflation was held in reasonable bounds. It patently was not. The facts seemed to fit the predictions made for so long by the American economist Milton Friedman. Governments could not affect the long-run level of unemployment. They were powerless. If they tried to reduce unemployment below the market-determined level it would simply produce inflation. Ideas only take root when the soil is fertile. In 1976 the soil could not have been better prepared for such an idea to take root.

The Labour government tried, initially with some success, to reach agreements with the trade unions to restrain wage increases. The government used social benefits, 'the social wage', as part of its case to persuade the trade unions to moderate their pay demands. Restrain pay demands and we shall be able to keep full employment and sustain the Welfare State, it argued. It worked in the short run but this was not 1940. In 1978/9 the attempt to continue to hold down public sector pay provoked massive public sector strikes. This 'winter of discontent' would live on in the folk memory and in political discourse. The policy and the government crumbled.

The failure of the incomes policy route left the Labour Party without a policy on full employment or inflation. No convincing answers appeared in the 1980s. It was the Conservative Party that adopted a new economic philosophy with enthusiasm.

Monetarism rules OK

Mrs Thatcher, in opposition, and her Conservative advisers became convinced that conquering inflation was the key economic goal and that Friedman was right. This conviction was to lay the foundations for the economic policy of the 1980s. Nor was the change of heart confined to the Conservative Party. Callaghan told the Labour Party Conference in 1976 that full employment could not be restored simply by boosting public spending. That might temporarily reduce the numbers of unemployed, but if the UK remained uncompetitive and if inflation went on rising, that remedy would be worse than the cure.

Unemployment rose from about 3 per cent in 1974 to 12 per cent in 1982/3. This was simply without precedent in the post-war world. Though other countries followed, accepting higher unemployment in an attempt to get inflation under control, none followed such a Draconian course through the 1980s. Heath, in 1971, had recoiled when unemployment figures rose above a million. The numbers out of work rose to more than 3 million in the early 1980s. Yet it did not bring the government down or lose it elections. Most people were not out of work. To most, 17 per cent inflation was more frightening than seeing other people unemployed, mainly in the industrial heartlands of the country. It took a decade of lower prices and finally unemployment hitting the middle class in the south-east of England, for that view to begin to change.

Social policy in 1945 had been founded explicitly on the assumption of full employment. Now that had gone.

The labour market and inequality

In retrospect we can see that unemployment was not the only structural economic change taking place at this time. Comparative economic analysis since has shown that a common trend of historic importance was beginning to affect first the United States and then the UK at about this time. For nearly a century, and certainly since 1945, the United Kingdom had experienced a slow but definite equalizing in incomes and living standards. In the late 1970s, before Mrs Thatcher, this began to change, as it had done in the United States in the early 1970s and was to do in many other advanced economies in the 1980s (Atkinson, 1993; Gardiner, 1993). The dispersion of earnings became more unequal not only because of the decline of old prosperous industries but because within existing industries the spread between the high- and low-paid became much wider. Part-time work became more common; most of the new jobs generated in this period were part-time. Female participation in the labour force rose sharply from 53 per cent to 65 per cent between 1973 and 1991 (though not in full-time jobs), while male labour force participation fell from 93 per cent in 1973 to 86 per cent in 1991.

Between 1971 and 1991 jobs in manufacturing nearly halved. At the same time roughly the same number of jobs were created in the services sector. While most of the jobs lost in the manufacturing sector were full-time and male, over a third of those created in the service sector were part-time. It was mostly women who gained the service sector jobs (Land, 1994). The trend to greater inequality was to be charted with devastating clarity by the Joseph Rowntree *Inquiry into Income and Wealth* (1995). It began in this traumatic period of economic change.

Taxes as a burden

It is not surprising to find these changes reflected in attitudes to taxation. In the period from 1951 to 1976 two-thirds of all Britain's economic growth had been devoted to increasing its public services. Other countries had done the same, but out of much higher growth rates, leaving their citizens significantly better off, privately, as well as publicly. Public opinion polls suggested that until the early 1970s most people in the UK were, however, reasonably content with this set of priorities. Conservative posters at the 1964 election had boasted 'the Conservatives are chalking up ten new schools a week'.

During the period of the 1964 Labour government, however, the percentage of the public supporting more spending on the social services fell from 44 per cent to 22 per cent. By the mid-1970s public opinion was receptive to cutting taxes, though support for the NHS and particular services remained high (Whiteley, 1981). The shift was scarcely surprising. In the mid-1970s average real take-home pay, after tax, actually fell for the first time since the war. In 1973 real consumer expenditure reached its post-war peak. It then fell in 1974 and again in 1975. It remained stable in 1976 and fell again in 1977. This was unprecedented since 1945. People were prepared to support improved public services as long as their private consumption patterns were improving too. That ceased to be the case from 1974 to 1977 and the repercussions for social policy were profound. The Conservative Party promised tax cuts at the 1979 election but did not propose any major changes in social policy to achieve them. The same political response to similar pressures happened in other parts of the world, from California to Denmark, at the same time.

Demography and home ownership

Other basic social changes were under way. The big increase in the child population, those born in the 1940s and 1950s, was now through school and into the labour force, paying taxes. The big rise in the number of the elderly had taken place from 1940 to 1970. Then the numbers of elderly stabilized and would not increase until the next century. The rising population was the middle-aged middle-class taxpayer. As Davies and Piachaud pointed out,

> Thus the dilemma arises that the households that are best off, and must be expected to bear the brunt of paying for improved social services, are the very households which benefit least from the social services. (1983: 52)

Standard rates of income tax were now affecting most families. In the 1940s only a minority of families were caught in the income tax system to any significant degree. By the mid-1970s nearly all families were in the income tax net. At the same time over half the households in the country were owning or buying their own homes. Early in married life, especially, this took a very high share of a family's income. Taxes threatened earners' capacity to house their families in ways to which they aspired.

So it is not hard to see why taxation and take-home pay now moved centre ground in home politics for demographic as well as economic reasons. Far from being seen as a boon to a family's living standards high taxes to pay for social benefits began to be seen as a threat.

On the eve of the election Callaghan, the Labour Prime Minister, confided to his political adviser, Bernard Donoughue,

> You know there are times, perhaps once every thirty years, when there is a change in politics. It then does not matter what you say or what you do. There is a shift in what the public wants and what it approves of. I suspect there is now such a sea change – and it is for Mrs Thatcher. (Lawson, 1993: 19)

A Thatcher revolution?

In the light of all these factors the shift that took place in tax and social policy in the 1980s should be no surprise. Nor should Mrs Thatcher's appeal. Yet was her victory in the leadership election as important a turning point in Conservatism as she and many commentators have suggested? Whatever the case made in other spheres the claim as far as social policy is concerned is less clear, especially in the period 1979–88.

Mrs Thatcher claims, in her account of her years at Number 10 (Thatcher, 1993), that Conservatism had gone profoundly wrong in making too many compromises with socialism in the post-war period. She had been a spending minister, like all the others, of course, pressing for expansion in education in 1972 (DES, 1972). So had Sir Keith Joseph. But, she claims, after the miners' strike, and Heath's defeat, Joseph and those around her went through an intellectual rebirth that rethought Conservatism in fundamental ways.

> Welfare benefits, distributed with little or no consideration of their effects on behaviour, encouraged illegitimacy, facilitated the breakdown of families, and replaced incentives favouring work and self-reliance with perverse encouragement for idleness and cheating. The final illusion – that state intervention would promote social harmony and solidarity or, in Tory language, 'One Nation' – collapsed in the 'winter of discontent' when the dead went unburied, critically ill patients were turned away from hospitals by pickets, and the prevailing mood was one of snarling envy and motiveless hostility. (Thatcher, 1993: 8)

The post-war generation of One Nation Conservative leaders – Macleod, Maude, Macmillan and Heath – had indeed left the stage. Remnants of that tradition saw this as a crucial turning point when dogma replaced pragmatism (Gilmour, 1992).

> Conservatives have never sought to produce equality, regarding it with Jeremy Bentham, as a 'chimera'. Yet, also agreeing with Bentham, they formerly sought to diminish inequality partly because they wanted to eliminate poverty and partly because they realised that, as David Hume put it 'too great a disproportion among the citizens weakens any state'. Since 1979 that humane and sensible attitude has been lost. (Gilmour and Garnet, 1998: viii)

A new social policy agenda?

Yet the Conservative Party did not come to power in 1979 with a shining new set of social policies. Its monetary policy *was* new, however, and it was pursued with a fierce determination no previous government had demonstrated. This had unexpected consequences on unemployment and hence on social policy. But for the most part, Conservative policy began in 1979 by returning to those principles thrashed out in 1947–50: home ownership, the right to buy council houses, and the concentration of public expenditure on those in need, combined with choice in education. R. A. Butler would have recognized it all.

What was different about the 1980s was that Mrs Thatcher did not need to temper these policies to meet hostile public opinion. She was moving with the grain. She was able to make a speech praising inequality, 'Let them grow tall' (Thatcher, 1979). It was happening anyway. Social and economic change were on her side. Most people were now working in non-manual occupations. Most people were now owner occupiers. Council house sales proved highly popular. Most people now had occupational pensions. Even so, once mainstream services that most people used came under the hammer, the public showed how deeply they had become part of the social fabric. This was above all true of the National Health Service. Mrs Thatcher did not dare to touch it until her third term. It is not until the end of Mrs Thatcher's period and her third election victory that fundamental structural changes were tried. Almost drunk with political self-confidence, one Cabinet minister was heard to say, at a dinner in 1988, 'There is nothing we cannot now do.'

But that was nearly ten years away. Mrs Thatcher's social policy revolution only unfolded slowly. There were other prior goals: inflation, the trade unions, the nationalized industries and foreign policy. Neither Mrs Thatcher's nor Nigel Lawson's long accounts of their periods in office (Lawson, 1993; Thatcher, 1993) contain any more than very brief discussions of social policy. Though the key changes begin in Mrs Thatcher's era the critical break with the past comes in 1976.

Labour 1976–9: Cuts and Fag Ends

Most of Labour's period in office after the IMF visit in 1976 was concerned with the battle with inflation, the statutory limits to pay and cuts in public expenditure. Many of these cuts were in fact no more than reductions to previously planned increases in spending but they were a sharp psychological adjustment for public sector workers and managers used to a world of regular incremental growth.

New ways to control public spending

The Treasury introduced changes in the way public expenditure was controlled. The Treasury reforms introduced in 1961 had largely survived intact. A department's expenditure plans for the medium term, five, then four, then three years, were argued over, cut and then approved. Once approved the department could, in normal times, be fairly sure they would be kept to. If any price or salary increases occurred an additional sum would be voted to meet the extra costs. This gave public sector managers a stable climate in which to plan and provide services, more stable than the private sector. It did mean, however, that managers could simply accept wage increases knowing the costs would be eventually accommodated. This

Table 8.1   Real public expenditure on selected programmes in the United Kingdom, 1976/7 to 1982/3

	1976/7	1978/9	1980/1		1982/3	
			Labour plans	Conservative out-turn	Labour plans	Conservative out-turn
Defence	102.0	100	107.7	106.5	108.0	115.3
Law and order	98.5	100	104.2	107.6	108.7	116.4
Education	102.4	100	101.8	98.5	102.3	95.5
Health and personal social services	97.0	100	103.5	102.0	107.8	105.3
Housing	124.3	100	109.8	90.9	114.4	62.2
Social security	87.1	100	104.9	105.8	107.7	119.1
Total public expenditure	101.6	100	106.1	101.8	110.7	104.2

Notes: The figures represent public expenditure in real (volume) terms with each programme indexed so that 1978/9 = 100. In this table, the programme figures for education and health and personal social services and housing relate only to expenditure in England; the law and order figure relates to expenditure in England and Wales; the social security figure relates to expenditure in Great Britain.

Source: O'Higgins, 1983.

was one reason for the steady rise in the share of public spending in the national income, the Treasury argued.

In the wake of the IMF visit a new system of control was introduced that set cash limits to a department's budget. It was set in ordinary money terms. If prices or salaries rose faster than the amount allowed for in the cash limit the department would not get any more money. It would have to make savings, cut staff or otherwise keep within its budget. Certain services, notably social security, were excluded from this arrangement because it was impossible to forecast accurately several years ahead what the level of unemployment would be, for example. The Conservative government later developed this into a tougher system of cash planning targets set for several years ahead but the first step happened in 1976. Cash planning has remained in place, with modifications, since (Harrison, 1989; Thain and Wright, 1995).

The first cuts

The Labour government's plans in 1976 set out to deliver a small rise in social security spending (see Table 8.1). In the end spending rose much more because of the increase in unemployment in the period. The government planned a very modest increase in health spending: 5 per cent over the remainder of its period in office. This was the kind of increase that had taken place each year in the past, not over the span of a Parliament. It planned a small real cut in education spending and stability in housing. In fact, councils cut their building plans for schools and housing because of the costs of borrowing money. Health charges were raised. There were no new policies or a new strategy. The government tightened its belt and hoped for the best.

At the end of this period of cuts and at the end of the winter of discontent, Mr Callaghan had to go to the country – and lost. The Thatcher era dawned.

Containment, Continuity and Tentative Change, 1979–88

Mrs Thatcher began with no overarching new social policy strategy beyond 'a strong set of gut instincts' (Timmins, 1995: 360). Few of her advisers had a close knowledge of social policy. The new Conservative think tanks like the Centre for Policy Studies took time to develop ideas, though the Institute of Economic affairs was still going strong. Most of the social policy academics were not sympathetic. Her government first returned to the principles established in the late 1940s: containing public spending, shifting the finance of services away from direct taxation, targeting social security, enforcing tenants' rights to buy their council houses. Structural change came later, not least because spending proved so difficult to check.

Containment

The economics of the mid-seventies found direct expression in the government's early pronouncements. Its first public expenditure White Paper began with the statement, 'Public expenditure is at the heart of Britain's economic difficulties' (Cmnd 7746, 1979).

In his first Budget speech the new Chancellor, Geoffrey Howe, painted a vivid and accurate picture of Britain's relative decline as a manufacturing nation. The answer lay, he claimed, in increasing personal incentives by reducing direct taxation and reducing the scope of state activity, 'to leave room for commerce and industry to prosper' (Hansard, 12 June 1979).

There were indeed dramatic shifts in tax policy. The second wave of tax reforms originally discussed in the 1960s were carried through (Daunton, 2002). The standard rate of income tax that most people paid on their marginal additional earnings was cut from 33p to 30p. In later Conservative Budgets this was to fall to 23p.

That reduction was paid for not by a reduction in spending, however, but by an increase in the tax on nearly all goods, the Value Added Tax, *and* by an increase in the National Insurance contribution. Over the period from 1980 to 1990 the Treasury contribution to the National Insurance Fund from general taxation was reduced from 18 per cent of the total to nothing at all in 1988/9. Indeed, before unemployment began to rise, the fund had moved into surplus (HC 617 1989/90). Pensions and contributory social security benefits were, by 1989, being paid for entirely out of contributions, just as Macleod and Powell had argued should be the case in the 1940s (see p. 75). What none of these measures did was actually *reduce* public expenditure. The government had inherited large awards (the Clegg awards) to public sector workers that had been necessary to get the previous government off its incomes policy hook. It had also come to power with promises to increase defence and police spending. Its tight monetary policy produced a sharp rise in unemployment and hence in benefit spending. Only very minor reductions in spending on the other social programmes were introduced. Housing was the one service where really massive reductions were made in capital expenditure and in subsidies to local councils. Education suffered with real cuts (see

Table 8.1). For the rest spending continued to rise. One commentator in 1983 concluded,

> beliefs that it [the Conservative government] would lead to radical changes in the welfare state are, so far, largely unfounded, not so much because the Government has changed its mind as because it has been unable to implement its rhetoric. (O'Higgins, 1983: 175)

Another long-term review

The Chancellor, Geoffrey Howe, was at that very time trying to induce the Cabinet to think big and long. Just like his predecessor, R. A. Butler, forty years before, he was struggling to make sense of a commitment to reduce taxation with no proposals to reshape social policy. The Treasury, as it had done on several occasions before, proposed a long-term review of public spending going well beyond the normal three-year period, looking at the coming decade and beyond. The task was entrusted to the Central Policy Review Staff, who then briefed Cabinet.

The results of this exercise suggested that unless something fundamental was done spending would go on taking an even higher share of the GNP than it had done under Labour. Various options were trailed (Lawson, 1993), including introducing education vouchers, replacing part of the NHS with private insurance. These were probably more by way of making the Cabinet think but in Lawson's words, 'The result was the nearest thing to a Cabinet riot in the history of the Thatcher administration' (Lawson, 1993: 303). The paper was shelved and to ensure its demise the 'wets' in Cabinet, so Lawson claims, leaked the paper to *The Economist*. Mrs Thatcher announced that none of the proposals were being pursued.

The Treasury did not give up, however, and after the election in 1983 a fuller, more cautious paper on the long-term prospects for social spending was produced and published as a Green Paper (Cmnd 9184, 1984). Lawson set a medium-term goal of stabilizing public spending in real terms and then modified it to a less impossible goal of a slower rate of growth than the long-term growth of the economy. But how to do it?

Social Security Reform

If spending constraints *were* to work, given Conservative policy on defence and law and order, they had to work on social security above all. It was the largest spending programme and rising the fastest. Here, the new Conservative government did make some early very important decisions.

Incentives to work

The first targets were the wage-related sickness and unemployment benefits introduced by the Labour government in 1965. These, at least higher unemployment benefits, had been introduced, it will be recalled, to make labour mobility more acceptable. The Conservative government believed that they merely reduced the financial incentive to seek work urgently and encouraged people to stay on sick pay for longer than necessary.

The fact that if benefits are sufficiently high they will at some point discourage people from returning to work is not really in doubt. It has been a basic principle of poor relief policy ever since 1834. The debate is about the level at which the disincentive to work effect begins to have a significant impact. The belief in 1979 was that the short-term benefits dating from 1965 were that high. In consequence, the earnings-related supplement for unemployment and sickness benefits was abolished from June 1982 and from the next month unemployment benefit and supplementary benefits paid to unemployed people (except the additions for children) were made taxable. This created 'clear water' between benefits and wages for all but the very poor. Did it have the desired incentive effect and increase employment?

As it happened a long-term study of the unemployed was taking place at the point when these changes took place and some answer can be given. For young people under the age of 25 there was some effect. Standardizing for other economic changes taking place, one group of leading academics concluded that the reduced benefits were associated with young people returning to work faster. For those with families and for older people, however, there was little or no effect (Narendranathan et al., 1983). The overall effect on employment was small.

Sick pay

The administration of sick pay was also changed. Until 1983 it had been paid, as Beveridge intended, as a cash benefit by the local office of the National Insurance or Social Security Department. The Social Security and Housing Benefit Act of 1982 made employers responsible for paying 'Statutory Sick Pay' for the first eight weeks of sickness, though the employer could recover most of the cost from the state by reducing the net National Insurance contribution paid. The period was later extended to twenty-eight weeks. (Some groups were excluded such as those under the lower earnings limit, the self-employed and those of pensionable age. It was not payable for the first three days off work.)

This change was presented as a simple administrative device. But many argued that it was a first step to making employers responsible for sick pay, as most have always been for higher-salaried staff. This prediction was borne out in 1994 when the government abolished its reimbursement of the costs of Statutory Sick Pay, leaving employers to cover all the costs of their employees' sickness absence (except for small employers). The reasoning was not just to save tax but to encourage employers to police sickness absence more closely. The concern of many critics was that it would encourage employers to be more selective in hiring staff. People with a poor health record or a chronic condition would find it difficult to get a job because they would be more costly. This had always been the case for a statutory scheme and general risk sharing.

Uprating

The most important change made in those early years of the new Thatcher government, however, was to alter the basis on which benefits were 'uprated', or increased on a regular basis. We have seen that in practice for most of the period since the Second World War social security benefits had been raised to match rises in the general level of earnings in the economy. Often this was delayed until just before an election, but by 1983 the real value of the basic pension for a married couple had more than doubled since 1948 and was at its highest point compared to the average after-tax income.

From 1982 the government was only to uprate pensions in line with prices. This meant that the basic pension became a lower and lower percentage of the average wage or average disposable (after-tax) income. It fell from over 23 per cent of average male earnings in 1981 to 15 per cent by 1995. On reasonable assumptions it would fall to below 10 per cent by the mid-century. The basic state pension would then become an irrelevance and could be abolished.

Similar trends have been followed with other benefits. The savings have been enormous in public expenditure terms: the cost of the basic pension has been cut by a third in a decade. None of this tackled the basic structure of social security, however, and Norman Fowler, the Secretary of State, initiated what was billed as the most thorough overhaul of the social security system since Beveridge – a claim that was to be repeated again in the 1990s and in 2006 as governments struggled to get some consensus behind change in UK pension policy.

The Fowler reviews

These were a series of four separate reviews of different aspects of the social security system, which were undertaken with painstaking care. Detailed studies were made using modern computerized modelling techniques. The economists in the DHSS produced studies of past trends in pensioners' incomes suggesting that old people had done better than many sections of the community if you took account of private pension income but those who had been hardest hit were young families (DHSS, 1985a). Improving their lot became part of the objective of the reforms. A Green Paper, backed by the results of the studies, was published (DHSS, 1985b) and a fierce debate followed. The process was a good example of the sort of informed policy debate that had characterized social security since Beveridge. It was a conscious attempt to live up to that tradition. It was also to show how difficult it is to change a complex system, not only because it serves many interested parties but because the problems it is trying to tackle *are* complex.

Targeting

This basic truth was best illustrated by the reviews' attempts to tackle the question of targeting. As in the Conservatives' discussions in 1947–50, the key objective was to save money by targeting and means testing benefits. What the review team found was that the UK already had one of the most targeted social security systems in the world, with a wide range of means-tested benefits that had grown up over the post-war period. The means-tested Family Income Supplement introduced in 1971 and the housing allowance a year later, had been superimposed on top of existing means-tested charges for services. This had created a fearsomely complex web. The consequence was that when people moved off these benefits, as their earnings rose, they had to pay full rent, full prescription charges and tax. At some points the loss of these means-tested benefits produced a 'tax' on earnings equivalent to more than the extra earnings gained. The Green Paper concluded, having reviewed the options,

A wholly means-tested approach to social security – including pensions and child benefit – would at best meet only one of the main objectives of social security: to concentrate help on those who need it most. This approach would, by discouraging self help and reducing incentives, undermine the importance of individual provision. (DHSS, 1985a, para. 6.9)

The dilemma of targeting could not have been more succinctly put.

Much energy and ingenuity was devoted by the review team to trying to reduce the effect of this poverty trap. Tapering off the means tests cost more money unless the basic benefit rates were cut. The politicians were not ready to do this. So a series of sensible but small adjustments were made which did improve the poverty trap slightly and did not cost too much but were nowhere near the hoped-for breakthrough to simplicity (see Barr and Coulter, 1990, for a discussion of this).

SERPS

The other major attempt to save money was the proposal in the Green Paper (DHSS, 1985b) to abolish the State Earnings-Related Pension Scheme (SERPS) introduced after such an anguished pregnancy in 1978 (see p. 114). Though it had then gained cross-party support the government now argued that the promises SERPS made to future generations of pensioners were too costly.

According to Lawson (1993) the civil servants on the review team came up with proposals that would have cut the costs of SERPS. This appears as one option in the Green Paper. Fowler, the Secretary of State, wanted to go further and abolish SERPS altogether. This option was included in the Green Paper as a second, but preferred, route. The basic flat rate pension should be retained, the Green Paper said, but,

> We should not place on our successors the responsibility for meeting all our financial expectations in retirement. Instead we should ensure that everybody is able to save and invest for his own additional pension. (DHSS, 1985b, para. 7.13)

To prevent people simply relying on the state to keep them when they retired, all workers would be required to contribute to a pension scheme of some kind a minimum of 4 per cent of their income. Tax reliefs would encourage people to opt into private schemes.

Lawson (1993: Ch. 47) describes a furious row that broke out between him and Fowler when Lawson realized that no one was costing the loss of revenue these tax reliefs would cost the Exchequer. He blames Mrs Thatcher for insisting that there must be incentives for people to join private schemes and that the government could not simply remove SERPS and not help in return. When the Treasury did do their sums they concluded that abolishing SERPS would actually *cost* the Exchequer £1 billion! Lawson also opposed the idea of making membership of private schemes compulsory, which would add to employers' costs.

This whole episode illustrates the key difficulty a government faces if it wishes to scale down its future pension responsibilities. The responsibilities for existing pensioners are difficult to abandon. On top of that such a government must also ask the present generation to spend more on its own future pensions (see p. 261).

The proposal to abolish SERPS and put the responsibility on to individuals and employers was almost universally opposed, among others by the CBI and the private pensions industry who did not relish having to cater for the lower-paid with poor job prospects. The campaign mounted after the publication of the Green Paper by the poverty lobby, groups representing the elderly, the CBI and the insurance industry stayed the execution of SERPS. It was retained but the pensions promised, above all to women, were cut. The government did also increase tax reliefs to those who joined private schemes.

The policy had close similarities to the failed legislation of the Heath era. Unlike Heath's scheme in 1973, occupational pensions were not the only, or the most favoured, alternatives. Instead, private, individually tailored 'portable' pensions, which an individual could take from job to job, were given particularly favourable tax treatment. The one option not seriously discussed was to raise the retirement age for women, primarily because Mrs Thatcher opposed it! It was proposed again in Kenneth Clarke's first Autumn Budget in 1993 and legislated when Mrs Thatcher had gone.

The Social Fund

Towards the end of the Labour government's period in office a committee was appointed to consider the tangle of discretionary payments that those on Supplementary Benefit could receive. A claimant might have special dietary needs or be in an emergency with no bedding or furniture. Claims were growing, as was the cost, but some offices and officers might be more sympathetic than others. The poverty lobby had pressed for clearer rights, and a team of officials set to review the scheme proposed that the guidelines that already existed could be tightened up and turned into statutory rules approved by Parliament (DHSS, 1978). This was done in 1980 by the new government. The scope for discretionary payments by officers was greatly limited but payments began to grow again and the application of statutory rights proved very expensive. When people's rights became clear they claimed them! The number of furniture grants given rose three and a half times between 1978 and 1983, the White Paper complained (Cmnd 9691, 1985: 37). The way to stop this rising expenditure on exceptional extras, the government concluded, was to give people money to meet the cost of new bedding in an emergency, but only to give it as a loan. A new fund was set up to meet these costs – the Social Fund – but it was not to be open-ended. Cash-limited sums would be made available for specialist officers in each local office to allocate in any year. The local office would set the priorities within guidelines. The fund would help with maternity and funeral costs and there would be community care payments for those leaving hospital, but other elements would move to a loan basis. Funeral expenses would be recovered from the dead person's estate where possible.

The Social Fund loans probably caused more dispute and anger than any other part of the reforms. Recovering loans made to poor people to cover emergencies seemed particularly harsh. The government claimed it would stop abuses of the system. The total sums of money involved, however, were quite small.

The resulting legislation, the 1986 Social Security Act, embodied these changes and smoothed out some of the perverse overlapping elements in the web of means-tested benefits that had grown up in the previous twenty years. Various changes were introduced during the passage of the legislation to mollify groups of losers, for example housing benefit recipients. It was *not* a brave new world but it was a slightly less idiotic old one. The provisions came into effect in April 1988.

The Social Security Act 1986

The main effect of the Act was that:

- Common rules were introduced to assess entitlements to all the means-tested schemes which had previously operated under different definitions and rules about income and capital.

- Family Credit was introduced in place of Family Income Supplement. It *was* more generous, and applied to low-paid families in work (24 hours a week reduced to 16 in 1992).
- Income Support replaced Supplementary Benefit. It had a simpler system of automatic additions to the basic rate to cover the costs of children or a disabled person.
- All recipients would have to pay a sum equivalent to 20 per cent of the rates and, later, the new poll tax. This was part of Mrs Thatcher's personal crusade to force local voters to recognize the cost of local services but it complicated the otherwise laudable attempt to simplify the Income Support scheme. This 20 per cent requirement was abolished after John Major became Prime Minister.

Results

The consequences of this complex and detailed set of new rules have been assessed by Evans et al. (1994). They conclude that little changed. Households facing a 'tax rate' of over 100 per cent did fall. In other words the number who were actually worse off when they returned to work fell. There was little change for those in less extreme situations. The number on means-tested benefits fell for a few years but then resumed its steady rise. As did the share of spending going on means-tested benefits (Evans, 1998). More help went to the elderly, to the long-term sick and to children, but less to the families of the unemployed. The Social Fund did result in a reduction of two-thirds in real spending on exceptional items. Spending on Family Credit did rise above the old FIS levels. The number claiming the new benefit rose from 3 per cent of all families with children, under the old system in 1986/7, to 5 per cent in 1990/1 under the new. A detailed look at which groups gained and lost suggests little overall effect on the level of poverty one way or the other. The main impact had been to churn up the incomes of the poor, some gaining, some losing. What it had *not* done was to reduce the social security budget.

Housing Reform

Council house sales

Undoubtedly the most popular and politically successful policy the government initiated in this first period was the sale of council houses. This had been on its agenda ever since the 1940s and individual councils had enabled their tenants to buy their council houses, but it had never been encouraged by Labour councils and it had never necessarily been an attractive option. What the government decided to do was to give council tenants of three years' standing a right to buy their homes at a generous discount under the 1980 Housing Act. The longer they had been tenants the larger the discount. The discount began at a third off the value of the house and rose by 1 per cent for each year up to a 50 per cent discount. By 1989 the discounts had been raised to 70 per cent in some cases. These were powerful inducements and they produced results. Sales reached a peak at nearly a quarter of a million a year by 1982. More than a sixth of the total stock of council houses was sold in the period 1979–87. Between 1979 and 2000 the share of the total housing stock owned by local councils fell from nearly a third to less than a fifth. Sales began to slow down as most of those who had the capacity to buy, and some that really did not, had bought their houses. This left behind in local authority and housing association tenure mostly the poorest groups in society. In 1974 just under half the tenants in social housing were in the bottom 40 per cent of the income distribution; by 1991 the proportion was three-quarters and only 40 per cent of them had jobs.

Diversifying social housing

Though councils did not get the full value of the houses they sold they did get some. But the government did not want the council sector they were busy reducing to grow again and stopped councils from spending most of their receipts on new building. It did, however, follow the trend set by the previous Labour government in switching financial support to non-profit housing associations. By the 1990s these had become the main suppliers of new social housing units for lower-income renting.

The final strand in the 1980s housing policy was to withdraw the subsidies councils received to keep down the level of council house rents. Councils were forced to raise their rents nearer to the fair rent levels set for private and housing association tenants. Poorer tenants, the great majority, could claim Housing Benefit from the Department of Social Security. This was still a subsidy from the central government but it came targeted on the poor and indifferent to the form of tenure. Housing Benefit was available to all tenants on a means-tested basis. The policy begun in 1972 had been taken to its full and logical conclusion.

Though making sense as a housing policy, it was steadily pushing up the social security budget and adding to poverty trap problems that social security reforms were wrestling with at the very same time. For a full account and an evaluation of the housing policy of the period see Hills (1998).

Continuities

The first two terms of Mrs Thatcher's government saw changes in direction and portents for the future but there was more continuity than change. In education the financial squeeze was tightest on the universities. Overseas students had to pay the full cost of their education, extending the logic of the policy begun previously. At one point, in 1984, Sir Keith Joseph proposed to make home students pay towards the costs of their university education. He saw this as a way of getting more money for the universities in his annual battle with the Treasury. Within weeks he had to withdraw the proposal in the face of outraged opposition from Conservative backbenchers. What would their middle-class parent constituents say and how would they pay for their private schools if they had to pay for university too? There was a wider political lesson. Touch those parts of the Welfare State that most benefit the middle class at your peril.

Keith Joseph had also become keen to introduce some kind of voucher scheme. This would have given parents the equivalent of a luncheon voucher that could have been taken to any school of the parents' choice, public or private, and cashed for their child's education. The DES officials patiently pointed out that for state schools this would have meant no advance on what could be achieved already if there were places available. There were few spare places and it would increase the administrative costs considerably. To extend the scheme to private schools would mean that parents who now paid for their children's education would become eligible for vouchers and public money. This would increase the education budget by 6 per cent at a stroke and the Treasury would never entertain the idea (for an account of the dilemmas see Blaug, 1984).

What did happen was a very limited scheme that went some way to replace the loss of support some direct grant schools had suffered after 1976. Parents with low incomes could apply to send their children to a restricted list of independent schools and fill a quota of 35,000 places in all. The state would then pay the fees on an income-related sliding scale. This was called the Assisted Places Scheme.

For the rest, though in straitened circumstances, the education system went on much as before, focusing on links with industry, criticized for its standards, beginning to lose custom to the private sector. For a detailed account and evaluation of the period see Glennerster and Low (1990). In the Health Service too there were changes designed to reduce costs and increase managerial efficiency. The complex layers of administration introduced in 1974, of regions, areas and districts, were slimmed down. Area health authorities went. Sir Roy Griffiths was brought in from Sainsbury's to advise on how to improve the management of the NHS. He could see no one in charge and proposed that there be a system of general management in place at each level to run hospitals and districts rather than leaving the service to be ruled by multiple professions. These changes took effect from 1983 on. Beyond that nothing fundamental changed in the NHS. What did was the fierce rigour with which cash limits and minimal growth were imposed. It was that which laid up problems for Mrs Thatcher's third, more explosive, term.

At the end of two terms in office, despite her dramatic confrontations with the Argentinians and the miners, large-scale privatization and trade union reform, Mrs Thatcher had still to tackle social policy in a radical way. The attempt to reform social security had been an object lesson.

The government wanted to achieve cuts in the largest programme of public expenditure but its own economic policy was increasing people's dependency on benefits. It wanted to increase targeting but it found that the extent of targeting was already considerable and was creating disincentives to work. It probably wanted to means test pensions but incautious remarks by the Chancellor to that effect caused such a hostile reaction that the idea was dropped. Social policy was an altogether harder nut to crack.

Questions to Answer

1 Why can 1976 be seen as a turning point in post-war social policy?
2 Looking back at council house sales from today's vantage point, what are some of its positive and negative effects? Why was it so popular?
3 This was a period when decisive changes took place in pension policy. Why did they occur? Why were they politically feasible? What impacts did they have on today's pension crisis?

9

New Directions, 1988–97

A Radical Manifesto
Housing Choice
Standards in Education
Student Loans
A Poll Tax
Health Service Reform
Community Care
Another 'Fundamental' Review
Taxation
Majorism
The State and the Family
Lone Mothers
Children
The End of an Era

Mrs Thatcher's third election victory was important for the institutions that deliver social policy in the UK, the National Health Service, schools and local government. The first priorities on the Conservatives' agenda had been accomplished. The trade unions had been tamed, the miners defeated, and inflation brought under control. Now, as their third election approached, the Conservative Party could contemplate something more radical. Mrs Thatcher's memoirs capture the logic:

The manifesto was designed to solve a serious political problem for us. As a party which had been in government for eight years, we had to dispel any idea that we were stale and running out of ideas. We therefore had to advance a number of clear, specific, new and well-worked-out reforms. (1993: 572)

There is a general and disturbing lesson to be drawn from these remarks from a consummate politician. Seeking to win votes by promising to spend more on social programmes was thought to be impossible and, in her case, undesirable. Parties cannot, however, merely promise to keep the status quo. It looks boring. 'New ideas' have to be put on show in each manifesto. Perpetual change becomes a consequence of the political market-place.

A Radical Manifesto

A series of policy groups had been set up in 1986 to prepare the ground for the next election, each chaired by ministers. The input from Mrs Thatcher's own Number 10 Policy Unit and through it, from external think tanks, was significant. Mrs Thatcher claims that, 'The manifesto was the best ever produced by the Conservative Party' (1993: 572).

In terms of its coherence around a central theme and the radical nature of its proposals, this is a not unreasonable claim. The first eight years of Mrs Thatcher's government can be seen as completing an old agenda that can be traced back to the period 1947–50. The 1987 election set a new agenda and a new direction for Conservative social policy.

It is usually claimed by political opponents and many social policy commentators that this change began the break-up of the Welfare State. For some in the Conservative Party this was probably the ambition. But it can be seen as the very opposite – the beginning of a revival in the social institutions that deliver social policy. Therein lay the political skill of the proposals. They appealed to both sections of the Conservative Party and had an appeal beyond. (For some varied assessments of the period see Pierson, 1994; Marsland, 2004; Glennerster, 2004; Land, 2004.)

On balance, the evidence is that it was the reformers and not the abolitionists who won. Middle England still needed the basic social services too much for a Conservative Party that wanted to win to abolish them. Timmins' (1995) account gets it exactly right:

At the end of the Thatcher era a remarkable paradox was apparent. A woman whose instincts were to unscramble the NHS and to increase charges, to roll back social security and social services, and to return schools to selection and fee paying had instead headed a government which found itself promoting reforms that, however controversial, were plainly intended to improve existing health, education and social services . . . the middle classes, instead of being encouraged to abandon those key services actually found their concerns being addressed. (p. 478)

Reversing long-run decline?

What Mrs Thatcher saw, with her populist insight, was that there was growing dissatisfaction with state services that gave little choice to their users, in which the professional view was dominant and the parent or patient in the waiting-room seemed to count for little. In a growingly sophisticated consumer society this compared poorly with the market sector. The Labour Party, in the 1960s and 1970s, had experimented with forms of consumer participation to remedy the same defects: a few token lay representatives were placed on consultative bodies. This had satisfied no one.

What had gradually happened was what Durbin had feared more than fifty years before. The professionals and service providers had come to be too insensitive to their clients. Services that lack an effective sanction against abuse will come to abuse. Ultimately, the most effective sanction is for the user to say, 'I have had enough. I am taking my custom elsewhere.' Institutions that lack such external discipline eventually decline, be they corporations, governments or social services (Hirschman, 1970). The cosseting of the British economy through imperial protection and the captive markets of the empire in the early part of this century may explain the long-run weakness of British firms. The same decline can be said to have afflicted the institutions of the Welfare State. It took a long time, but by the 1970s some of the signs were on the wall.

Some of the earliest were visible on the vast public housing estates built in the 1960s where the 'consumers' had least capacity of all to make their voices heard or to exit. Until the 1940s, at least, council housing had been both much sought after and well managed. Then, as politicians saw success and votes in building houses, regardless of the quality of the living environment, or the capacity of the councils to manage the stock, standards fell. Housing managers, caretakers and other staff left the estates for cosy central offices and left the tenants and the stock to fend for themselves (see Power, 1988, for a vivid description of this process of long-term decline). The tenants left behind, especially after the encouragement of owner occupation, had even less leverage and purchasing power. Some estates became hard to let, despite a housing shortage, and provided an environment of squalor and crime that made them social ghettos. This was happening long before the right to buy policy came into force (Glennerster and Turner, 1993).

Education also had its warning signs. One of the most dramatic and well publicized concerned a primary school in a poor area of Islington.

> In the autumn of 1973 William Tyndale was an ordinary enough junior school in a run down part of north London; within just two years the school had fallen apart and striking teachers, angry parents and helpless politicians were confronting one another through the headlines of the national press and the current affairs programmes of television. (Gretton and Jackson, 1976)

The poverty of the area and the extreme difficulty of appointing good staff on the salaries available were the predisposing factors at work in this school. Yet it also showed how powerless the system and parents were when a school fell into the hands of teachers who took the law and the children into their own hands. The politicians had given up exercising control, the inspectors only advised, the governors were ineffective and the parents powerless. In the end, there was an independent inquiry and teachers were dismissed, but the whole episode alerted the wider public to the fact that there was something very wrong with a system that could let this happen. Gretton and Jackson, in their powerful account, concluded,

> All these issues we have mentioned – the powers and responsibilities of local authorities, the control of the curriculum, the criteria for assessing a school's efficiency, the aims of primary education, the need for testing, the role of the inspectorate, the function of managers and the professionalism and accountability of teachers – are proper subjects of consideration by the Secretary of State for Education . . . After William Tyndale [he – though all his predecessors have] can no longer pretend that it is all happening somewhere else. (1976: 125–6)

This 'scandal', like the Ely Hospital scandal of the 1960s (see p. 126), shook a complacent system. It came on top of the publication of a very influential set of papers by Conservative academics – the Black Papers (Cox and Dyson, 1969) – highly critical of modern methods of teaching and standards in state schools. This theme had been picked up by the previous

Labour Prime Minister James Callaghan, in a famous speech at Ruskin College, Oxford in 1976. Work had then begun within the DES on devising a National Curriculum.

Lawson's account of the origins of the education reforms is worth noting. He, too, perceived that voters were worried about standards.

> When I became Member for Blaby . . . I found the biggest single issue to be parents' dissatisfaction with the standards of education and conduct in the schools most of their children were obliged to attend. (Lawson, 1993: 602)

Nor was Blaby unrepresentative. As Halsey concludes, in his review of a series of public attitude surveys in the 1980s, 'Public perceptions of the performance of secondary schools in particular are decidedly gloomy' (Halsey, 1991: 57). There was comparative evidence from abroad to support such instincts (Green and Steedman, 1993).

The continuing concern for education standards was later illustrated by the considerable attention given in the press and television to a critical speech made to the British Association by Sir Claus Moser in 1990 about the standards of British education. The result was private support to set up a National Commission on Education, which reported in 1993. It contains the best review of the education system as it was in the 1990s.

Lawson and Thatcher had thus listened to middle England when the Labour Party was still tuned to the wave length of the NUT. Education, after health, was next to top priority for voters (Halsey, 1991).

Radical ideas

When the policy groups reported in 1987 and the Conservative manifesto emerged it contained radical proposals on housing and education. There was nothing on the National Health Service. No radical ideas had crystallized and Mrs Thatcher decided that it was too hot a political potato to handle anyway in the manifesto (Thatcher, 1993: 571). Nor was there any fundamental change to the policy on community care. Both were to come later.

Housing Choice

> Municipal monopoly must be replaced by choice in renting. (*The Next Moves Forward*, Conservative Party, 1987)

It was clear by 1987 that there was little extra mileage in the sale of council houses to individuals, at least as a way of significantly reducing the size of the council sector. The remaining tenants were too poor. Why not give tenants the right to transfer the ownership of their house to a private landlord or housing association if they were dissatisfied with their council? If the estates were so bad that no one wanted to buy them a central government agency could take them over, improve them and sell them off.

Ultimately, if there was to be real choice the private landlord market had to be revived and this meant giving landlords the right to let at free market rents. The tenant would have some security at the end of the lease, the right to appeal if a rise in the rent was unreasonable or beyond a normal market increase. This last provision was an improvement on the situation in the 1957 Act, which had no provision for appeal and no element of security. Taken together these ideas amounted to the most coherent housing policy the Conservatives had had since 1953.

These were the ideas embodied in the manifesto and the 1988 Housing Act:

- Rent control in the private sector was removed. New tenancies would be either assured leases with renewal rights or short-hold.
- Central government could designate an area of public housing and create a Housing Action Trust to manage the houses, eventually disposing of them.
- The notion that individual tenants could get a landlord to take over their house was dropped as impractical and replaced by an arrangement which put the onus on private landlords or housing associations. They were given the right to bid to take over an estate or part of it and the tenants had a right to vote on the proposal and veto it, under some complex voting rules.

Under the 1989 Local Government and Housing Act local councils lost their right to subsidize council rents out of local revenue.

Housing outcomes?

This was a comprehensive package of housing measures driven by a clear philosophy and the intention of giving more market power to tenants. The difficulty was that really no market for poor tenants' custom existed. There were no private landlords who could get sufficient return to make the political risk worthwhile. Very few housing associations wanted to get into the business of taking on large estates of very poor tenants. The danger to their reputations of owning such problem areas made that an unattractive prospect. Tenants themselves feared that new landlords would put up rents and might want to move them out of their houses. When proposals to buy were made, few gained tenants' support.

Only six Housing Action Trusts were created for very much the same reason. The Department of the Environment, even at one remove, did not want to be lumbered with managing the most deprived and crime-ridden areas in the country. That promised to be a civil servant's and a minister's graveyard.

Much of the 1988 Act, for all its radicalism, remained a dead letter. That is not to say that social housing was not changing. Little by little housing associations of varied kinds and sizes came to be the new main providers of social housing. The range of landlords for poor and vulnerable people was far more varied than it had been and the new housing associations were managing their property effectively. The monopoly of social housing had been broken and the quality of management had been improved by action taken by both Labour and Conservative governments from 1974 onwards. For a careful evaluation of the whole period see Hills (1998).

As against that the social problems that were accumulating on the most deprived estates were worsening by the year. This was the reverse side of the very success Conservative housing policy had had in extending owner occupation to the great bulk of the population. Many people, and the most active, now had the capacity to leave. It was also the consequence of the government's economic policy that had led to the sudden collapse of jobs in many industrial areas in the 1980s. The growing concentration of poverty worried the government, which began to respond through special schemes like the Single Regeneration Budget – a pot of money for which local authorities could bid to help revive the worst areas.

It is not until the major parties really come to terms with this problem that it has any hope of solution. Yet it only affects a small minority of the population, most of whom do not vote. As the Welfare State comes to be concerned increasingly with the poor and only the poor, will the ordinary voter have any interest in what happens to them? Housing is the first test case. The issues are remarkably similar in whatever European country we look (Power, 1993).

The prospects are not all bad. Governments of both main political parties in the UK have supported concentrating efforts on the worst estates, improving the quality of management and decentralizing it. The Priority

Estates Project was an initiative begun by the Labour government in 1979 and continued, after some initial doubts, by the Conservative government, through the 1980s. Estate Action and a number of projects followed. All had some success (Glennerster and Turner, 1993; Power, 1988). Yet in the end they could do little on their own to reverse the tide of growing and extreme deprivation that was afflicting such areas.

Standards in Education

The ideas of a National Curriculum and some kind of national standard-setting had been around in the old Ministry of Education in the 1950s. The then Minister, Sir David Eccles, had bemoaned the fact that this was forbidden territory for politicians. A proposal to set up a Curriculum Study Group in the ministry had been seen off by an outraged National Union of Teachers and others in 1962. But the tide of opinion had turned in the early 1970s, for reasons touched on already, and this had been accelerated by the economic crisis of 1976. The prime ministerial initiative by Callaghan to take the standards issue seriously in 1976 (see p. 170) was the first public step. The DES could also see that it would be possible in this new climate to press for a new role.

In the 1950s and 1960s the old Ministry of Education had been brilliantly successful in expanding education through a series of reports that levered more money out of the Treasury. It was probably the lead promotional department and was an exciting place to work. It was admiral of a large fleet of smaller local authority vessels. It determined where local schools would be built, what organizational form they should take, what pace and form the expansion of higher education should take.

After 1976, for a period, there was a halt to educational expansion, only a tiny new building programme to allocate between local authorities, little opportunity to interfere with the design of local schools. What were these civil servants to do! What more natural than to see an enhanced role for the centre in curriculum design.

A series of discussion papers was produced exploring what might be in a national curriculum, though it was initially presented as a voluntary move to harmonization between schools. This had continued from 1977 to the mid-1980s.

By the time ministers were preparing for the 1987 election, in the midst of a long-running teachers' strike that was damaging teachers' credibility and support, it was possible for ministers to feel they could go the whole way, that is, to a statutory National Curriculum. There was broad agreement across the political spectrum on this. Teachers were in no position to resist, or so it seemed.

The proposals in the manifesto were to go well beyond a curriculum. There were to be assessment targets. Schools were to be judged on their performance in these tests. It was this step that lost the consensus that existed on a National Curriculum. Most teachers supported some core common syllabus for the key subjects. The Department of Education wanted to go several bridges further. Mrs Thatcher did not. It proposed a detailed curriculum for most subjects, regular testing of children at the ages of 7, 11, 14 and the last year of schooling, and the publication of the results for parents to make informed choices between competing schools. The result was a long-running battle between the teachers' unions and the government that was not resolved until the mid-1990s when resistance waned. For an account of this story see Timmins (1995: 437–46). Disputes continued about the principle of testing and the content of the National Curriculum. Scotland and Wales were to take a different view about testing, as we shall see in Chapter 10.

Choice and decentralization in education

The idea of giving vouchers to parents to buy education for their children had attracted Conservative intellectuals since Milton Friedman (1962) had advocated it in the early 1960s. We described in the previous chapter why it came to grief in the first Thatcher period. Greater rights of choice had already been given to parents using state schools. Perhaps there was mileage in extending this idea. Two strands of policy that were already well developed in a number of local authorities were added.

The first was decentralizing financial responsibility to the schools themselves. The extent to which state schools had devolved responsibilities had varied. Some had the power to spend their own small budget on books and small equipment as they wished. In other cases virtually everything the school used had to be purchased through the central local authority office miles away and with considerable delay. Local authorities paid the salaries of the teachers, allowing each school a quota of teachers of different ranks. This tended to mean that favoured schools in attractive areas kept their teachers, who progressed up their salary scales. As a consequence they did better in cash terms than schools in poor areas (Glennerster, 1972). A number of authorities tried to remedy this situation by giving more cash to schools in poor areas. This money could be spent on whatever the school wished. The Inner London Education Authority took this the furthest and gradually extended the principle. It was a Labour authority. Another more Conservative area, Cambridgeshire, took the experiment the whole way and gave each of its schools a total budget out of which they could employ what teachers and what other equipment or books they chose. It improved their capacity to react quickly and freely without LEA approval, and it was popular with these schools (Burgess, 1986). It was a new idea and it was not the voucher idea that the DES saw so many objections to. The government decided to extend the scheme to all schools. The 1987 manifesto contained a pledge to give all secondary and some primary schools their own budget. Governors and managers of schools had for a long time been pressing the government to give these bodies more freedom and to require the representation of parents on these bodies. A committee set up by the previous Labour government had proposed increasing community and parental representation on bodies that at one time had been entirely political appointees. Most authorities were going down this road. The government was proposing to go with the tide.

The second strand of policy was more controversial. Previous education Acts had increased parents' right to choose a school and gave powers of appeal if they were not given that choice. The 1987 manifesto went further, proposing to remove local authorities' right to limit the size of a popular school. Schools' budgets would be set according to the number of pupils they could attract on a formula basis: so much per pupil attracted to the school.

Taken together these elements amounted to a voucher scheme operating in the state system. Schools would compete for custom. When a pupil signed up, that would attract a sum of money, in exactly the same way as would happen under a voucher scheme.

More controversial still was the idea that some state schools should be able to become independent and supported by central government funds, recreating the direct grant schools in effect (Thatcher, 1993). In the event this proposal was modified to become the grant-maintained or opted-out schools scheme. Parents dissatisfied with their local authority could exercise collective exit powers. This paralleled the similar powers given to tenants in the Housing Act of the same year.

The Education Reform Act 1988

This Act embodied these ideas and was the first really large structural change to the education system since the 1944 Act and the comprehensive school reforms of the sixties. Despite the Act's importance the process of consultation was minimal compared to the careful crafting and compromises reached in 1944. A few brief typewritten consultation documents were circulated during the summer vacation of 1987 with replies required by the end of September or the middle of October. The debates that ensued were furious, again in contrast to the passage of the 1944 Act. There was little consensus in the education world especially on the setting of attainment exams from 7 on, the detail of the National Curriculum and the abolition of tenure for university teachers.

The key elements in the Act were:

- It laid a duty on the Secretary of State to establish a National Curriculum for all state schools setting out targets of knowledge children should have reached by 7, 11, 14 and 16: 'attainment targets'.
- Pupils would be tested on these at those ages in a uniform national way and the results would be published by each school.
- A standard number of pupils would be fixed for each school by central government.
- A formula would be set to allocate budgets to each school by each authority but it would be approved by the Secretary of State.
- Schools could opt out of local education authority control if the majority of parents voting approved. The schools would be funded directly from central government and would be called grant-maintained schools.
- Polytechnics became independent, not run by local authorities. Later they were to become universities.
- A new University Funding Council was given powers 'to make grants (to universities) subject to such terms and conditions as they think fit' (Section 131(6)) and tenure was abolished. This was the most sweeping extension of state power over universities seen in the post-war period.

Student Loans

The 1987 manifesto had cautiously referred to the review of student finance that was under way. Burned once, the government was going to be very careful. The eventual scheme was caution itself. Fees were left untouched. There was to be no contribution to university fees paid by the ordinary home student. They would continue to be paid by the local authority on his or her behalf. Instead the student maintenance grant would be frozen but students could top it up with loans. The original idea had been to administer these loans through the banks but no one thought to ask the banks first, and the National Union of Students made it clear that it would call on students to boycott any bank that co-operated. None did.

The scheme was significant only in that it established the principle that students should repay part of the costs of the education that would benefit them financially. The scheme would cost the Exchequer *more* in the first instance because the loans were made out of public money. It would be into the next century before the revenue from the repayments would significantly outweigh the extra cost. (For a contemporary critique see Barnes and Barr, 1988).

A Poll Tax

A third major element in the 1987 manifesto was the proposal to introduce a flat rate poll tax to finance local services. Ever since the Second World War local authorities had been given extensive new responsibilities to provide social services without anything but an unpopular property tax – the rates – as a way to finance them. Increasingly central government had to finance services that it willed through grants to local councils. In the 1980s, when central government tried to cut local grants, it found local councils willing to raise the rates to try and sustain services. Furious that its attempts to cut spending were being frustrated, central government tried increasingly interventionist ways of stopping the process. Rates were capped or limited by Parliament. Then, in desperation, councils were given a form of revenue – the poll tax – that was oppressive to administer and was not related to people's ability to pay (the inside story is brilliantly told in Butler et al., 1994). This was meant to restrain high-spending councils but its evident unfairness rebounded on the government instead. It was implemented first in Scotland. It was there that rising rates, sparked off by revaluation of property, had begun the whole attempt to reform the rating system, it proved so unpopular that it contributed to Mrs Thatcher's downfall and was replaced by the council tax in 1993. (For the story in more detail: Gibson, 1990; Glennerster et al., 1991; King, 1990.)

Though the council tax proved more acceptable it left the basic weakness in the finance of local services unresolved. Much of social policy is delivered locally by political bodies who only raise a small part of what they spend. This leaves accountability for service quality uneasily spread between central government, who pays, and local government, who runs the services. The weakness of such a situation was lucidly argued in a report by the Layfield Committee in 1976.

Health Service Reform

There had been no mention in the 1987 election manifesto of any funda-mental changes to the NHS. In 1988, however, the consequences of the cash constraints on the service applied in the early and mid-eighties began to have their effect. Between 1983 and 1987 the real purchasing power available to the NHS had barely increased. Yet the demands on it from an ageing population, let alone other factors, were increasing by about 1 per cent a year. The result was that the resources available per head of population, weighted for age, had declined in each of those years (King's Fund Institute, 1988). The consequence of this fierce control on spending was that waiting lists grew and well-publicized consequences on services followed. Districts were running out of money well before the end of their financial year. A child was unable to gain access to intensive care for lack of staff and the case became a national story. The Prime Minister was put on the defensive regularly in the House of Commons, an unusual phenom-enon, and she reacted in characteristic style. She contacted a former member of her Number 10 staff, David Willetts, and asked him to under-take a secret review of the NHS (Timmins, 1995: 460). In January 1987 she went public on TV during a *Panorama* interview much to the surprise of Department of Health civil servants and ministers alike.

Instead of relaxing the spending constraints she called for the whole future of the NHS and its finance to be rethought from scratch. A com-mittee was given a year to come up with an answer. It was no ordinary committee but a 'ministerial group' that Mrs Thatcher herself was to chair. It seemed to her that 'the NHS had become a bottomless financial pit' (Thatcher, 1993: 608). Given the success of containing spending in the previous four years that was a revealing remark.

Change the basis of funding?

Two main approaches to funding the service, according to Mrs Thatcher (1993), dominated the early discussions. One was to move the NHS to a system of health insurance with a specific health insurance contribution alongside the social security contribution. The NHS would then have been self-financing and outside the public spending round. This would have been fine for the Health Service but not for the Treasury and would have produced more, not less, health expenditure. The other idea was to expand the contribution private finance could make and ways to boost private health insurance were explored. According to Willetts, who saw the Cabinet papers throughout, 'none of these ideas really got past first base' (Timmins, 1995: 460). The NHS had found an unexpected ally – Nigel Lawson the Chancellor. In his memoirs (Lawson, 1993: Ch. 49) he claims to have been convinced that the basic way the Health Service was financed was correct and that here was one area where the private market simply did not work. Indeed, the NHS was performing remarkably well compared with other countries. If you wanted to contain public expenditure on health, the Treasury argued, the NHS was the best system on offer.

Lawson, and as far as we can tell the Treasury, proved staunch defenders of the basic idea of the NHS not because it was popular but because it made economic sense. This is largely supported by Mrs Thatcher's account. She was clearly furious at the Treasury's line!

The purchaser–provider split

Ways of introducing private finance to solve the problems of the NHS largely dropped out of the discussions. How could the system be made to produce more for the same money? An early idea, later watered down, was to float off all the hospitals as independent or privatized units. In its watered-down version this became the proposal to give hospitals the right to trust status rather like the old voluntary hospitals. Here the Conservative Party was proposing to return to a pattern it had supported in 1945. A more original idea was to give the public the right to choose to belong to different local Health Maintenance Organizations, or funds, who would buy care for their patients.

As time went on this idea got narrowed down to making district health authorities the bodies that would buy care from the semi-independent hospitals. This would introduce a 'purchaser–provider split'. Hospitals would compete for the right to win contracts from the districts. If a hospital went on performing badly it would lose its contract. The district would get 'exit' power on behalf of its population. The principles, applied in the case of education and housing, were to be applied to the NHS too.

Mrs Thatcher was getting worried that the review was not being radical enough. Her own policy unit at Number 10 were critical of the way the discussions were going. They were unhappy that the idea of *patients* having choice had been lost. Hospitals would have to compete for districts' contracts but districts would not have to compete for patients' custom. They returned to an idea that had been canvassed before: making GPs the purchasers of hospital care for their patients. Patients would have choice of GP and therefore who would purchase on their behalf.

Later on in the proceedings John Moore, whom Thatcher thought was performing poorly, was replaced by Kenneth Clarke. He had been a junior minister in the department when this idea had been discussed before. It was revived and introduced almost as a late appendix to the main part of the reforms, as the GP fundholding scheme. (For an account of its origins and progress see Glennerster et al., 1994. For an account of the politics of reform see Butler, 1992, and Timmins, 1995: 453–72.)

The White Paper

At one point it seemed as if the discussions were getting nowhere but Mrs Thatcher insisted that the original timetable be kept. A White Paper would be published one year from the date the review was announced. The result was a paper that was typical of this period and very different from the Fowler reviews of the previous era. Bold radical changes were proposed in outline with little or no detail. The civil servants and the local managers would make up the rules and the details of the scheme as they went along. The White Paper, *Working for Patients* (Department of Health, 1989b), provoked the most furious public and professional reaction. The Labour Party portrayed it as proposing the privatization of the Health Service and the internal market as introducing commercial principles into health care. The British Medical Association, ironically in view of its opposition in 1946–8, threw its weight against the reforms and in favour of the NHS as it was. It financed a nationwide poster campaign to this end. Clarke, who liked a good fight, stuck to the government's guns as Bevan had done, and passed the legislation largely unchanged.

The government, however, shaken by the Opposition and the public support it was getting, did slow down the pace at which the reforms were implemented. It told its local managers to change as little as possible before the coming election and it increased spending on the service substantially. Emphasis in ministerial guidance moves from promoting competition to collaboration and maintaining 'a steady state'. As Butler (1994) points out,

In retrospect, however, it is clear that as Mrs Thatcher's grip on office began to weaken, so ministers and their officials began to distance themselves from the stance they had been taking . . . 'Buyers' become . . . 'purchasers' and then 'commissioners'. 'Sellers' become 'providers'. General practice 'budgets' become 'funds' . . . 'Marketing' becomes 'needs assessment'. (p. 22)

All this shows how far the public and the profession had absorbed the non-commercial ethic and philosophy of the founders of the service. Despite the service's failings any suggestion that it was to be 'privatized' touched a raw nerve. So, too, did the idea that some patients would get preferential treatment.

The National Health Service and Community Care Act 1990

The Health Service sections of this Act amounted to the biggest change in the structure and logic of the service since the 1946 Act.

- Hospitals and community services could opt out of direct control by their district health authorities. They would become autonomous trusts run by trustees who own the assets with a debt owed to the Treasury. They would manage the hospital directly. If it could not attract the custom to survive, in theory, it would contract or close. The trusts were to be directly accountable to the Secretary of State.
- District health authorities would cease to be responsible for managing trust hospitals and would assume the primary task of determining the health needs of their area. Having done so they would purchase or make contracts with hospitals and community services, inside or outside their area, to provide the services the district thought it could afford. The district would be financed by central government, via regions, on the basis of the population size, age structure and relative health status.
- General practitioners with more than 9,000, later 7,000, patients could choose to hold their own budgets to purchase non-emergency treatment from hospitals (and later community services too). These GPs would also be given a budget to meet the costs of the drugs they dispensed. If they saved on that they could use the savings to spend on hospital treatment or vice versa.

Outcome of the health reforms

In the event the outcomes were neither as terrible nor as positive as the protagonists had forecast. The government sharply increased its spending on the NHS in the years before and immediately after the reforms. Long waiting times were significantly reduced.

But, as we saw, the full rigours of competition were not enforced. One of the elements in the reforms that had most impact, in the narrow but important field to which it applied, was GP fundholding. It redressed the balance of power to some extent towards GPs, giving them some sanction over hospital consultants whom they felt were doing less than a good job. For an overview of the whole period and the outcomes see Le Grand and Vizard (1998). For an assessment of all the research done on the reforms see Le Grand et al. (1998).

To a large extent those in the NHS have continued to do what they always had done. Doctors and NHS managers were resistant to thinking in competitive terms. They were not encouraged to do so when it might mean hospital closure. So the changes did not produce as much improvement as its initiators had hoped. Yet, as the professions got used to the changes there was growing agreement with them.

Community Care

The community care reforms had little to do with community care as such and a lot to do with saving public expenditure, and provide an interesting counterpoint to the other reforms.

Under the old Supplementary Benefit rules it was possible, in very exceptional circumstances, for an old person to have his or her fees in a private old people's home paid out of the social security budget. An old person might run out of savings but it then might not be in his or her best interests to be moved to a local authority home. Such cases were very rare. In 1979 the total cost of such payments amounted to £10 million. In the early 1980s, as the Supplementary Benefit scheme was put into the form of explicit regulations, this facility became better known. The old person's fees could be paid by the local social security office at the going local price for homes.

Several things began to happen. People began to rid their elderly relatives of their assets and claim Supplementary Benefit to cover the costs of their being in the home. Local authorities, under pressure to cut spending, began to see that if they closed homes or privatized them the old people could still be looked after in residential care and the central government would have to pay for them through the social security scheme. Private home owners began to realize that if they increased fees locally in line with other homes the social security scheme would have to pay up. There could be no better example of the way individuals will change their behaviour in fairly ruthless ways to avail themselves of public money.

The paradox was that this was an almost perfect voucher scheme that had grown up by accident. Families could choose a home for their elderly relative and the state would pay. This maximized choice and consumer power. Unfortunately, it also maximized the growth of public expenditure on this group. It exposed the latent demand for the care of elderly people that local authorities and families could not manage. Faced with what seemed like an open cheque-book, many people used it. In the period between 1979 and 1991 the level of social security spending on residential care rose from £10 million to £2,072 million.

Not surprisingly the government was desperate to limit this spending. It also ran counter to declared public policy, which was that of enabling old people to stay in their own homes. A series of official reports struggled with solutions and analysis (Audit Commission, 1986; Griffiths Report, 1988; House of Commons, 1984/5). It was Roy Griffiths who probably finally convinced Mrs Thatcher that, to stop the outflow, powers to give public money for the care of the elderly should be taken from the social security system and given to local authorities. A way had to be found to sugar the pill for Mrs Thatcher, who was so opposed to giving local authorities any more money. The answer lay in insisting that local social services departments become largely purchasing agencies – 'enabling authorities'. The extra money they were to get would not necessarily or mainly be spent on local authority services. The government would insist that the great bulk be spent on the private sector. Since there was no real private sector except for the residential homes, much of the money was to find its way back to the same private homes, in the early stages of the reform. The reform of community care thus fitted into what was now emerging as the common pattern of social policy reforms in the Thatcher period – continued state funding but a variety of forms of private and public providers.

The community care element in the NHS and Community Care Act 1990

Legislation included the following main changes:

- From April 1993 the social security system would cease to provide support for new residents in private or voluntary homes.

- Local authorities had a duty to assess the needs of any person they believed required community care. They must provide services either themselves or by buying them from a private or voluntary agency.
- They must prepare a community care plan.
- They must set up an arm's-length agency to inspect premises in which care was being provided.

Outcomes of community care

As with the health reforms the government was anxious to smooth the changes, both by urging authorities not to act too radically too soon and by making a transitional special community care grant available, with tight rules on its spending. As with health the language from the centre has been softened from 'purchasing' to 'commissioning'. Just as in the case of the NHS reforms those working in the services have been very uncomfortable with the whole idea of introducing markets and competition and with local authorities becoming mere enabling authorities (Wistow et al., 1994; Lewis and Glennerster, 1996). But change it did. By the end of the 1990s half or more of all residential home places were in private homes, many funded from public funds. A much wider range of organizations were providing care in people's own homes than a decade before.

Another 'Fundamental' Review

Even before Mrs Thatcher was defeated in the leadership election of November 1990 the tight strings on public spending were being loosened a little to find money to ease the NHS and the poll tax reforms. John Major's election as leader and the run-up to the general election of 1992 produced a temporary increase in public spending. The share of the GDP going to social policy purposes rose from 22 per cent in 1990 to 26.7 per cent in 1993. This was higher than in 1979, when it was 23 per cent. So much for the reforms' capacity to get more out of less.

The Treasury was not amused. The scale of borrowing was getting out of hand. That autumn, Kenneth Clarke, the new Chancellor, in the newly combined spending and tax Budget, was going to have to raise taxes substantially. The time had come for another attempt to get public spending down. In February 1993 Michael Portillo announced a fundamental review of the long-term prospects for public spending and a no-holds-barred look at the spending of the social ministries of social security, health and education.

Here we were, again, back in the same exercise as R. A. Butler in the early 1950s, Thorneycroft in the late 1950s, Callaghan in the mid-1960s, Healey in the mid-1970s, Howe and Lawson in the early 1980s. Once again ministers looked at ways of cutting back the growing social security budget. Once again they drew back from fundamental change. They did agree to cut back on the growth of spending on the long-term unemployed and what was seen as the abuse of the system of disability benefits. The old contributory unemployment benefit, dating back to 1911, was abolished. It was replaced by the Job Seeker's Allowance in 1996. The contributory element would continue for six months but applicants were not merely required to be 'available for work' but also to enter into a contract to 'actively seek' work or enter appropriate training. The Blair government was to take this approach much further after 1997.

Taxation

Taxes and the poor

Through the 1980s the Conservative government had reduced the headline marginal rates of income tax. When they came to power the standard rate of income tax was 33 per cent. When they left office the main rate covering most people was 23 per cent with the first band of earnings taxed at 20 per cent. The standard rate of tax was, Clarke boasted, 'the lowest for sixty years' (HC 90, 1996/7). The overall burden of taxation was not very different, however. As we saw earlier, higher Value Added Tax and social security contributions together had filled the revenue gap. They had fallen disproportionately on poorer households.

In the run-up to the 1992 election, though public expenditure had been increased, taxes had not and this meant rapidly increasing levels of public borrowing to cover the shortfall. Two budgets in 1993, the first introduced by Norman Lamont and the second by Kenneth Clarke, very substantially increased the level of overall taxation. They set in train a programme of tax increases that would raise the percentage of the national income taken in taxes and social security contributions from 34 per cent in 1993 to 38 per cent by the end of the century. No wonder some Labour MPs privately called Clarke 'the best socialist Chancellor we have had'. However, Conservative voters were not amused. They were to severely punish the Conservative government for breaking their promise not to raise taxation made in the 1992 election. Once again many of these increases took the form of more indirect taxation. The most unpopular of these was the attempt to extend VAT to domestic fuel. Though it was defeated in 1994, the result was other increases in indirect taxation. Looking at the changes in tax and social security between 1985 and 1994 Giles and Johnson's (1994) analysis, however, suggested that,

> Worst hit were unemployed couples with children, followed by lone parent families, with over three-quarters of the former, and nearly two-thirds of the latter losing from the changes over the decade . . . Two earner couples gained much more frequently than single earner couples, reflecting higher total incomes and twice the opportunity to gain from direct tax cuts. (p. 14)

More precise figures show that 78 per cent of unemployed couples with children were worse off as a result of the tax changes of the period, on aver-age losing 2.7 per cent in net income. Earning couples with children more often lost than those without children. Of couples with children and only one earner 62 per cent lost, and of two-earner couples with children 42 per cent lost. Here was a family policy of a kind expressed through tax changes.

Taxation, women and the family

From the 1970s the new Equal Opportunities Commission began to bring pressure on government to think about the gendered nature of the tax system. A married woman was treated merely as a part of her husband's income and property for tax purposes. Incomes of both were aggregated and married men received an additional allowance for being married. This applied whether the wife was wholly dependent or not on the husband's income. The husband therefore received more *net* pay per pound earned than a woman, making a nonsense of the equal pay provisions. Critics asked, why should a husband receive extra money for supporting his wife (through paid work) instead of the wife receiving money for supporting her husband (through currently unpaid work)? The government did move to begin a public discussion on some of these issues in 1980 by publishing a Green Paper, *The Taxation of Husband and Wife*.

This floated a number of proposals. It suggested replacing the married man's allowance with a system that enabled a non-earning spouse to transfer her personal tax allowance to her husband. This would have encouraged more women to stay at home or at least increased the incomes of single-earner households.

It suggested the replacement of the lone parent allowance, which was equivalent to the married man's allowance, by a higher lone parent payment. The payment of benefits is generally seen as less desirable than giving tax allowances. The reason given is that benefits appear as public expenditure and allowances do not (i.e. a book-keeping strategy). So it was uncharacteristic to support higher benefits to lone parents. Land suggests (1983) that this would have given government more control over who got these payments. This proposal was not in fact taken up.

It took many years for these proposals to bear fruit but in 1989 two changes were introduced. The married man's allowance became the 'married couple's allowance'. Either partner could claim it. Also they could opt for separate assessment. This later became automatic. Husbands and wives are now treated as separate individuals for tax purposes.

The 1993 Budget began to reduce the importance of the married couples' allowance by only permitting it to be offset against the 20 per cent tax rate.

Majorism

What if, anything, did John Major's government contribute to social policy? (For a detailed assessment see Kavanagh and Seldon, 1994.) To a large extent it was concerned with implementing the reforms of the late Thatcher period. Major did seem genuinely to want to improve the standards of social provision like the NHS. His contribution was to insist, in 1991, that all public services produce a charter of rights and standards for consumers of those services. Few people seem to have heard of these or to use them for redress. As a means to an end, it was a step back to the world of performance indicators and indirect sanctions rather than the vigorous competitive market between public and private providers that was Mrs Thatcher's preferred model.

Yet, half-way through his period in office, and worried by the power of the right in his party over Europe, he appeared to give the right its head at the Conservative Party Conference in 1993. A revival of an old theme tune began: renewed stress on a return to traditional family values, complaints about the abuse of the social security system and public housing by single parents. If there was something new about this period, it was the flavour of these speeches and the policy initiatives that began to follow. Government had already become concerned with the consequences of broken marriages and the cost to the Exchequer.

The State and the Family

Conservatives under Mrs Thatcher were encouraged to be unashamed economic liberals. Yet they also remained defenders of the traditional family and favoured strong government action and incentives to sustain this institution. This was not as contradictory as it seemed. If the state was to withdraw from its major role the family had to take on more responsibilities. Yet, if the 1970s and 1980s were any guide, the family seemed less and less capable of fulfilling that role. Commonly, debates on the issue of government intervention in the family tend to polarize between the argument that state intervention *supports* the family by lightening its burden, and the argument that state intervention *weakens* the family by stripping it of some of its functions. Post-war policies upheld the general notion of the privacy of the family, but provided greater welfare services both for individuals, and more directly, for families (free school meals, preventive family casework, family allowances, etc.) in order to help families survive greater pressures.

The post-1979 Conservative government took the opposite tack. The New Right attack on a 'dependency culture' is fought on economic and moral grounds. Moral decline is seen as the cause of economic decline. The argument is that the Welfare State has displaced the role of the family as the main provider of welfare; children no longer look after their elderly parents, parents cannot control their children, fathers abandon their families; without a role model of a nuclear family teenage boys become 'yobs' and teenage girls become unmarried mothers; when the state, and not the family, becomes the first port of call in times of trouble the result is increased public expenditure and a growing tax burden which is a disincentive to industry. Increased expenditure is directly affected by 'the breakdown of the family' because of increasing numbers on benefits, and indirectly is the result of the perceived link between lone parenthood and crime. Single parenthood was damaging, moreover, and should be discouraged anyway (Dennis and Erdos, 1994). American influence on Conservative thought here became particularly important, though the policy regimes and incentives were very different (Murray, 1984). These arguments were contested by other social scientists (Burghes, 1994).

Family relationships cannot be managed by government, but the hope was that a withdrawal of state support would push families to look after their own. There were several examples of this, some dating from the Thatcher administration and accelerated under Major. From 1980 local authorities were no longer required to provide school meals. In 1988, Income Support was made unavailable for 16- to 18-year-olds at the same time as child benefit was no longer available for those of them who were no longer in full-time education. In 1986 benefits were reduced for 18- to 25-year-olds. In 1996, when the Job Seeker's Allowance replaced Unemployment Benefit, 18- to 25-year-olds faced a 20 per cent drop in benefit. The Child Support Act reasserted parental responsibility. The introduction of student loans, and the withdrawal of benefits from students, increased their dependence on their families. The Criminal Justice Act introduced the idea of parental responsibility for a child's crimes. A parent can be required to pay a 'bind over', which is forfeited if the child commits another offence.

While all these measures were designed to put more responsibility on the family, the government was forced to respond to pressures from the EU and the labour market which were demanding more female labour market participation. In order to achieve this, concessions were made to working mothers. In 1990, employers could offset the costs of providing workplace child-care against tax. In 1993, in response to an EC Directive (though not implemented until October 1994, the latest possible date), maternity provision was made as soon as a woman started work, and was extended for part-time workers. Although these measures were funded by government, it could be said that the government was more concerned with helping women to enter and to stay in the labour market, than with improving conditions within it. This is apparent in the light of the abolition of Wages Councils in 1993, which was presented as necessary in order to maintain the number of jobs. This attitude was also clear in 1994 when Michael Portillo, Employment Secretary, resisted the European changes regarding parental and paternity leave. Any such arrangements, he said, should be made privately between employer and employee; government legislation would be inappropriate and would restrict competition. This policy was to be reversed by the Blair government after 1997.

Lone Mothers

The problem of the single mother exploded into one of the nastiest of social family policy issues in the 1990s. It also went to the roots of one of the apparent contradictions in modern Conservative thought.

There were well over a million lone parents, making up 14 per cent of all families with dependent children. Sixty-six per cent of these were dependent on Income Support. This figure had increased from 330,000 in 1980 to 770,000 in 1989. Sixty per cent were divorced, 33 per cent never married and 7 per cent widowed.

At the end of the 1980s a degree of agreement had emerged between those acting as advocates of single parents and government that something should be done to ensure that natural fathers be required to support their children. For the government this would have two advantages. First, it would reduce the burden on the Exchequer. Second, it would bring home to a man who left his wife the financial consequences of his actions and hence act as a deterrent. For the single parent left behind it would mean that the state was taking on the responsibility of getting maintenance out of the father. As the 1990s unfolded the government's attitudes hardened.

> They [lone parents] were no longer seen as victims with special needs for financial support and, in the case of young unmarried mothers, for case work, but rather as irresponsible and probably, again in the case of unmarried mothers, manipulative people willing for example to have a baby in order to jump the queue for social housing. (Lewis, 1994)

Privatizing maintenance

Not only were there more lone mothers but, through the 1980s, fewer were employed. More became dependent on social security. The number in receipt of Income Support grew from 320,000 in 1979 to a million in 1991 (DSS, 1993b).

The government began to underline the father's responsibility for maintenance. First, it imposed limits on the process of 'diversion' which had guaranteed the value of maintenance payments to women on Income Support. This was only made available to women whose husbands had defaulted in the last six months or who had suffered violence. Under the liable relative formula, where the DSS administered the maintenance, the father had to pay something towards the parent with care. These measures were taken further in the Child Support Act 1991. This extended the boundary of the state significantly.

Child Support Act 1991

Under the Act all lone mothers on either Income Support, Family Credit or Disabled Worker's Allowance must authorize the Secretary of State to take action to recover maintenance from an absent father. The body set up to administer the system was the Child Support Agency. It took over from the courts all aspects of the assessment, collection and enforcement of child maintenance for children whose parents live apart. Public law has effectively replaced private law in this area. The Agency and the policy proved to be a disastrous failure. The original principles behind the legislation had attracted widespread support. Fathers should support their children and lone mothers receive adequate income. Taxpayers should not support sexual indiscretion. Different sections of the population supported different parts of that argument but taken together these principles attracted broad support. However, ministers and civil servants, notably in Her Majesty's Treasury, then proceeded to make a series of strategic blunders from which the Agency never recovered (Brook-Lapping Productions, 1999, *Can't Pay: Won't Pay*, Channel Four Documentary). The model from which ministers began was American. That in itself is an interesting commentary on social policy in this era. In Wisconsin the Liberal reformers had seen their prime objective as securing an income for lone parents, albeit at minimum cost to the public purse. To gain mothers' co-operation in seeking out the father they recognized that she had to be financially better off as a result. The Department of Social Security, with its long experience of administering benefits to lone parents, recognized this too. They argued that a significant portion of money extracted from the father be disregarded in setting benefit levels. The Treasury wanted it all clawed back in reduced benefits. Mrs Thatcher was called upon to adjudicate and found in the Treasury's favour.

The Treasury also insisted that the Agency pursue fathers who had already settled their financial responsibilities in the courts. They would become liable to make payments at the level the Agency set. It was this that provoked the outrage of men who thought of themselves as responsible law-abiding citizens. The state was breaking private contracts and doing so retrospectively. A powerful press campaign, non-cooperation and worse began. Women saw no point in cooperating and many men actively obstructed the Agency.

Matters were made worse by an over-elaborate attempt to be fair to those now responsible for a second family. Hugely complicated regulations covered their required payments, taking account of family responsibilities and income. These brought the Agency to its knees and meant that women did not get their money, at least without huge delays. Those in most need were put off while the Agency tried to raise money from easy cases.

The Agency, which began work in 1992, became the most vilified public body in the land. In January 1995 Peter Lilley, the Secretary of State, was forced to announce changes and new legislation – the Child Support Act 1995. It allowed the Agency to take account of previous clean-break settlements between couples. That mollified few. The next government would have to try again.

Family Law Act 1996

In November 1995 the Queen's speech included a promise to radically reform the divorce law. The 1969 Family Law Reform Act (see p. 160) had introduced the notion of 'no fault divorce' but had maintained the proofs of breakdown based on fault, and these had proved the most commonly used since the use of such facts, adultery, for example, or desertion, speeded up the divorce process. The Act was designed to 'save saveable marriages' and to reduce acrimony between divorcing couples by encouraging them towards mediation rather than litigation. This would reduce the distress to couples and their children and improve post-divorce relationships, it was hoped.

Under the Act a divorce could not be granted until the post-divorce arrangements had been approved. Paramount consideration was the welfare of the children. It encouraged privately agreed post-divorce arrangements. It also made some provisions for victims of domestic violence. The central part of the Act was not to be implemented until 2000. As we shall see in the next chapter that was not to be. Yet the Act and the discussions on it go to the heart of the dilemmas that face modern governments legislating for an institution that has changed, is changing fast and about which there is no clear value consensus.

The modern 'family' began to attract renewed interest from sociologists and demographers in the 1990s (Giddens, 1992, 1998; Beck and Beck-Gernsheim, 1995; Morgan, 1995; Smart, 1997; Smart and Neale, 1997; Kiernan et al., 1998). Two broad schools emerged. One was a continuation of the doom and gloom of the 1980s. The traditional family was collapsing and the state was largely responsible. The other newer and more positive strand argued that people were increasingly not adopting predetermined roles but were working out their own interpretations of 'family' life. They were 'doing families' in a variety of ways. This was no bad thing. Past family practices had been inherently unequal (Giddens, 1998). Women's greater participation in the labour market and the growth of women's education and cultural capital was making such inequality untenable. The 'traditional family' idealized in the 1950s was no more than a transitional phase. Beck and Beck-Gernsheim (1995) saw new family structures as a natural response to changing social forces and to personal growth. To quote Giddens (1998):

> There is a widespread yearning for the family to provide stability in a changing world, but realistically it is as likely to reflect other qualities of this world as to compensate for them. (p. 94)

The law had to accommodate these changes. It could do little to prevent them. As Jane Lewis (1998) put it:

> The importance attached to morality from within and the relational aspects of marriage effectively subordinated the traditional emphasis on the duties of marriage to the quality of the relationship, which came to mean achievement of personal satisfaction. It was this profound shift in the conceptualization of marriage, as much as a change in the law that accompanied it, that helped to promote the change in the marriage system in the late-twentieth century. (p. 96)

The 1996 Act reflected some of this modern view of marriage. The workings of intimate relationships were not susceptible to judicial arbitration. If, after a period of reflection one partner concluded that the marriage had irretrievably broken down, that was proof enough. Mediation was to be encouraged instead of arm's-length negotiation between lawyers. Post-divorce relations need not be translated into court orders. Responsibilities to children must be secured and old accounts between the parties, about property, for example, had to be sorted out. The law should help people move on with minimum cost to the children or the couple.

The Act had been proceeded by a thoughtful review of the law by the Law Commission (Law Commission, 1988) and a Green Paper by the Lord Chancellor's Department (Cm. 2424, 1993) as well as the White Paper (Cm. 2799, 1995).

> It has to be accepted that, although the law can lay down the formalities for marriage, it cannot prescribe the expectations with which individuals enter marriage and so it cannot enforce them. (Cm. 2424, para. 3.3–4)

The Conservative Lord Chancellor put it with compelling force in the debate in the House of Lords.

How can it be said that a requirement to make allegations of fault provides the law with an underlying moral base when in fact to commit a wrong – such as adultery – actually means you can be divorced in less than six months? (HoL *Debates*, vol. 567, col. 701)

Modern, perhaps, but too modern for many Conservatives.

to make of marriage a licence to cohabit, terminable at one year's notice by husband or wife, is likely to destroy the significance of marriage. (Lord Coleraine, HoL *Debates*, vol. 567, col. 733)

Many backbench Conservatives opposed the bill and it caused one of the biggest revolts of the period. John Patten MP asked:

Were the proposals in our 1992 Manifesto? No. Have there been big demands at Tory Party Conference for instant action? No. So where does the law come from? It comes from some lawyers and the Law Commission in particular. (*Daily Telegraph*, 19 September 1995, p. 12)

As a result of this revolt the Labour Opposition was able to get concessions on greater protection for victims of domestic violence. The government needed votes; backbenchers had forced the government to abandon a bill on domestic violence (Dobash and Dobash, 2000).

In its passage through Parliament the reconciliation features of the bill were strengthened and implementation was put off for four years while experiments with mediation were carried out. A study of the problems mediation had caused in American courts might have given Parliament more pause (Mason, 1999). Many of the official documents published prior to the bill talked about it as a kind of therapy. It would allow couples 'to address together what had gone wrong with their marriage' (Cm. 2799, 1995: 2.17). Mediators pointed out that they could not do the job of lawyers nor were they therapists. Lawyers were happy to leave discussions about children to mediators but where property and money were involved the legal process was a better safeguard of individual rights, especially for women (Roberts, 1993; Walker, 1996; Davies et al., 1994; Mason, 1999).

Children

There was one other piece of social legislation that had cross-party support as well as opponents in this period – that on children. The Children Act

1989 marked a watershed in legislation on children and the state's treatment of intra-family relationships.

In the 1980s there had been parliamentary and Law Commission reports on children's issues following three deaths of children as a result of abuse and the Cleveland affair (Butler-Sloss, 1988). Here social workers had been criticized for interference while other reports called for more state intervention to prevent abuse.

Families, rather than the wider society, were usually treated as the objects of blame in these discussions. The Act tries to balance two sets of contradictory pressures: greater child protection with greater parental rights, and greater state power to intervene in family autonomy. As the 'Introduction to the Children Act' notes,

> The Act seeks to protect children both from the harm which can arise from failures or abuse within the family and from the harm that can be caused by unwarranted intervention in their family life. There is a tension between those objectives which the Act seeks to regulate so as to optimise the overall protection provided for children in general. (para. 1.31)

The Act marks a shift of emphasis from parental rights to parental responsibilities. Never-married mothers and married parents of a child automatically have parental responsibility. Others, non-married fathers or those who have been looking after a child as if it were a child of the family (grandparents, say) can *apply* for parental responsibility. The welfare of the child is 'paramount' in all court proceedings. Where parents are living apart neither party has sole power and authority. There are instead residence orders, contact orders, specific issue orders and prohibited steps orders to settle disputed claims.

Through various provisions of the Act it stresses that wherever possible children should remain with their families, provided this is consistent with their welfare. Where a local authority does have to care for a child,

> This should preferably be under voluntary arrangements with the parents who will retain their responsibility, acting so far as possible as partners of the local authority and the substitute carers. (para. 1.9)

There can be no better illustration of the dilemmas that face modern social policy legislators. They would like to leave individuals and families to cope without interference and taxpayer responsibility. Yet modern life is becoming more complex and families more vulnerable. Society, or rather voters, are not prepared to let government simply walk away. Unwilling as they may be, governments will continue to be deeply involved in families.

The End of an Era

Dogged by sexual and financial scandals, bitterly divided on its attitudes to Europe, with its will to govern draining away by the day, the Major government stumbled to the end of its term. Yet, the eighteen years of Conservative rule had changed the political landscape in ways that the previous continuous Conservative administrations of the 1950s and 1960s had not. Social policy would never be the same again. The centre of gravity had shifted.

Questions to Answer

1 What common threads run through some or all of the legislation of this period? How much of a break with the past was it? How far has it laid the foundations of current approaches?
2 What did the Conservatives do to support the traditional family? Discuss what happened to social policy as it affected women in this period.
3 Why was the poll tax ever passed? What does it tell us about British government and the checks and balances of the legislative process?

10

Sixty Years On

A New Start?

In May 1997 Tony Blair was elected Prime Minister with a majority that outstripped even that of 1945. He was the youngest person to hold that office since 1812 and subsequently won two more general elections. Inevitably this electoral achievement and the size of his majorities invite comparison with the Attlee period with which we began. There were to be no fundamental changes of the kind that both Attlee and Thatcher achieved, beyond the devolution of social policy powers to Scotland and Wales. But it was to be a decisive period for social policy. Here I differ from those who see Blair's term as a mere extension of the Thatcher era or part of a 'new consensus' (Lowe, 2005: 433). It was a decisive period, in my view, precisely because it marked both a break with some of the founding principles of the Thatcher years and a break with previous Labour orthodoxies. Gone was the presumption that there is 'no such thing as society' or that the scale of state activity had to be progressively reduced. These were essentially Mrs Thatcher's starting points and the Blair years reversed them.

But gone, too, was the 'Old Labour' presumption that large-scale state monopolies were the best way to deliver social services. Here Blair gradually came to accept that state welfare monopolies had to be challenged if they were to improve their quality and maintain their electoral appeal. Work became a central feature of social policy. Unlike the Attlee period this was not just seen as a matter of economic management, but of designing benefit policy to create incentives to work. Work was the inclusive cement of society. It brought dignity and self-respect. Moreover, voters would only support benefit generosity if they thought welfare recipients were being required to work if they could. More fundamentally still, lax benefit administration was reducing the chances of achieving full employment and low inflation. Labour MPs from Attlee's time would have been hard put to recognize many of these principles. Particular legislation, as we shall see, provoked unprecedented backbench rebellions.

More traditionally Old Labour was the big spender on health, education and the personal social services. There was a building boom in schools and hospitals not seen since the 1960s. Most money went on higher pay for those who had seen their relative earnings fall through the Thatcher years like teachers, nurses and doctors. Yet, despite this largess, many of those in these services became restive, frustrated and angry. The government repeatedly changed its mind. White Papers, Acts and 'organizational churning' came thick and fast. In the end, we shall argue, many of the changes were necessary but came late on and were poorly implemented. Whatever this was it was not Thatcherism, nor consensus, nor Old Labour. Social policy had entered a new phase. (For a balanced but critical account of Blair's term in office see Seldon and Kavanagh, 2005. For evaluations of the New Labour government's social policies see Powell, 2002; Lowe, 2005; Hills and Stewart, 2005.)

Institutional Change and its Sources

Modern political scientists of the 'institutional school' have emphasized the relative stability of institutions like those of the Welfare State. They cater for so many people at crucial times in their lives that political support for them is high. Only particular conjunctions of events and the skilful use of incremental strategies can make change possible (Pierson, 1994; 1996). Existing institutions are supported by powerful interests, like the professions who work in them and the set of ideas civil servants and experts carry around with them. All these forces interact and make countries dependent on the institutional path they have originally set for themselves.

It is true that Britain's 'Welfare State' is still recognizably that of 1945–8 in many ways. But, as we have argued in earlier chapters, something began to change in British politics after the economic crisis of 1976. Sexual attitudes, what constituted a family, marriage and 'partnership', women's working lives, all changed. Major social as well as economic changes were under way providing fertile ground for change (Heclo, 1974; Hall and Taylor, 1996; Beland, 2005). Hall (1993) distinguishes change at the highest level, in the ideas or purposes of policy, in the mechanisms by which policy is delivered and change in detail, like benefit levels. The Blair/Brown government undertook changes at all three levels. In family policy there were changes in purpose. In health and education and social care there were big changes in accepted ways of achieving old purposes. There were major changes in benefit policy too. The reasons, I suggest, lie in the scale of social and economic change the society had experienced and was passing through, and they were not confined to the UK (Taylor-Gooby, 2004). Hence, in what follows, I try to link policy changes over the long haul with the structural changes to which they were in some way a response.

A Dual Premiership?

Before doing so it is worth reflecting briefly on the constitutional oddity of this period. Prime Ministers have always, given the right conditions, had particular powers to drive the policy agenda if they wished to do so. But this tendency has grown, notably since Mrs Thatcher set the pattern. Post-1997 policy was also driven from the top. But there were twin peaks.

This was a period of near 'dual premiership'. Blair left not only economic policy, but parts of social policy too, to Gordon Brown at the outset. Some have suggested that Blair tacitly handed 'overlordship' of social policy to Brown. (Kavanagh, 2005 discusses this notion but does not entirely support it.) The truth is more nuanced and changed over time. The Treasury led on social security and employment policy from the outset, but Blair intervened in detailed ways, through a large Number 10 staff, on health, education, long-term care, Home Office affairs and much else. Much good policy was hammered out in combination between these two centres of authority – the upper and lower millstones grinding away some rough edges. But departments and ministers were told what new policy initiative to embark on, and when, by this dual centre. That would have been unthinkable in the Attlee period.

Changed Economic Circumstances

The country's economic record since 1945 had been disappointing. In the 1940s the UK had had the highest income per head in Europe. By the 1990s it had one of the lowest. Only countries like Spain and Portugal were below it and were catching up fast. Even that one-time poor relation, Ireland, had overtaken the UK. It was this state of affairs that prepared people to accept Mrs Thatcher's attack on traditional institutions, the brutal medicine she prescribed for the less efficient parts of British industry, the weakening of trade union power and the subsequent rapid growth of private services. The humiliating exit from the European Exchange Rate Mechanism reduced the value of the pound and made British goods cheaper abroad. A clearer monetary policy strategy then evolved in which the Treasury and the Bank of England targeted a low rate of inflation as the key goal of monetary policy. This change was to prove of fundamental importance. Every Labour government since the Second World War had begun its period in office with high social policy ambitions. Each had had to scale these back in the face of economic crises (Tomlinson, 2004). This Labour administration reversed that pattern. It began with modest social ambitions and scaled them up as the economy proved more successful than most expected.

In 1997 Brown's first and most important act was to give the Bank of England charge of monetary policy with the power to set the bank rate and hence guide other interest rates. The detailed task was actually undertaken by the Bank's Monetary Policy Committee, composed of leading economists chosen by the Chancellor. Instead of monetary policy being set with an eye to winning elections in a destabilizing way, the Bank charted an extremely successful non-political path. During his first two years as Chancellor Brown himself began very cautiously with spending plans that kept to limits the Conservatives had set. Inflation, world-wide, subsided. In addition, as we shall see, the Chancellor restructured the UK's social benefits and tax system to encourage people into work. This mix of policies, building on the more flexible labour market he inherited, proved very successful. In the 1980s and early 1990s the UK economy had run into accelerating inflation and other problems as soon as unemployment fell below 10 per cent. Then measures to slow the economy had to be introduced. By the new century this figure had fallen to 5 per cent or so (Nickell and Quintini, 2002).

So, through a combination of policy inheritance from the Thatcher era, some cautious economic judgement and some good luck, the Labour government from 1997 to 2006 experienced good economic fortune. It saw national income grow without interruption at a faster *sustained* rate than it had done since 1945. By 2005 citizens in the UK were enjoying an income per head *higher* than most other countries in Europe – excluding the Scandinavians and the Irish.

There was room to expand public spending again. Brown did this in a series of Comprehensive Spending Reviews undertaken every two years. The last, due in 2006, was deferred until 2007 and will set spending targets up to 2012 and beyond. The pace of growth in public spending will fall back to just below that of the whole economy. Were a Conservative government to follow, the pace of expansion would probably be slower still. So the early years of the twenty-first century were good for social policy. In the period we are studying here public spending on social policy grew at a rate not experienced since the 1960s, especially in the case of health, social care and education (see Figure 10.1).

This spending had to be paid for, of course. In 2006/7 UK taxpayers will be paying 3 per cent more of their (larger) incomes in taxes of all kinds than they had been in 1996/7 – 38 per cent compared to 35 per cent. Social surveys suggested that voters were content with this small rise but they had little stomach for further big increases (Taylor-Gooby and Hastie, 2002). On the other hand the most recent research on views about tax suggests people are very supportive of tax and spending policies that are quite strongly redistributive – a point to which we shall return (Sefton, 2005).

Figure 10.1 Welfare spending,[1] 1900 to 2004

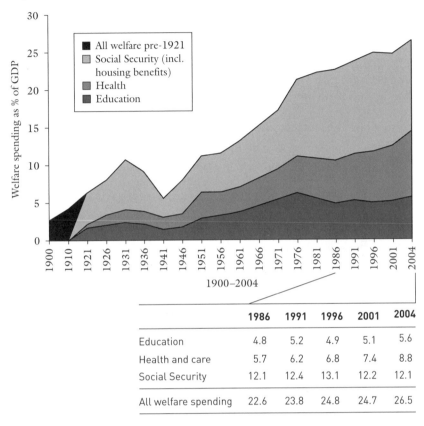

	1986	1991	1996	2001	2004
Education	4.8	5.2	4.9	5.1	5.6
Health and care	5.7	6.2	6.8	7.4	8.8
Social Security	12.1	12.4	13.1	12.2	12.1
All welfare spending	22.6	23.8	24.8	24.7	26.5

[1] This includes the old Poor Law, modern Social Security, Housing Benefit and its predecessors. From 1987 some small items are included from agencies like the criminal justice system. They formed 0.5% of GDP in 1987. Social care spending has been removed from the official figures on social protection and added to health care for consistency with previous figures. Housing capital is excluded.

Sources: Glennerster, 2000; HM Treasury, 2005

Devolution

The devolution of government to Scotland, Wales and Northern Ireland was a change of major constitutional importance. It had important implications for social policy. Years of growth in Scottish Nationalist representation and Scotland's detestation of rule by Thatcher's Westminster led to a sea change in moderate opinion both in Scotland and in England. Some kind of devolved power to a Scottish Parliament might well be the only way to save the Union.

Blair inherited promises to create a Scottish Parliament and devolve powers to a Welsh Assembly from the time of the previous Labour leader, John Smith – a Scot. In Northern Ireland the Good Friday Agreement promised a return to devolved government as long as there was power sharing with the nationalist parties. There were referenda in all three cases. The Scottish Parliament and the Welsh Assembly, with less power, began life in June 2001. In Northern Ireland the Assembly came and went as Unionists refused to cooperate until the IRA satisfied them that the armed struggle was over and weapons were destroyed.

The days of 'British Social Policy' seem numbered. Education, health, social care and housing policy became the responsibility of the devolved legislatures. They used their powers to forge a very different set of priorities, defying Blair's agenda, as we shall see. (For an account of devolution, subsequent policy divergence and the unfinished agenda for independent funding see McLean, 2005; McLean and McMillan, 2005.)

Changing Families

One of the most important and far-reaching changes in British society since 1945 has been in the traditional family and in women's role more generally. We saw in Chapter 2 that Beveridge's social insurance plan was grounded in a highly traditional view of the family and that the UK continued for some time to conform to a 'male breadwinner model' of social provision (Lewis, 1992b; 2002). In the 1940s the Labour government closed down the extensive network of day nurseries that had been created to enable women to work in munitions factories and other wartime employment. They were seen by trade unionists as a threat to men's employment. As Lewis argues:

> The male breadwinner model family worked in practice for most families for only a very short period in the years following the Second World War. But as a set of normative prescriptions, accepted in large measure by people as well as policy makers the model proved powerful and long lasting in some Western European countries. (2005: 61)

The UK moved to something nearer a one and a half earner model. By 2005 more than half of women whose youngest child was under 3 were in some kind of paid employment and this rose to three-quarters of those whose youngest child was over 8. Many were in less than full-time work but the need for more child care and longer school hours, for example, had been evident since the 1960s. Such shifts took place in the Scandinavian countries and the Netherlands between the 1970s and 1990s, but not in the UK.

Marriage and partnering had been altering, too, as we have seen in past chapters. In the first sixty years of the twentieth century few births occurred outside marriage. By the 2001 Census, 40 per cent of all live births were registered outside a legal marriage – many to cohabiting couples. Three-quarters were registered by two parents and three-quarters of those were at the same address. But many women were bringing up children on their own. One in five of those children born in the early 1970s were living with their mother alone by the age of 16 (Kiernan, 1998). Marriage, partnership and parenthood had changed profoundly. Yet, for many years the presumption of a male breadwinner couple with children was embedded in our legal structure and policy framework. This explains why politicians found it difficult to accept, let alone promote, change (Lewis, 2000).

Early in its term the new government produced a consultation paper called *Supporting Families*. Families were inclusively defined – cohabiting, single, separated – something of a departure in itself. While accepting the scale of the changes that had happened, the paper made it clear that in the government's view 'marriage is still the surest foundation for raising children' (Home Office, 1998: 4). The government was straddled, like the electorate, between old and new notions of the family. (See Maclean, 2002 for a discussion.) It took the view that promoting good parenting and easing the trauma of divorce for children should be its most important role. There should be more advice prior to marriage and mediation when things began to go wrong. A National Family and Parenting Institute was created to give advice to parents <http://www.nfpi.org.uk>. All this was highly tentative but it was the first ever government paper on 'the family' and, as such, testament to the fact that 'family policy' was now, for good or ill, in the realm of politics. (For helpful discussions of issues being faced by many other societies see Katz et al., 2000; Carling et al., 2002; MacLean, 2005).

Perhaps public policy was itself to blame for the growth of single parenthood as many claimed in the US. British Income Support had always dealt with single mothers relatively unstigmatically, not least because Income Support was nationally administered and widely used by the respected and 'blameless' poor unlike US 'welfare'. Work requirements had never been imposed. From the 1940s on it was thought mothers were better off bringing up their children at home whether single or married. As a result:

> modern welfare policies have permitted the transformation of traditional family forms and the formation of autonomous households by lone mothers while at the same time attempting to enforce assumptions about men's obligation to maintain – a Janus-faced [policy]. (Lewis, 2000: 82)

Welfare Reform

In the US President Clinton had used 'welfare reform' to distinguish his brand of New Democrats from the spendthrift 'Old Democrats' and it had been successful. Blair and Brown, much influenced by American ideas, took this as a model (Deacon, 2002). It was not just a political gimmick. Both men had become convinced that the benefits system had tipped too far towards emphasizing rights not responsibilities. It gave too few incentives to return to work. If the public merely associated 'welfare' with layabouts, more generous benefits would be difficult to sell. Blair turned to someone who had expressed such views in print (Field, 1995; 1996). Frank Field, sometime secretary of the Child Poverty Action Group, was a maverick thinker, critical of the Titmuss tradition of social policy, which he claimed ignored the impact of incentives on ordinary people's actions.

He was first given charge of thinking about policy while Labour was in opposition and then given the job of Minister for Welfare Reform. That title was not what it seemed. He was a junior minister in the Department of Social Security housed in a small office with barely any staff. It became clear that the real minister for welfare reform was the Chancellor himself. The Treasury became the driving force for that part of social policy which interacted with the labour market.

Field believed passionately that incentives to cheat and not to work, not to save for retirement, lay in the excessive means testing that had grown up under the past government. The Treasury believed, as they always had done, that targeting was necessary to limit the impact on the public purse. Added to that was Brown's belief that if redistribution and poverty alleviation was the goal means testing was essential. This fundamental divide delayed action and muddled it.

A poor start

The government's first attempt at welfare reform was to prove a disaster. Just before the election the Conservatives had frozen the lone parent premium that was added to a range of benefits if you were a lone parent. It had been introduced in the 1980s on the grounds that such parents faced higher costs. The other view was that this rewarded single parenthood (Morgan, 1995). Ministers agreed. Reversing the cut the Conservatives had proposed would send the wrong message. Extra help should go to all poor families not just lone mothers.

But lone mothers were not the black welfare mums of US demonology. Backbench Labour MPs were appalled that their government had singled out some of the poorest families for benefit reductions as the first social policy act of government. The result was one of the biggest backbench revolts since the IMF debates in the 1970s. As later attempts to encourage lone mothers into work were to show, British women, like their Dutch counterparts, were not keen to enter the labour market full-time while their children were young, whether they were single or married. Nor were politicians prepared to make them.

The blueprint for welfare reform was delayed and delayed. In the end the document that emerged contained measures announced already by Brown and a lot of high-minded waffle. It is remembered today only for the phrase that encapsulated New Labour philosophy and was contained not in the main document but in Tony Blair's preface:

> Work for those who can: security for those who cannot. (Cm. 3805, 1998: iii)

The two ministers directly involved, Harriet Harman and Frank Field, lost their jobs. It was not an encouraging start. Yet, in the end, the row may have had a salutary effect. If we trace the sequence of benefit increases that followed, notably the big rise in Income Support levels for children, we find that lone parents were relative gainers. A lone parent on half average earnings saw their net real income rise by nearly a quarter between 1997 and 2003. A couple with two children on average earnings saw only a 13 per cent rise (Stewart, 2005: 147).

Work for those who can

> The new welfare state should help and encourage people of working age to work where they are capable of doing so. (Cm. 3805, 1998: 23)

Brown had been convinced by the argument encapsulated in the Social
Justice Commission Report (1994: Ch. 5) that work for all, including
women, was central to achieving social justice. Benefits could never bring
the self-respect and independence that went with income from work.
Benefits paid by taxpayers would always be niggardly and carry stigma.
Work was the route to social inclusion. But work had to be adapted to
the needs of the new family. In many ways that chapter in the Social Justice
Commission Report provides a coherent thread for many of the New
Labour policies that followed.

The Chancellor's and the Treasury views also owed much to the economic evidence presented by LSE's Professor Richard Layard and others
that the UK's unusually high level of long-term unemployment was the
result of lax administration of benefit policy (Layard, 1997a, b). People
could remain out of the labour market, making no real effort to return
and with little encouragement to do so. Once out of work for more than
six months they were unlikely to return. Active measures to reintegrate
them, of the kind that the Scandinavians used, were lacking. The previous government had begun to tighten the rules and replace the old
unemployment benefit by a Job Seeker's Allowance which required more
active job search but that was not enough. What emerged, despite the
initial debacle over single parents, was a restructured benefit administration
designed to encourage return to work for particular target groups who
might be tempted to remain idle – young people, those out of work for
a long period, those over 55 who might find work difficult to come by,
the disabled and single parents. It was a process still developing in 2006.

The strategy combined sticks of a kind that Mrs Thatcher might have
approved of, weak though they were, with carrots, of which she would
not. Benefit administration and job advice were combined in new Job
Seeker Plus offices. It was a strategy that was distinctively New Labour
and it is one that is likely to remain a permanent feature of social policy.
It is to be found across European welfare states. New Labour copied many
aspects from our Scandinavian and Dutch neighbours as well as Australia
and New Zealand, rather less from the US (Lodemel and Trickey, 2000;
Banks et al., 2005).

Sticks and advice

Those aged between 18 and 24 were the first targets of experimental
programmes introduced in July 1997 and January 1998. The national
programme began in April 1998. Those who had been receiving the Job

Seeker's Allowance for six months without getting a job were required to attend an interview and be assigned to a personal adviser to assist them in getting a job. This person would give advice on suitability for particular jobs, help with job applications, preparation for interviews. For others it would mean improving skills, workplace trials. This phase – the Gateway – would last up to four months. If no job was forthcoming there would be four options:

- A job offer with a designated employer who would receive a subsidy for six months plus an additional training subsidy. The subsidy amounted to 40 to 60 per cent of the typical wage so it was relatively generous with the training subsidy on top. The employer had to promise to continue the employment so long as the person was performing satisfactorily and to pay at least the minimum wage (see below).
- Full-time education or training for up to twelve months with no loss of benefit.
- A job for six months with a voluntary sector employer paid a subsidy.
- A job on the Environmental Task Force cleaning up open spaces or other similar tasks.

The education option proved the most popular (nearly two-fifths) with the other options evenly divided.

Some elements of this approach were then gradually extended to other groups:

- Those over 25 out of work for two years, which later became eighteen months.
- Those over 50.
- Disabled persons.
- Those with repeated periods off work.
- Lone parents.

Given backbench and popular reaction to ideas floated about curtailing benefits to single parents the government approached reform very gingerly. New Labour strategy was to tackle the issue from both ends – to raise in-work benefits and rely on advice and encouragement. US, Canadian and European experience suggested that a combination of advice and financial incentives worked better than penalties alone. Begun with pilots in 1997 the national programme, called New Deal for Lone Parents, developed from the next year in gradual steps.

- In April 1998 all new applicants with children over 5 years 3 months were invited to participate in an advice session about returning to work.
- From October 1998 this applied to all existing claimants with children of that age.
- From May 2000 this included those with the youngest child aged 3 or more.
- In 2001 work-focused interviews were required for those where the youngest child was aged 13 to 15 as they were for new claimants with young children.
- In 2002 interviews were required for those with children aged 9 to 12.
- In 2006 it was proposed that these mandatory interviews be held every three months for those who had been claiming Income Support for at least a year and whose children were at least 11. (Cm. 6730, 2005)

Thus, by 2006 entitlement to benefit for those making new claims for most benefits depended on attending 'work-focused interviews' at 'Job Centre Plus' offices. These were administered by an agency of the Department for Work and Pensions. They were followed up by more interviews if no progress was being made in getting a job. These requirements also applied to partners of claimants.

Carrots

A series of measures were taken to raise the incomes of low-paid workers and especially those with children. The taxpayer was to help with the costs of child care for low income families in paid work. All of this represented a major shift in attitudes towards subsidized wages, means testing and extending the participation of women in the paid labour market which the Labour government of the 1940s would have rejected.

The government used the tax system to distribute the benefits, another innovation designed to link work and reward and to make means testing more acceptable. It also had presentational advantages for the national accounts. These new benefits mostly showed up as reductions in taxation not as additional public spending! Consequences for families were another matter as we shall see.

The work incentive carrots took the following form:

- A minimum wage was introduced. Unlike many European countries and the USA, the UK had never had one. Wages Councils once set minimum wages for particular low-paid industries but even they had been abolished by Mrs Thatcher. A Low Pay Commission was created to recommend a minimum hourly rate of pay. It carefully examined experience in other countries and came up with cautious levels designed not to price workers out of jobs, especially young workers. The basic adult worker minimum was set originally at £3.60 an hour. Despite fears to the contrary such a minimum had a negligible impact on employment. So the level was raised in small steps to reach just over £5 an hour in 2005. Quite apart from its direct impact on poverty, which was not great, it set a floor to wages which enabled more generous wage supplements to be introduced.

- The starting point for paying National Insurance contributions was raised along with the income tax threshold.
- Child benefit for all first children was raised by 25 per cent in real terms.
- The existing cash benefit to low income families was replaced initially by a Working Families Tax Credit (WFTC) in October 1999. Families in low-paid jobs with children but not paying tax could claim the equivalent in cash. The more children the higher the credit. To be eligible someone in the family had to work more than sixteen hours a week and those working over thirty hours got more. As the family income rose the level of support reduced.
- From April 2003 the WFTC was replaced by two separate tax credits – the Working Tax Credit that applied to all low-paid workers and a separate Child Tax Credit which gave income-related benefits to the mother or whoever claimed them.

Results

Overall levels of unemployment amongst young people fell steadily, though mostly because job opportunities improved. Careful evaluations comparing those in the programme with matched samples outside it suggested a positive but modest direct impact of the programmes themselves (Blundell et al., 2003). But the extent of long-term unemployment, the focus of all these measures, has fallen significantly since 1997. It has fallen most in those countries that introduced measures of the kind New Labour did (Nickell et al., 2005).

- Overall the percentage of men and women of working age who were wanting jobs but remain jobless fell steadily from the mid-1990s to 2005. The unemployment rate in 2006 was under 5 per cent, half that in France and Germany.

- However, the number of inactive men withdrawn from the labour force on long-term sick and disability benefits continued to rise and became a focus of policy for Labour's third term.
- Employment among lone parents rose but not as fast as the government's targets (McKnight, 2005; Gregg and Harkness, 2003). In 1997 45 per cent of lone parents were in employment. In 2005 the percentage rose to 55 per cent, short of the end of decade target of 70 per cent but a rise nevertheless.
- Most important for the long term was the fact that the UK economy seemed to have changed in a fundamental way as a result of the combination of Thatcher and Brown reforms. As we have seen, when unemployment fell below quite high levels the UK economy regularly ran into inflation and balance of payments crises. The authorities had to slam on the brakes. By the early years of the new century the 'equilibrium rate of unemployment' at which the economy could be left alone to expand had fallen sharply. This was a hugely important change.
- The use of the Inland Revenue as a benefit-giving agency to distribute tax credits nevertheless caused problems. It was a huge new task. It involved merging staff from the Benefits Agency, steeped in a social security ethos, with the Revenue staff. The merging of cultures and administrative traditions, let alone information systems, proved difficult. The Revenue underestimated the volatility of income over the year for the families dependent on these benefits (Hills et al., 2006). This resulted in over- and underpayments. The Revenue sought to recover overpayments from families in financial crisis. It is one thing to recover taxes from well-off households who have underpaid, quite another to recover cash from families in crisis. The complexity of the system overwhelmed both clients and staff. Families experienced long delays. The Revenue came in for stiff criticism from the House of Commons Committee on Public Accounts (HC 412, 2005/6). In December 2005 the Chancellor announced that increases of income up to £25,000 in a year would be disregarded. This should reduce the need to reclaim benefits.

Disability and work

While there had been some success in reducing the numbers of unemployed and lone parents the numbers of Britons on long-term sickness or disability benefit continued to rise. See Figure 10.2.

In 1985 the prevalence of disability among those of working age was 6 per cent. A decade later this had doubled and over the period 1997 to

Figure 10.2 Numbers of people on benefits, 1979 to 2005

Source: Cm. 6730, 2006

2005 the figure had risen to 15 per cent, though the data sources differ (Berthoud et al., 1993; Rigg, 2005). This was initially thought to be the result of deliberate government policy to keep down the numbers of 'unemployed' in the 1980s. Officials had been encouraged to get people on to sickness rather than unemployment benefit. However, incentives for people to remain on such benefits continued. They were more generous than the new Job Seeker's Allowance. On the other hand many were older workers, genuinely unable to regain a footing in the new labour market or depressed by absence from regular work. The balance between these explanations has been strongly contested (Burchardt, 2000) but the scale of long-term sickness absence was a matter for growing Treasury concern. The Disability Discrimination Act 1995 was intended to limit discrimination in general and facilitate access to employment. The Labour government set up the Disability Rights Commission in April 2000 to help people obtain the rights given in the 1995 Act.

Shortly after being elected in 1997 the government sought to encourage more of those who could return to the labour market to do so. It did so by tightening the medical checks on incapacity and by extending the new deal pattern of advice to disabled people and improving the financial incentives to work in the form of a tax credit. The New Deal for Disabled People was introduced nationwide in July 2001.

Take-up of this new deal has been very low and inactivity rates remained high. Seventy per cent of men between 55 and 64 with a limiting illness or disability remained out of work (Faggio and Nickell, 2003). So, in February 2005 the government announced a national expansion in the Pathways to Work Programme, a pilot scheme of intensive advice and help back into work. In 2006 the latest phase of measures were set out in a White Paper (Cm. 6730, 2005). The problems that remain, the government claimed, were that:

- Little was done to prevent people moving on to incapacity benefits
- The entry point was badly managed – claimants were receiving benefit before satisfying the main medical test.
- There were perverse incentives – the longer a person was on benefit the more they received, hence trapping people on benefit.
- Nothing was expected of recipients and little help offered to return to work.

The government proposed measures to tackle these.

- Measures to improve workplace health and the management of long-term sickness absence by employers. Advice for GPs on ways of dealing with high sickness absence as an alternative to simply signing repeated sickness notes.
- No one would be eligible for a higher level of benefit than Job Seeker's Allowance until they had completed a Personal Capability Assessment and that would be improved to make sure it reflected mental health conditions more sensitively.
- From 2008 a new benefit would be introduced – the Employment and Support Allowance, replacing existing benefits. It would apply to all except those with very severe disabilities. There would be a careful assessment phase. Applicants would need to participate in regular work-focused interviews and a rehabilitation and return to work plan. Existing claimants would remain on existing benefits.
- Those with the most severe conditions would not be subject to this regime and would receive higher benefit.

Just what effect these steps will have remains to be seen.

Parental leave

Paid maternity leave was increased first to six months, and will increase to nine months in 2007. A period of twelve months is promised later. A statutory right to ask to work flexibly for those with young children was introduced and extended to carers of adults. Paternity leave of two weeks began in Labour's first term and extended in its third to six months if the mother returned to work after six months. Gradually social policy was changing to catch up with the big changes in family patterns of work. That extended to schools and pre-school education.

A national child care and pre-school strategy

The government embarked upon the first major extension of the welfare state since 1945 – the goal of providing universal early years education for all 3- to 5-year-olds, together with day care facilities from 8 a.m. to 6 p.m. Activities during school holidays were also expanded.

If women were to be encouraged into the labour force more child care was necessary. Feminists had been arguing this from the 1960s. Research both in the US and the UK showed how important these early years were in determining future life chances (Waldfogel, 1998; Feinstein, 2000). It was symptomatic that the crucial task, pulling together the evidence and drafting the strategy, was undertaken by a team headed by an ebullient senior Treasury official.

Parts of this programme were begun in the poorest areas of England, under the label Sure Start, in 1998. It was one of the most popular things the government did. Prior to the 2005 election a plan to extend the scheme nationally was announced for England (Treasury, 2004; Labour Party, 2005).

- Children's Centres in every area offering information, parenting support, and child care.
- Fifteen hours a week free care for thirty-eight weeks a year by 2010 with a goal of twenty hours. Out-of-school child care for all 3- to 14-year-olds between 8 a.m. and 6 p.m. each weekday by 2010.
- The child care element of the Working Tax Credit covering 80 per cent of costs up to £300 a week.

Child care provision is also being extended in Scotland and Wales (Scotland Office, 1998; National Assembly for Wales, 2005).

Teenage Pregnancy

This was an early concern and the subject of one of the first Social
Exclusion Unit reports (Cm. 4342, 1999). It pointed to some deep causes,
notably poor and declining success for some girls at school with little to
look forward to but unrewarding jobs in poor areas. The government
committed itself to halving the number of pregnancies by 2010. Improved
sex education in schools, a national helpline and access to family planning advice were promised. So, too, was a tougher stance towards teenage
fathers. Young mothers who could not live with their parents were to
be offered supervised hostel accommodation rather than council flats.
Teenagers who did become pregnant should be encouraged to return to
education. To this end Reintegration Officers were funded in eighty-nine
local education authorities. But the deep causes were more difficult to
reach. In fact, teenage pregnancy rates did fall but not at a rate that meant
the government's target would be met (Burchardt, 2005).

Children at Risk

We saw (p. 64) how the murder of two brothers by those who had
been charged with their care in the 1940s led to the creation of
Children's Departments in 1948. In 1970 these agencies were merged
into Social Services Departments. In 2004 a new Children Act required
local authorities in England to take a step back to the 1940s and appoint
a Director of Children's Services, this time with responsibility for bringing together a range of local services to 'improve the wellbeing of children'. Slightly different arrangements applied to Wales. Why the turning
back? The reason was yet another child's death. The whole story gives
us a glimpse into the underworld of social policy in modern Britain and,
indeed, Europe.

Victoria Climbie had been born in the Ivory Coast, one of seven
children. Her aunt suggested she come back to France with her and be
educated there. She did go, and attended school briefly, but she soon came
to the notice of French social workers and she was then taken to the UK,
the aunt claiming Victoria was her child. The pair then drifted from one
kind of temporary accommodation to another and the aunt moved in with
a male partner and gained a job in a hospital. Her childminder observed

injuries to the child. She was taken to hospital, more than once, and to social services who assigned her a social worker. Despite this Victoria underwent months of neglect and abuse and finally was taken to hospital in a dreadful state and died there.

Lord Laming's report (DoH, 2003; <http://www.victoria-climbie-inquiry.org.uk>) should be read by anyone who wants to know how this could happen and what life on the edge of society is like for a helpless child who began life in Africa as a lively girl who was good at school. It is a damning account of public agencies' failures to collaborate and the failure of professional staff, unable to read the signs or take action.

Out of this dreadful story came the Children Act 2004. Local authorities were required to appoint a Director of Children's Services, a lead elected member and to produce a local plan linking all services for children and young people by April 2006. These formal arrangements for joint working were to be called children's trusts. The Department of Education and Skills became the lead department in Whitehall. Directors of Children's Services are in many areas past Chief Education Officers, now responsible for both education and children's services, <http://www.everychildmatters.gov.uk>.

How exactly this collaborative machinery to 'purchase' children's services will work is far from clear at the point of writing, especially as arrangements will differ between areas. The salutary memory is that we were trying to remedy just such failures sixty years ago.

Child support again

In the previous chapter we described the debate which led to the creation of the Child Support Agency. The complexity of its procedures and poor administration led to lone mothers waiting long periods for financial support. Some fathers objected vociferously to its very existence. The agency's failings became a political issue. The financial rules were simplified in Labour's second term but the agency remained unpopular and inefficient. The reasons lay in the fundamental weakness of its original design. In July 2006 the government announced the end of the agency and a 'redesign of child support' that would take effect from 2008 (Cm. 6895, 2006). It would increase the amount of maintenance parents with responsibility could keep and encourage couples to reach their own agreements.

Institutional Reform: From Monopoly to Diversity and Choice

This was the second distinctive theme of the Blair years. Again it was a break with the past. Consumers' expectations of their public services had changed since 1945. In the immediate post-war world, as we saw, most goods were rationed. It was only possible to shop with one grocer and one butcher who held your ration book. You queued for a tiny bag of sweets, as I vividly remember. It was not surprising that the same was true if you needed to go to a hospital. You were told where to go and you queued. Medical care was free, which was an enormous relief. But by the twenty-first century such passivity was not normal. Couples spent their weekends shopping. Or they used the internet, which offered more information and alternatives galore.

To suppose that people would go on being prepared to be told which hospital or school to use and to wait for the privilege was becoming wholly unacceptable, at least to the voters Blair needed to capture. The middle class were beginning to vote with their feet. The rapid rise in the use of private health insurance in the 1980s and the similarly rapid rise in private education spending was a warning that old-style social services were in danger. Yet, almost by accident, as we saw in the last chapter, the previous Conservative administration had stumbled on ways to improve the performance of these services. They hoped this would avoid having to spend more. But what the voters clearly wanted in 1997 was both better and more.

The New Labour government initially only partially accepted this new approach. It accepted more choice and diversity in schools and in social care but it baulked at doing so for health. It had been so critical of the Tory reforms and talked of 'saving the NHS' in its 1997 election campaign. But events forced it to change direction – in England. After devolution the story was to evolve in very different ways in Scotland and Wales.

Schools

By 1996 the main elements of the changes legislated in the 1988 Education Reform Act (see p. 200) were in place.

- National tests for 7-, 11- and 14-year-olds were taking place in all English state schools and the results were published.

- Schools were following the National Curriculum.
- All schools now had their own budgets.
- Each child who chose that school triggered a sum allocated to that school.
- The governing body with parents, staff and local representatives on it decided how the budget should be spent and the curriculum delivered, managed the buildings and appointed senior staff.

Some schools had opted out of local authority control under the Conservative Act – the grant-maintained schools. One of the new government's first steps was to reintegrate these schools into the pattern of local provision, giving them somewhat more independence like the voluntary church schools. They were now called foundation schools. With this one exception the new government accepted the Conservative's devolution of power to individual schools. But it stopped the extension of academic selection. And it sharply increased spending after what had been a real terms standstill and a decline in spending as a percentage of the GDP. More of the money LEAs received had to be passed directly to schools. The Secretary of State, David Blunkett, set ambitious targets for schools to increase the percentage of children reaching 'expected levels' of achievement in maths, English and science at 11.

Pioneering work that had begun in the Conservative period and proved successful in schools in poorer areas became a national programme – the literacy and numeracy hours. These required teachers in primary schools to spend an hour a day on both 'literacy' – reading and writing and 'numeracy' – maths. It also advised them on best-practice ways to spend the time. A television channel is now devoted to examples of best practice across all age ranges and subjects.

Why were these regulation hours needed? A personal note may help. My wife, who taught maths for most of her career in Inner London comprehensives, for a period taught primary school teachers to teach maths. Most had struggled with maths themselves and as a result spent little time in their classes on it. All kinds of seemingly good reasons were advanced for not doing maths today. Now they had to. Neither the tests nor the elaborate record-keeping were popular with teachers. But they were with parents. A sample of parents from the poorest areas in the country were asked regularly, as part of a wider survey by colleagues at the LSE, about the best and most important changes they thought were happening in their local area. What is happening in the schools was the answer.

Results

A range of quantitative evidence also suggests that something significant happened in English schools after about 1996. For twenty-five years there had been little improvement in the levels of mathematical attainment gained by British schoolchildren, indeed some small decline. Much the same can be said of most of the other leading nations despite higher spending all round (Gundlach et al., 2001).

The test results of English children after 1996 suggest a change was taking place. In that year the percentage of 11-year-olds reaching the expected level of maths for their age was 54 per cent. By 2000 this had risen to 72 per cent. By 2005 it was 75 per cent. Other subjects showed a similar, if not quite so striking, trend. Taking science, maths and English together, 43 per cent of children reached the expected level in all three subjects in 1997 and 57 per cent in 2005 and pupils in poorer schools improved more than in average schools. Those in England gaining five or more A to C grades at GCSE rose from 45 per cent in 1997 to 55 per cent in 2005 (Glennerster, 2002; DfES, 2005a, b). International studies suggested significant relative improvement by Britain (OECD, 2001).

For various statistical reasons, and because the first set of results might reflect mere growing capacity to do tests, we may need to discount the scale of the improvements somewhat (Tymms, 2004). Even if we do so the improvement remained substantial. But there was much slower improvement after 2000. The improved results gained in primary schools seemed not to be following through to the same degree in secondary schools. The international studies suggested that while on average schoolchildren's performance in the UK was higher, it still had one of the largest differences between social groups (OECD, 2001). This old legacy was proving very difficult to shift. Though schools with most poor children in them were improving their performance faster than other schools the gap between children actually on free school meals and the rest had widened a little since 1998. Both had shown substantial improvement but the gap had not narrowed.

Yet another type of school

The government tried again (Cm. 6677, 2005). It proposed:

- There should be more scope for new independent not-for-profit schools to come into the local education market to challenge local complacency where existing local schools were failing. Quicker action would be taken if a school was seen to be underperforming.

- Local School Organisation Committees, which advised on whether new places or new schools were necessary and which operated in the interests of existing schools, would go. There would be no new local authority community schools.

- New Trust Schools would have more independence from Local Education Authorities and do their own selection 'taking account of' national rules that were designed to prevent selection by ability of the old eleven-plus kind.

- A number of quite sensible measures already in process to help schools single out children making little progress and focus special measures on them.

This produced a highly unusual rebellion which went far beyond the traditional Old Labour opponents of Blair. What concerned many was the possibility that these new schools would reintroduce selection by the back door. Others worried that local authorities would lose their power to set the local framework for the range and type of schools in their area. Many saw no need for yet another type of school with an even more complex governing structure and with less parental representation. Above all the idea that the problems of poor children in deprived areas could be solved by fiddling about with the governing structure of schools seemed to many, including the author, misguided.

Not only did the rebels produce their own alternative but, to its credit, so did the House of Commons Education and Skills Committee (HC 633-1, 2006) in a report that made a lot more sense than the original White Paper. It argued for stronger controls on admissions. Local authorities and admission forums should have stronger powers to oversee school admissions policies and report them to an independent adjudicator if the national code was being ignored. To ensure that selection procedures were not disadvantaging children from less advantaged homes, benchmarks should be set for a socially mixed intake and the success of schools in achieving this should be regularly reviewed. The need for another type of school was dismissed.

In the eventual legislation the government accepted most of these arguments except the case against a new type of school. Local authorities were given clear powers over the structure of local schooling but were required to achieve 'variety' and allow new schools to be set up. Selection on ability and interviews for selection were banned. This was not enough for many rebels. The government needed Conservative support to get the bill through.

The row was instructive. Bad memories of the old eleven-plus and the ideal of socially mixed local schools that took root in the 1960s seemed to have a continuing appeal for many in the Labour and Liberal Parties. Even Conservatives were hesitant to go back to overt selection. The really tough question of how to cope with the hard core of low achievers still remains unanswered and the answer lies, in large part, beyond schools.

Higher education

We saw in the previous chapter that higher education had been expanded sharply by the previous Conservative administration in its later years. It had done so on the cheap. Expenditure per student on post-school education fell by a half in real terms between 1974 and 1995. Class sizes rose and individual tutorials I once gave and enjoyed had gone. The system of maintenance grants to help with living expenses on a means-tested basis had been steadily withdrawn making university more expensive for students from poor families. Several universities were in serious financial difficulties. The main parties tacitly agreed to kick the problem into touch for the 1997 election and a committee of inquiry was set up to consider future funding for universities and to report after the election.

The Dearing Committee (1997) reported shortly after. It stated very clearly that standards were slipping. The universities needed money quickly. UK science was suffering from outdated laboratories. Yet the Labour government had frozen its education budget to levels determined by the past government in its first two years. One solution discussed by the committee was to increase spending now but recover the costs later through a graduate tax or system of loans. Another option it set out was to charge fees on a means-tested basis. The difficulty for the government was that universities needed hard cash now. The outcome was a compromise that got the universities a little extra but was unpopular too.

- Students would, from 1998, pay a flat fee of £1,000 if their families' incomes were in the top third of the income range. The next third would pay £500 and those from the poorest families would pay nothing.
- Students could get a loan to cover living expenses at a higher level than the old maintenance grant and old loan but they would have to repay it later through the Inland Revenue.

This became an issue at the new Scottish parliamentary elections. The resulting Lib–Lab coalition was faced with a difficulty. The Liberal members had campaigned to abolish fees. The result was a compromise. Tuition fees would be paid by the state but bursaries would be available to poor young students and the cost recovered through a 'Graduate Endowment' or graduate tax paid after graduation on a sliding income scale. Scotland was going its own way again.

At the 2001 election university fees in England were manifestly unpopular. Blair returned to 10 Downing Street determined to try to do something to modify the scheme. But awaiting him was the opposite pressure. The leading university Vice Chancellors made it very clear to him that their universities could not continue in the front rank internationally without more resources. The only way out, they argued, was permission for them to be able to charge even *higher* fees.

Some kind of fundamental rethink was required and Blair set it in train. Ranges of options were tried but after a year little progress had been made. Blair ordered a White Paper to be produced with a solution by January 2003. The Secretary of State Estelle Morris resigned and her replacement, Charles Clarke, had a month to finalize the White Paper on which the Higher Education Minister Margaret Hodge had been working.

They and Blair's office became convinced that the only way to put in place a long-term sustainable flow of income for UK universities *was* to permit universities to charge higher fees but for students to pay those fees when they had left university when their incomes were high enough. The Student Loans Company would pay the university the fees when the student entered college, but the student would only repay through the income tax system when his or her income rose above £15,000 a year and on 9 per cent of their income over that limit (Cm. 5735, 2003). The gap would be filled by that company borrowing the sums involved. Upfront fees would be abolished. Most of the total extra spending would not appear as part of public expenditure. If universities were to have the right to charge fees they would have to accept the duty to make sure students from poorer families were not put off applying, indeed they should try to ensure that more did so. A regulator was appointed to make sure this happened. Maintenance grants would be reintroduced for those from poorer families.

Since some colleagues and I had been espousing such a solution for many years, the reader should recognize some bias here! But to me this represented a flash of enlightened courage. (For an account of the intellectual case made over the years for such a policy see Barr and Crawford,

2005. For the opposite view the reader should consult the NUS website
<http://www.nusonline.co.uk>.)

The battle to get the proposals through the Commons was a very close-
run thing. Backbench MPs demanded concessions which increased the
generosity of the policy towards students from poor homes. But pass
it did, despite defections on the Labour side and opposition from the
Conservative and Liberal Parties. The hope was that once universities
began to benefit from the additional revenue such a scheme would
become entrenched. The new Conservative leader elected in 2005, David
Cameron, suggested that the Conservatives would indeed accept this
fundamental shift as inevitable.

Health care

The Labour Party in opposition had bitterly fought attempts to introduce
an internal market to the NHS. Yet, as the reforms took hold, most of
those managing the services came to agree that separating the funding and
planning of services from the day-to-day running of hospitals was a good
move. What bitterly divided many in the service, and became the Labour
Party's pet hate, was GP fundholding. Over half of GPs had their own
budgets to buy services for their patients and they were reluctant to give
up that power. What emerged was a compromise (Cm. 3807, 1997).

- The 'purchaser–provider split' was to stay.
- Hospital trusts would stay.
- Fundholding would go. But Primary Care Groups, later larger Primary
  Care Trusts, would have most of the NHS budget devolved to them.
  They would have significant representation of GPs and would be
  responsible for making long-term agreements with hospitals and other
  providers to supply services. They would be given a fixed budget that
  would have to cover virtually all the services patients used including
  the cost of prescriptions. For the first time a single body would be
  in the position to set priorities between services at a local level and not
  have the budget tied up in separate untouchable packets. Such at least
  was the theory.
- The Department of Health would, after discussion with the Royal
  Colleges, academics and the wider professions, produce 'evidence based
  National Service frameworks' setting out best-practice approaches to
  priority areas of care. Cancer, heart disease and mental health were the
  first examples.

- Two bodies were set up to give professional advice to push for more consistent and effective clinical standards. One concerned advice on cost effective clinical practice, new drugs and procedures. This was the National Institute for Clinical Excellence (NICE). In 2005 it merged with the Health Development Agency to form the National Institute for Health and Clinical Excellence. A comparable body in Scotland was NHS Quality Improvement.
- Separate inspection regimes for health and social care providers were created. The Healthcare Commission inspects public providers of health for quality and value for money in England and Wales. It reviews Trusts' performance and rates them. It also inspects and regulates private providers to ensure minimum standards. A Commission for Social Care Inspection does the same for social care facilities. The two bodies are to be merged.

Despite these structural changes the NHS was working within the very tight spending limits the Conservatives had bequeathed. Bed shortages, rising waiting lists and an influenza epidemic in 1999 coincided to bring a crisis reminiscent of 1987. As then, the Prime Minister felt obliged to go on television and be seen to be doing something about it. This time the response was not more reorganization but more money. Blair promised that health spending would rise to the European average in the next decade. We get some insight into the role the Prime Minister played here from the reminiscences of the then chief economic adviser to the Department of Health. He recalls being phoned before Tony Blair was to give his *Frost* interview and being asked how much it would cost to raise the UK's level of health spending to the European average. He was the only person available with the figures to hand at home at the weekend!

A full-scale Treasury analysis then followed chaired by an outsider – the Wanless Review (Treasury, 2002). It estimated what NHS spending would have to be on various scenarios about changes in the population's health and age. It proved important in convincing the Treasury that more resources were needed. Over the whole period since the NHS had been created, real (after inflation) spending had risen on average by 3 per cent a year. In Labour's first term it rose by 4.8 per cent a year. In the second it rose by 7.4 per cent per annum. By 2008 the NHS will consume 2.5 per cent *more* of the Gross Domestic Product than in 2000, about 9 per cent in all. For long-time watchers of the NHS, like the author, this has been nothing less than extraordinary. The great tragedy was that such largess was handed out before any serious attempt was made to increase the efficiency of the service.

A big discussion was launched to decide how to use the extra funds. It pulled in people working in the service and outside groups to discuss practical changes that could be made to improve the quality of services. Out of this came a whole range of useful initiatives but also targets that came to irk professionals.

- Maximum waiting times for in-patient treatment of six months by 2005 (later three months by 2008).
- Patients to see a primary care practitioner in twenty-four hours and a GP in forty-eight.
- A four-hour maximum wait in emergency rooms.
- Detailed plans for improving cancer treatment and health inequalities and much more.

The whole was contained in something called *The NHS Plan* (DoH, 2000).

A long series of negotiations began with the medical and nursing professions to change their contractual obligations to the service and their ways of working. They were not completed until just before the 2005 election. The aim was to tie consultants more effectively to their local hospital and to extend general practitioners' roles, widening the scope of testing, treatment and monitoring that could be undertaken within primary care and in the local surgery. The latter especially is happening but the price of these contracts has been high. The British medical profession is now better paid than almost anywhere else except America.

Secretary of State Alan Milburn, and Blair, were becoming increasingly frustrated by the slow progress being made in reducing waiting lists and meeting the other targets. Seeking to run the NHS in England as if it were some national corporation, with regular telephone calls from the centre to under-performing hospitals, was just not working. Attention began to return to mobilizing market incentives and introducing competition from new entrants to the health market.

One idea was to give local hospitals more independence if they were doing well, financial freedom to borrow money and sell land. Milburn and his adviser had in mind a new form of not-for-profit body responsible to the local population. That was not how many Labour MPs and the public sector unions saw it. To them this meant privatization. The Treasury's worry was that it would lose control of public capital expenditure. Brown put his foot down. Foundation hospitals would have limited borrowing powers and all hospitals would gradually reach foundation status. In order to ensure competition was real it could not be confined to existing NHS providers. There had to be a quick infusion of new capacity where the NHS was failing and always had failed most – providing routine operations for non-emergency cases. Competitive contracts to do the work in specialist treatment centres were offered and won by many new independent providers.

The real change of strategy, however, went largely undebated at the time (DoH, 2004). Its significance began to become evident later. Hospitals, like schools, would get their money by successfully attracting patients. Money would follow the patient. (The whole scheme was given the odd title 'Payment by Results', the name given to the late nineteenth-century system of funding schools.) Patients, advised by their GP, would have the right to choose their hospital or other care provider, including a private hospital. The hospital would be paid a set 'tariff', or price, for each patient treated, given the condition and its severity. (The provider would be compensated for higher local labour market costs.) There would be no price competition, in other words, providers would compete only on quality and speed of treatment. This was a huge change in the whole approach to NHS funding, which dated back to 1948. It would become in the interest of hospitals to treat more patients faster. They would get paid more if they did so. In this respect it resembled the way most other health care systems in the world worked. Even the tax-funded health services of Sweden and Denmark had moved in this direction.

It was easier to see how the chosen model would work with clear-cut treatment episodes, having a hip joint replaced for example, less easy for people who suffered from chronic diseases that continue for long periods and required many agencies to work together. Completely new billing systems would be needed and financial control of a hospital's budget would be more difficult (Audit Commission, 2005). So it proved. Hospitals could not be permitted to run up deficits with other budgets raided to rescue them, as had usually happened in the past. The Treasury demanded that hospitals' books balance before the new regime took effect fully in 2006. Shock-horror stories of hospitals in deficit filled the papers in early 2006. This major and technically difficult change was being simultaneously compounded by more structural change as primary care trusts and strategic health authorities above them were amalgamated. The depressed feeling amongst managers and senior staff was palpable in 2006. If these kinds of changes had been implemented gradually from 1997 on, the transition would have been smoother. But that was probably politically impossible. There were only so many shifts New Labour could have attempted all at once.

To many all these changes were a betrayal of the original 1948 ideal (see for example the letter to the *Guardian* on 24 September 2005 from many leading health professionals, academics and historians). To others the government's changes were necessary if the NHS was to win the political battle for survival with demanding consumerist voters. Whoever turns out to be right it is now difficult to see the NHS ever being the same again – at least in England. Not so in the other countries that make up the United Kingdom. Scotland and Wales did not follow this move to the market. There health policy returned to its pre-Thatcher roots (Greer, 2004). The close ties between the medical professional elites and the political elite in a more closely knit Scotland led politicians to rely on trust and cooperation between local professions to achieve results. The internal market was abolished and left unresurrected. In Wales the prime focus was on public health and local public services. Again, the strength of public service workers' interests in the political arithmetic of the province helps explain this.

The comparative impact of these different reform strategies is difficult to measure yet. England did well on waiting times but other outcomes were difficult to compare (Alvarez-Rosete et al., 2005). Despite falls in the number of hospital beds in every country England continues to have just over *half* the number of beds per head of population as Scotland. Scotland has one-third more GPs and more of most other kinds of staff. The Scottish budget, like those of the other countries, is simply much higher, as in other areas of social policy (McLean and McMillan, 2003).

Health inequalities

The countries of the UK also differed in the way they approached health inequalities. The whole issue had been largely banished from discussion for most of the Conservative period. The last Labour government, just before it was voted out, had commissioned the Black Report (DHSS, 1980) which reported early in the new Parliament in an almost clandestine way. Its members included two close colleagues of Richard Titmuss, Professors Jerry Morris and Peter Townsend, who were not about to let the report be buried. It was published as a widely read Penguin (Townsend and Davidson, 1982) and became something of a symbolic work for the left. Black's most quoted finding was that the gap between the life expectancy of the lowest social class males and the highest social class group had widened through much of the post-war period despite free health care. Its causes lay in wider society.

There were disputes about the findings. Numbers in the lowest social group were much smaller than they had been and the figures said nothing about women. But even Black's critics agreed that on their own measures health inequality had begun to widen in the 1990s, responding to the sharp widening in overall inequality (see below). Early in its first term the new government set up a repeat of the Black inquiry under a former Chief Medical Officer, Sir Donald Acheson. His report's (DoH, 1998) findings were much the same as Black's, with even more evidence. It made sweeping recommendations encompassing pretty much the whole of social policy, far beyond the remit of the Department of Health, and it was not costed, so it did not win many friends in Whitehall. Precisely because it did reach deep into almost every area of public policy and private activity, it was difficult for highly compartmentalized spending departments to get their heads round it.

To its credit the government did respond. The Treasury undertook a cross-departmental review to see what options might be most effective. Health inequality targets were included in the public service agreements with local government and cross-departmental machinery was created to follow up a 'Programme of Action'. The goal set was to reduce inequality in life expectancy at birth and in infant mortality by 10 per cent by 2010 with a range of other indicators chosen. Responsibility for oversight lay with a subcommittee of cabinet chaired by the Deputy Prime Minister. No other country in the OECD had set up such machinery.

There were some positive outcomes – narrowing the absolute gap between rich and poor areas in circulatory heart disease, for example. The first progress report (DoH, 2005a) is well worth study. But overall progress was slow and very patchy. The causes of health inequality are as deep as inequality itself.

In England the government was forced into a complete ban on smoking in public places, following Scotland, after a free vote in the House of Commons.

Long-term care

It had always been the case that older people who entered a local authority residential care home were expected to pay according to their means. In practice, however, most old people did not own their own houses in 1948 or for many years after. For them care was free and it came to be seen as a right, no different from the NHS. Then gradually this capital test began to apply to the middle class and they did not like it. They received free hospital care. If they then had to move into an old people's home they had to pay. If they had a district nurse come into their home it was free because she or he was employed by the NHS. But if they went into a nursing home they had to pay for this nursing.

This became a political issue in the run-up to the 1997 General Election. The Labour Party simply said it would appoint a Royal Commission to consider the whole issue of long-term care and its funding. They did and the Sutherland Commission reported in 1999 (Cm. 4192). The trouble was that the government did not like what they were told.

- The majority report argued that the boundary lines between long-term care and health care were so unclear that people were right to see the different funding of each as unfair.
- The market failures involved in long-term care insurance were so serious that the private market would never be a major player. (As has proved to be the case.)
- The solution was to make both nursing and personal care, like feeding, dressing and bathing, free. Both should be funded from the same source as the NHS, central taxation. Since it was impossible to draw a boundary between health and social care, or nursing and personal care, both should be funded from a single budget.
- The costs of food and accommodation should be the individual's or their family's responsibility. For the poor this would be paid out of Housing Benefit and Income Support as it would be if they were at home.

The minority report (short and well worth reading), mostly written by David, now Lord, Lipsey, strongly disagreed.

- The majority's solution would be far too expensive. If it were made free, personal care by spouses and families would cease or they would demand payment. The result would be 'a Croesian flood of expenditure' (Cm. 4192, 1999: 119, para. 34).
- The middle class would be the main beneficiaries. If they owned houses they could afford to pay. Their complaints were merely to preserve middle-class inheritances. Old people should insure themselves for the risk of needing care.

The English government rejected the majority report but moved some way towards it. It said nursing care should be 'free' in homes that provided it. In practice this meant using NHS funds to subsidize homes providing nursing care for all those deemed in need of nursing support. The sum paid depends on an assessed level of individual need.

In Scotland the Parliament took a different view. They accepted the majority view and introduced free personal and nursing care. Under the Community Care (Scotland) Act 2002, residents in care homes were assessed by a social worker to see if they qualified for free care. 'Free' means that the Scottish government makes a contribution to that care – so much for personal and a larger sum for nursing care. However, the Westminster government in England has increased its spending on nursing care much faster than in Scotland and graded it in line with three levels of severity. For those in the highest need category, spending was roughly twice that in Scotland in 2005 (Bell and Bowes, 2006). Scots in care homes also lose rights to attendance allowance. The King's Fund (2006) in a major study again recommended abolishing means testing, local government guaranteeing a minimum level of personal and nursing care for all; individuals could then add to that basic care package with government matching the sum up to a given ceiling.

Social care

The Conservative strategy had been to encourage, indeed, force, local authorities in England to use more private providers of both residential and domiciliary care. The Labour government removed that compulsion but merely required local authorities to determine what was 'best value'. That did not check growth in the use of private providers. In 1993 95 per cent of home support contact hours were provided by local authority staff. By 2003 64 per cent were provided by the independent profit-making sector.

A new industry of private care providers had grown up – 3,000 had registered by 2003. In 1980 80 per cent of places in residential homes were provided by local authorities, by 2005 the figure was about a quarter. Resulting standards were often low, as many complained to a King's Fund Commission (Robinson and Banks, 2005). Since 1990, younger disabled people have been able to take cash, or a 'direct payment', from a Social Services Department in England to pay for their own care. In 2000 this was extended to older people. A Green Paper proposed extending the idea (DoH, 2005b). Individuals could be assessed for need and a sum set aside for publicly funded support. The individual and carers could decide how to spend it.

Ageing and Pensions

One of the biggest social changes to have taken place since the Second World War was the longer life people were enjoying with improved health. How different societies have responded to this change tells us something about the way they think about older people. Much of British discussion of this change is dominated by ideas of growing burdens and income poverty. Other countries have seen their elderly more positively (Thane, 2000).

The great bonus of longer healthy life does carry financial and economic implications, especially if that trend is accompanied by reduced child-bearing. Fertility rates, the number of children each woman has in her lifetime, have been falling steadily. For women born in 1947 their child-bearing phase of life ended with their having produced just over two children. Each new cohort since then has had fewer children. It is now assumed that the average completed family size will end up at a little over 1.7 in England and rather fewer in Scotland. This means fewer workers to support those who are no longer working.

In 1950 the average cohort life expectancy for 65-year-old men was about twelve more years. The 2003-based projection for 2010 was that such a man would live for twenty more years and that figure would likely go on rising (Pensions Commission, 2005, Appendices Figure E.1). (To check the latest figures go to <http://www.gad.gov.uk>.)

It is these two trends taken together that have transformed our capacity to fund old age – more old people and fewer young workers. Retirement requires us to move resources created by workers to those who are not working. In the period immediately after the Second World War there was the 'baby boom' we have discussed before. It meant that far more young people became available for work. For a time this hid the impact of an ageing population. Then that birth boom faded and reversed. Fortunately, from the 1950s through to the present, more women have entered the labour force, again increasing the output that could be spread to the older non-working population. That trend is also slowing though more women could work full-time.

There are only two ways for the working population to have their out-put transferred to the non-workers – through higher taxes that take away their consumption or higher savings that transfer potential demand through the private pension market into the pockets of pensioners. Politicians hoped the voluntary route would suffice. Indeed, politicians of both parties congratulated themselves on the extensive private occupational pension schemes the UK had.

Through the 1980s and early 1990s this seemed to be working. As we saw, the previous Conservative government had ceased to increase the value of the basic state pension in line with earnings so that it fell as a percentage of average earnings year by year. That government had also reduced the generosity of the State Earnings-Related Pension (SERPS) and encouraged people to opt out into private schemes with generous tax relief. Just before the 1997 election it produced an even more radical plan to phase out the state basic pension altogether, requiring membership of a private scheme. When Labour came to office it had no pension plan. Frank Field had been appointed to think afresh on the issue but his ideas were unacceptable to the Chancellor. The Treasury won. It came up with a solution that readers of its memoranda in the 1940s would have found familiar.

A new second pension

SERPS, that had been the main pension contribution of the previous Labour administration, was recast. British willingness to tear up pension schemes at will every few years leaves foreign observers gasping. This Second State Pension was introduced, though old SERPS rights were preserved within it. It was designed to help those unable to finance their own retirement, then felt to be a small proportion of the population. It would gradually become another flat rate pension on top of the old flat rate Beveridge one. For the low-paid it would be worth roughly double what SERPS would have paid for those earning £9,000 a year (40 per cent of average earnings at that time). For those earning more it became less and less a good deal. The higher pension promised to future low earners was made possible by the state putting in substantial additional contributions for the lowest-paid. As an individual moved out of a low-paid occupation, he or she would, if they had any sense, opt into a private scheme. Such was the hope.

For someone in the scheme for life it would just take them above the means-test pension level on retirement. However, since that pension was not to rise with earnings after that point and the means-tested support level would probably rise, the likely result was that individuals would fall back into means-tested support not long after retiring. Many women with more transient jobs or with caring responsibilities would never get above the means-tested pension level (Rake et al., 1999). These deficiencies were to come home to roost later.

Stakeholder pensions

A second plank to the government's pension plan was a scheme to encourage moderate earners to take out private pensions. Over a third of employees at that point had no occupational scheme. These new private pensions would be simple to understand, have low administrative start-up costs, would enable people to start and stop payments and be moveable between jobs. Employers would have to offer access to such schemes but would not have to contribute to them themselves.

The scheme was a complete flop. The following succinct summary by the Pensions Commission (2004: 92), of which more below, puts it clearly:

> The vast majority of small company Stakeholder schemes are empty shells with no contributing members. Sixty-five percent of companies with 5–12 employees have nominated a Stakeholder supplier, but only 4% are making contributions. And the 'new premiums' which have gone into Stakeholder Pensions include a large element which previously was going into other types of pension scheme. There is little evidence of a net increase in ongoing pension contributions flowing into [private pension schemes] as a result of the introduction of Stakeholder pensions.

'Improving' the safety net

As so often in the past, when faced with the political demand to do something to help the elderly, the government made the means-tested safety net more generous rather than fixing the future. It changed the name of the benefit as its predecessors had done – from National Assistance to Supplementary Benefit and then to Income Support. Now the means-tested safety net was to be a 'Minimum Income Guarantee' for the elderly and then later 'Pension Credit'.

The old Income Support levels were raised significantly for the elderly and this lifted more than a third out of poverty, but it caught more people in a savings trap unable to benefit from the small savings they had made. So, then, the government allowed more income from savings to be ignored for the purposes of means testing. This produced a two-tier means-testing regime. The 'Guarantee Pension Credit' tops up the income of someone who is 60 or over to a given level, and then reduces the sum as income rises on a pound-for-pound basis. This guarantee was just short of £110 for a single person and £167 for a couple in 2005/6. The savings credit made the cut-off less harsh for those just above and just below the Guarantee level. It only comes into force when someone is 65 or over. Even this highly simplified account makes it clear how complex a structure successive governments had created. Those who were receiving occupational pensions built up in the good years or those on SERPS were not doing too badly. The big losers were those who had worked for small employers, women and those in more marginal jobs.

Then, at the turn of the century, perceptions began to change. Some major pension companies were not able to honour their pension promises. Many had mis-sold pensions to ill-informed buyers. Most important of all it became clear that the employer schemes on which successive governments had relied were in serious trouble. New accounting rules required companies to show their pension liabilities, their promises to future pensioners, as part of their main company accounts. The boom in the stock market that had hidden their debts now reversed. Realistic estimates of the growing age of their future pensioners showed how longevity had been underestimated. Debts on many company pension schemes made many companies appear unprofitable.

Their response was to reduce their pension coverage. Companies began to change their schemes from ones that promised, for example, half the pay an employee was earning on retirement (defined benefit schemes) to ones that simply paid a given sum into a pension scheme and let the market decide how much the savings were worth when the individual retired (a defined contribution scheme.) That transferred the risks from the firm to the employee.

Two-thirds of final salary schemes were closed to new members by 2003 (Pensions Commission, 2004: 85). The estimate was that only 1.6 to 1.8 million people would be members of defined benefit schemes on which so many hopes had been placed a few years before. Employers also reduced the amount they were contributing to these pension schemes despite the fact that their employees were living longer.

The government had made things worse. It had reduced the income tax advantages such schemes had enjoyed. The more generous means-tested credits system previously described brought more people within means testing. The continuing decline in the basic pension relative to future earnings would bring more and more people within that means-testing regime as time went on (over 70 per cent of pensioners by mid-century according to the Pensions Commissions, 2005, Figure 1.22). That seemed incompatible with the goal of relying on private savings to fund pensions. Most people will know that some of their savings, at least, will be 'wasted'.

(For an historical account of how the UK came to get itself into this fix see Pemberton et al., 2006.)

This combination of bad news led the government to appoint an independent body to look at the issue of whether pension contributions to private schemes should be made compulsory. The result was the Pensions Commission appointed in December 2002. It was a team of three chaired by Adair Turner, Vice Chairman of Merrill Lynch Europe and a former Director of the Confederation of British Industry. He had been the chair of the Low Pay Commission which recommended the minimum wage and had undertaken a review of the NHS for Tony Blair. Turner was supported by Professor John Hills from the LSE and Jennie Drake, at the outset President of the TUC, then reverting to her post as Deputy General Secretary of the Communication Workers Union. Like Beveridge before them they decided that the specific narrow question of compulsion they had been set could not be discussed without looking much more widely. They produced an analytical review of the problem in their first report (Pensions Commission, 2004). It is one of the best examples of public policy analysis of any state paper since the Second World War, in my view. Their conclusion was:

> If we do nothing, many people, in particular of middle income levels, will reach their planned retirement age with inadequate pension funds, and will then have to accept lower than planned pension income, or keep working longer than they intended. (p. 170)

So either:

- pensioners would become poorer;
- taxes or national insurance contribution would have to rise;
- private savings would have to rise; or
- average retirement ages must rise.

A year later it produced its policy recommendations (Pensions Commission, 2005), just sixty-three years on from Beveridge's publication. The Commission recommended that to prevent the first option of growing pensioner poverty it was necessary to follow each of the other three routes in combination.

- Like Beveridge they wanted the state to provide a secure unmeans-tested platform on which private savings could be built. That required future governments to raise the value of the old flat rate basic pension and that of the second state pension, so that in combination they would lift most people above the level of means-tested income support.

- To make the basic platform work for women and carers the old Beveridge scheme would gradually move from a contribution basis to one earned by an individual's right of residence. From a given date rights would accrue by virtue of being resident in the UK not from social insurance contributions. This would amount to a fundamental change of principle and would make the eventual result a citizen's pension. The Second State Pension would have more generous credits for caring responsibilities.

- Somewhere down the line these two pensions would no doubt merge, though to do so in the short term leaving no losers would be very expensive and complicated.

- To pay for all this taxes/contributions would have to rise. In the short run the reduced pension costs derived from raising women's pension age to 65 would reduce the impact. In the longer run the cost would be met in part by raising the age at which these state pensions would be paid. They could rise gradually to 68 by 2050 assuming life expectancy rose in line with estimates at the time. This would keep constant the share of a person's life they could expect to be retired. Some increase in actual retirement ages has already been under way. For those who are long-term sick it would be possible to draw a means-tested credit earlier. Reducing the inequalities in life expectancy needed tackling more successfully, as we have seen already.

- On top of this platform individuals would be strongly pressured to save for retirement along with their employers. A National Pension Savings Scheme (NPSS) would be created to which all employees would belong unless they were already in a good employer's or other pension scheme or unless they expressly opted out. A percentage of their pay (4 per cent) over a threshold would be taken off through the Pay As You Earn tax system or some parallel mechanism. Employers would have to contribute the equivalent of 3 per cent and tax credits would add another 1 per cent, doubling the employee's contribution. US evidence suggested few would opt out of such a scheme.

- These sums would then be available for investment in a range of approved schemes. The NPSS would transfer a sum regularly to the pension scheme of choice. The low administration costs (the Commission recommended 0.3 per cent) would significantly increase the value of the private pension. Their value would be 30 per cent higher than the low-cost stakeholder pensions and greater still compared to other schemes. The selling side of the industry complained that this was too low a figure. It began to lobby and suggest that voters would not want their money handled by a 'government quango', the real point being that they stood to lose a lot of money in handling charges! It offered to set up its own scheme – with higher charges.

In May 2006 the government responded to these proposals (Cm. 6841, 2006). In the words of Lord Turner, it 'accepted 90–95 per cent' of his recommendations. More important,

> The basic architecture of the package contained in the government's pensions white paper appeared last night to have won widespread support across political parties, on both sides of business and industry and within the pensions movement. (*Financial Times*, 26 May 2006: 1)

If anything like that consensus is sustained through to final legislation and beyond it will be one of the major social policy achievements of the post-1997 period, despite the government's early pension mistakes.

There were differences from the Turner model hammered out in the end, the *Financial Times* tells us (26 May 2006: 4), after long one-to-one discussions between Blair and Brown.

- The basic state pension would rise in line with average earnings from 2012, with a Treasury caveat – 'subject to affordability . . . but in any event by the end of the next Parliament' (Cm. 6841, 2006: para. 37). Taken together with changes to the pension credit and the second pension, this would reduce the eventual dependence on means testing from a potential of three-quarters of all pensioners to about a third by 2050.
- The full state pension age would rise to 66 in 2006, to 67 in 2036 and 68 in 2046, slightly faster than the Commission suggested.
- The idea of moving gradually to a citizen's pension based on residence did not survive but the contribution rules were to be changed to be far more favourable to those with caring responsibilities. People would qualify for the state pension after thirty years' contributions. There would be a new weekly credit for those caring for children and a contributory credit for those caring for severely disabled people. This went a long way to achieving the same results.
- There would be transition arrangements helping employers adjust to their new matching contribution requirements.

- The arrangements for handling the National Pension Savings Scheme and choosing between private schemes would involve more discussions with the industry.

Housing and Urban Policy

As the careful reader may have already noted we have come a long way in the story of the Blair government without mentioning housing policy. It had been Bevan's great dream and Macmillan's great achievement. It had dominated the early years of Harold Wilson's government. Ending rent control in the 1950s had been a major political dispute. Mrs Thatcher's most popular policy had been the sale of council houses. But building more houses was no longer a focus of political heat, except for those in green belts and the south-east, who objected to new building. The potential for unrest and racial tensions which tended to flair up in large public housing concentrations were a worry. But that had to do with law and order in people's minds, not housing policy. Some commentators asked 'does housing policy have a future?' (Bramley, 1997; Malpass, 1999; Kleinman, 1999). One of the most important measures begun by Clarke and finished off by Brown was the ending of tax relief for owner occupiers. This reduced a large subsidy to the middle class and pushed up house prices. Its abolition was a major advance. Housing benefit, that complex and often poorly administered system of subsidized rents of poor households, was simplified a little but remained largely intact. For the rest housing became part of wider policy for poor communities and the wider debate about what future we wanted for our cities.

Neighbourhood renewal

The Social Exclusion Unit (see below) developed a 'National Strategy for Neighbourhood Renewal'. It did so after lengthy visits and consultation with residents and local staff and negotiations across government. It resulted in the creation of the Neighbourhood Renewal Unit within the Office of the Deputy Prime Minister, which oversaw the dispersion of a Neighbourhood Renewal Fund. This gave funds to local schemes in eighty-eight of England's most deprived areas.

The New Deal for Communities scheme focused on whole areas and attempted to 'put the residents in the driving seat' of changes to the physical and social structures of the area.

The Welsh Assembly began with 'People in Communities' and subsumed that into 'Communities First' in 2001. It tries to pull together varied streams of funding for poor areas. In Scotland Social Inclusion Partnerships focused more directly on problems of poor housing, ill health and low educational achievement. There were other schemes to give communities more say and integrate services better.

Urban policy

Lord Rogers, a well-known architect of the day, was appointed to chair the Urban Task Force (1999). It recommendations included:

- Planning measures to ensure the government met its target that 60 per cent of all new dwellings be built within existing cities on 'brownfield sites' – old, abandoned or poorly used land.
- Building new houses does not attract VAT but refurbishing old ones does. That incentive should go. VAT should be charged on all house-building activity.
- More resources should be devoted to regenerating poor areas in terms of not just housing but the whole environment.
- Developing more mixed social and private housing schemes and giving tenants more choice of dwelling.
- A range of planning recommendations for improving the design of streets, spaces and buildings to support the local community; increasing density to moderate levels; more frequent buses and general improvements to public transport.

The important recommendation on equalizing VAT was not implemented nor was major additional support given for urban regeneration through public funds. Much else was done. The Urban Policy Unit began work in 2001 to follow up the Task Force's recommendations. In 2003 the government set out its recommendations on how to meet the growing housing pressures and protect the countryside (ODPM, 2003). Many felt this was giving in too easily to the pressures for development in the south-east but that was where many of the UK's new jobs were being generated.

Impact

Colleagues who have studied the impact of these varied schemes on a sample of local areas saw little change in the physical character of the housing stock, except the demolition of some of the worst buildings. However, the efforts to improve the local environment, transport and social facilities did seem to be having a positive effect on tenant confidence and sense of wellbeing, especially the longer-term plans. Many northern cities in particular were making a strong comeback. The general economic climate was making a difference but so was long-term investment in the areas. The most effective measures were those which made people want to stay and others to join poorer local communities (Paskell and Power, 2005; Lupton, 2003; Lupton and Power, 2005).

The Task Force itself, reassembling in 2005, saw progress, too, but also too little emphasis on environmental priorities and design quality. It wanted to push the target for building on brownfield sites up to 75 per cent (Rogers, 2005).

New build again

Net inward migration, more people coming into the country than leaving it, rose in 2005–6 to levels not seen since the 1960s. The resulting stresses, especially in London and the south-east, were partly blamed for the showing of the far right in local elections and ministers began to turn their attention back to the supply of social housing.

Inequality: Turning the Tide?

Social exclusion

The 1997 government came to power against a background of worry about growing divisions in society and a period of growing inequality. One of the first steps Blair took was to set up a cross-departmental unit, the Social Exclusion Unit, that reported directly to him and the Cabinet on social exclusion. This group had a close likeness to the Central Policy Review Staff that Heath had created. However, this time the focus was on extreme social deprivation. 'Social exclusion' was originally a French term used to mean exclusion from the normal workings of their social security system. Its meaning had widened to cover those excluded from the normal activities of society by virtue of poverty, disability, prejudice, area or other isolation.

The Unit was headed by a young woman, an ex-Treasury civil servant, and staffed by a mix of young high-fliers and some drawn from outside government. The working parties it set up crossed departments and included those from local government, voluntary agencies and, unusually, those affected, tenants in poor areas, for example. It produced a series of very good early reports on poor neighbourhoods, school exclusions and truancy, on family disruption and young people, for example (Cm. 4045, 1998; Cm. 4342, 1999; Cm. 4405, 1999). Later, in 2002, it was subsumed into the Office of the Deputy Prime Minister. After a Cabinet reshuffle in May 2006, Hilary Armstrong was made Minister for the Cabinet Office and Social Exclusion. She was meant to revive the emphasis on tackling social exclusion and to chair a new Social Exclusion Cabinet Committee. That was to be supported by staff from the now disbanded Unit and from the Prime Minister's Strategy Unit. Especially in its early days, the Social Exclusion Unit had been a force for good, encouraging departments out of their narrow boxes and putting the problems faced by the most deprived on politicians' desks in a way that normal departmental interests and briefs rarely do. By the same token it never had big departmental clout. Losing the Prime Minister's early special interest made its work more difficult. This small story is a testament to how difficult it is to impose a cross-departmental strategy in government.

Asylum and ethnic factionalism

The Attlee administration never had to worry about the impact of big world movements of population driven by war, disorder and labour mobility encouraged by an enlarged European Union. Numbers of new migrants grew steadily especially after 1997. The issue grew, too, in political salience. At the 2005 election it was a major topic pressed by the Conservative Party and it struck home on the doorstep. Though in many places newcomers had grown well into local communities, in many others they had not and local politicians had not given sufficient attention to growing separation in living circumstances and in the schooling of different ethnic groups (Amin, 2002; Burgess et al., 2005; Phillips, 2005; Burchardt, 2005). This was going to be one of the key challenges of the new century. Two American authors (Alesina and Glaeser, 2004) argued that poor relief and social policy institutions are less likely to develop when the ethnic composition of the population is diverse, more likely if it is cohesive and similar. If the poor are seen as 'others' and the society fractured ethnically and religiously, poverty relief is marginalized. As Europe becomes more ethnically and religiously diverse welfare states will lose support. This thesis is contested (Taylor-Gooby, 2005). The UK has not been without significant population influxes. Its past strong labour movement and value system reinforced by its established universal institutions may be powerful enough to survive such changes. Recent evidence suggests that British people are willing to see newcomers benefit from social services so long as they stay, work and pay their way (Sefton, 2005).

Homosexuality and same-sex partnerships

The Labour government in its first term did take a number of measures to change the law relating to homosexuals.

- The previous government had required local authorities not to 'promote homosexuality'. Section 28 of the Local Government Act 1988 had caused considerable confusion about what teachers could say in class about the subject. If they were even-handed and did not denounce homosexual behaviour were they 'promoting it'? The proposal to repeal that section provoked an angry response from some bishops and social conservatives. The Lords rejected it.
- In April 1999 the Lords threw out proposals to equalize the age of consent to sexual intercourse between men to that which applied to that between men and women – the age of 16. Both measures were subsequently passed.
- In November 1999 the government announced a new code of conduct covering sexual activity for homosexual and heterosexual personnel in the armed forces.
- Homosexual partners have been discriminated against in public housing. In October 1999 the Law Lords ruled that a man who had been living with his partner was part of his partner's family (*Fitzpatrick* v. *Stirling Housing Association*).
- Under the 2004 Civil Partnership Act those in same-sex relations could register as partners from December 2005 and gain the same rights and responsibilities as married couples. This followed long campaigns by the gay and lesbian communities. It followed the pattern of similar legislation in Denmark as early as 1989, Norway in 1993, Sweden in 1994, the Netherlands in 2001, Belgium in 2003 and Spain in 2005. With that one exception such changes in Europe have been confined to the northern less Catholic welfare states. Many in these countries, too, consider this an attack on traditional marriage and the privileges and duties that go with it. Registration is not formally 'marriage' as in some other countries but the effect is the same.

Poverty and income distribution

At bottom any Labour government is likely to be judged on what it has done about poverty and the spread of incomes, especially so for this government which came to power following such a sharp widening of inequality. Unfortunately the story is not a simple one to tell. (For a simpler account see Glennerster et al., 2004: 92–160. For a longer-term and deeper analysis see Hills, 2004.)

- Overall inequality at least stopped growing on most measures and it reduced on others.
- Numbers of families living under the poverty line fell, measured in both relative and absolute terms for the elderly and for children, if not in relative terms for those in work with no children.
- It fell by considerably more if we take 1996 policies as our comparator. In other words things would have got worse without the policies pursued after 1997.
- Was British society markedly less unequal in 2006 than in 1997? No.

Tony Blair used the occasion of his being asked to give the Beveridge Memorial Lecture in 1999 to announce a goal that surprised his audience. The government would aim to end child poverty in a generation.

> Our historic aim . . . is to end child poverty and it will take a generation. It is a twenty year mission but I believe it can be done. (Blair, 1999)

That long-term goal was translated into a shorter-term one – reducing child poverty by a quarter by 2005. The original goal was measured in terms of the then widely accepted measure of poverty – 60 per cent of average earnings. It was later modified to a more complex measure, also taking some account of improvements in absolute standards enjoyed, or suffered, by the poor and a measure that included gauging material deprivation by lack of particular items (DWP, 2003). (For a discussion of various measurement approaches see Hills, 2004: 39–47; and Lister, 2004 for thinking about what we mean by poverty.) The government did not quite meet its ambitious target of reducing poverty, on the 60 per cent of the median definition, by 25 per cent over the period 1998/9 to 2004/5. It reduced it by 22.5 per cent.

However, colleagues who modelled the impact of the post-1997 policies compared to what would have been the case if prior policies had

Table 10.1 Impact of policy on poverty levels, 1997 to 2005

	Relative poverty rates (below 60% of median income)		% change
	1997 policies (price indexed)	2004/5 policies	
Children	27	15	−44
Pensioners	27	19	−30
Working adults without children	13	13	0
All	20	14	−30

Source: Sefton and Sutherland, 2005

simply been rolled forward suggested that by 2005 child poverty had been reduced by over 40 per cent and elderly poverty by a third (Sefton and Sutherland, 2005). But those without children and in work had not been affected significantly. The impact of the minimum wage had been offset by rises in the average wage. That did not mean that the absolute standard of living of the poor remained the same. The number of children in poverty measured by 1997 living standards halved.

The impact of social policy on income inequality over time

This question was first studied seriously by a PhD student of Nicolas Kaldor at the LSE during the Second World War. Like his supervisor he was a Hungarian refugee from Hitler. Colin Clark (1938) had raised the question in the 1930s and this student decided to follow it up. His name was Tibor Barna. His PhD essentially pioneered the way we think about the subject today. Although he did not have the survey material we do, he pieced together material from the Inland Revenue returns for the higher income groups and administrative data about who got what kind of benefits and services (Barna, 1945). The subject was returned to by an American student from Yale (Cartter, 1955), by Alan Peacock (1954) and then by Nicholson in the Central Statistical Office in the late 1950s

(Central Statistical Office, 1962). He used the then Family Expenditure Survey we have discussed before (p. 117) to attribute the value of benefits in cash and kind, like free schooling, to families with different incomes and calculated the taxes they paid including those on goods in the shops. This is still done annually by the Office of National Statistics.

I have reworked Barna and Cartter's raw data to put them on the same basis as the modern surveys. For the technical detail see Glennerster, 2006. This enables us to see how far the spread of incomes earned in the market-place has changed since 1937 and how much post-war social policy, taxes and benefits in cash and kind have modified that original inequality.

To do this we have to choose how to measure inequality and there are many ways in which this can be done. The most used is a measure invented early in the last century by an Italian economist, Gini. It goes by the name Gini coefficient and it takes perfect equality as 0 and a situation where one person had all of society's income as 100 or 1.0. Barna and later followers measured inequality in incomes when they came into a household's collective pocket, ignoring, as we still wrongly do, transfers within the family. That aside, he measured how unequal household income was after families had received state benefits, then after income taxes were taken off, then after indirect taxes were paid, like our VAT, and then assigned the value of services like free education which the family would otherwise have had to buy. The final measure of inequality was taken after all the intervention of the state, excluding the impact of the police or roads in which all are assumed to benefit, clearly questionable but immeasurable. Today we call this households' 'final income'. We now take account of family size to produce 'equivalized' household income. I did the same with the early data and used the Gini, which the early authors did not.

The first row of Table 10.2 shows us that in 1937 income inequality in original incomes was reduced by four points as a result of the range of state benefits then available. It was reduced by a further four points by income tax. Indirect taxes did not affect inequality and the services in kind like education and health insurance reduced it only by a further 1 per cent. Overall the effect of the Welfare State and tax regimes of pre-war years was to reduce inequality by nine points.

What we see for 1949 is that original incomes had been massively equalized. There was a fully employed economy, labour shortages and a powerful trade union movement able to push up manual workers' wages. But the decisive difference was in the labour market and original incomes. Why was the impact of the new Welfare State not greater? The answer is that which Abel-Smith (1958) gave and we quoted earlier in this volume. The

Table 10.2 Inequality before and after taxes and benefits, 1937 to 2003/4

	Gini coefficient expressed as a percentage						
	Original income	Gross income after benefits	Disposable income after direct taxes	Disposable income after direct and indirect taxes	Final income	Reduction of inequality	
						absolute	%
1937	37	33	29	29	28	9	24
1949	26	21	16	16	14	12	46
1977	43	30	27	29	23	20	47
1996/7	53	33	34	38	31	22	41
2003/4	52	37	34	38	31	21	40

Note: The ONS do not think it is appropriate to equivalize the final income measure because this contains notional income from benefits in kind. The equivalence scales used in the original articles are based on household spending and do not therefore apply to such items as notional income for education. They are correct but it makes little difference in practice.

Source: Author's calculations and personal communications with Office of National Statistics (ONS)

way the Attlee government chose to fund many of those changes was very regressive – flat rate, poll tax-like contributions, and high indirect taxes on smoking and drink. The very high marginal rates of income tax hit few people.

By 1977 the economy was already generating a much more diverse level of original incomes. The maturing of the benefits system was doing more to raise incomes of the larger elderly population. Then came the big increase in inequality generated in the Thatcher years. Social policy mitigated some of that growing inequality but final incomes became more unequal too.

In the late 1990s that trend to higher inequality in original earnings faded. The Gini coefficient used in Table 10.2 has its deficiencies as a measure. It gives a quite high weight to high incomes at the very top. If we take another widely used measure – the ratio of the incomes of the top 10 per cent to the bottom 10 per cent – we find a slightly more equalizing outcome. In 1990, at its peak, the richest 10 per cent were receiving nearly five times that of the poorest 10 per cent after taxes and cash benefits. In 2003/4 the figure had fallen to just over four to one (Jones, 2005).

So Blair's government, with its emphasis on getting people into work, and economic events that were in train before it arrived, may have checked the tide of inequality in incomes but it did not turn the tide. Perhaps no government could in an open economy and with an electorate not keen to see very big increases in taxation. At least the poor shared more or less equally in the rising prosperity that the UK enjoyed for ten years. That had not been true for the previous twenty.

Did the cash and benefit system do more to reduce that inequality after 1997? It did not, despite the impact it had on reducing poverty of children and old people. How is that possible? The reason lies in the shift in spending priorities and the fall in unemployment. The 1980s and early 1990s were periods when many people fell into the safety net. Saving them falling further is costly and redistributive. That was less necessary by 2005. Most of the extra taxes raised had gone into health and education, which are spread much more evenly across the population.

Sixty Years On

The share of the nation's resources being devoted to social policy as we have defined it in this volume is three times what it was in 1945 (see Figure 10.1). In terms of absolute real spending social policy is seven times the scale it was in 1950 (see Figure 10.3).

If those absolute numbers seem rather dry and meaningless, some personal memories may help. I have clear recollections of my state elementary school. For some reason I have a sharp memory of the ritual after the register was called. The teacher would write up on the board in a little square at the top the number of pupils in the class that day. Those numbers varied between forty-seven and fifty if I am not mistaken. We wrote in chalk on slates. At the end of the lesson we would all shake out little woollen knitted cloths with which we had erased our work. The air filled with chalk dust and in my asthmatic state I dreaded the end of every lesson. Having failed the eleven-plus I attended the same senior elementary school my father had and spent many hours doing woodwork and metalwork. In the autumn we lined up to enter lorries to go and pick potatoes in the nearby fields. As I watched my children and grandchildren pass through modern comprehensive schools I can only marvel at the improved standard of life and education they have enjoyed.

Figure 10.3 The size of the Welfare State, 1951/2 and 2004/5

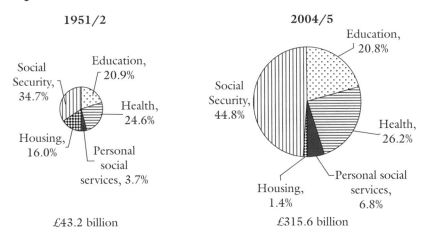

1951/2

Social Security, 34.7%

Education, 20.9%

Health, 24.6%

Housing, 16.0%

Personal social services, 3.7%

£43.2 billion

2004/5

Education, 20.8%

Social Security, 44.8%

Health, 26.2%

Personal social services, 6.8%

Housing, 1.4%

£315.6 billion

The sums are in billions of pounds expressed in 2004/5 prices and on a UK basis

Source: Glennerster, 2000; HM Treasury, 2005

Sixty years on from 1945 social policy has become even more central to politics than it was then. I once undertook a content analysis of newspapers of that time. By far the most column inches were devoted to imperial and international issues like the coming independence of India, the communist threat to Eastern Europe and the shortages at home. Yet the Welfare State that emerged in those years has captured the support of the British people in its deep principles if not always in its day-to-day administration. The support for basic state-secured standards in health, education and old age remains very strong, as does support for redistributive tax and benefit regimes (Sefton, 2005). The Welfare State emerged from the Thatcher and Blair years re-engineered and, its new architects hoped, better suited to the demands of a consumerist population. But the need for some state role in health and pensions, in education and the care of the elderly, is not now in serious dispute. Indeed, with a fast-ageing population and major failures in the private pensions market, not to speak of the unabating demand for better health care, the state's role looks more likely to grow than to decline. In what way it does so will be as contentious as it was in 1945.

Questions to Answer

1 What were the achievements and failures of Blair's term
  in office as far as social policy is concerned?
2 What big shifts in ideas about social policy, its goals and
  its institutions, have there been since 1945?
3 How robust a future does social policy have?

Appendix: Social Policy Ministries and Ministers 1940–2006

Ministry	Prime Minister	Chancellor of Exchequer	Home Secretary (1)	Minister of Health (2)	Minister of Education (3)	Minister of Housing and Local Government (4)	Minister of Social Security (5)
May 1940–May 1945 Coalition govt	Churchill	Wood Anderson	Anderson Morrison	MacDonald Brown Willink	Ramsbotham Butler	—	Womersley (6) Jowitt (7)
May 1945–July 1945 Caretaker govt	Churchill	Anderson	Somervell	Willink	Law	—	Womersley (6) Hore-Belisha (7)
July 1945–Oct. 1951 Labour govt	Attlee	Dalton Cripps Gaitskell	Chuter Ede	Bevan Marquand	Wilkinson Tomlinson	—	Griffiths Summerskill
Oct. 1951– April 1955 Conservative govt	Churchill	Butler	Maxwell Fyfe Lloyd George	Crookshank Macleod	Horsburgh Eccles	Macmillan Sandys	Peake
April 1955– Jan. 1957 Conservative govt	Eden	Butler Macmillan	Lloyd George	Macleod Turton	Eccles	Sandys	Peake Boyd-Carpenter
Jan. 1957– Oct. 1963 Conservative govt	Macmillan	Thorneycroft Amory Lloyd Maudling	Butler Brooke	Vosper Walker-Smith Powell	Hailsham Lloyd Eccles Boyle	Brooke Hill Joseph	Boyd-Carpenter MacPherson
Oct. 1963– Oct. 1964 Conservative govt	Douglas-Home	Maudling	Brook	Barber	Boyle	Joseph	Wood

Period / Government				Dept of Health and Social Security	Dept. of Education and Science (9)	Department of the Environment (9)	
Oct. 1964–June 1970 Labour govt	Wilson	Callaghan Jenkins	Soskice Jenkins Callaghan	Robinson Crossman (8)	Stewart Crosland Walker Short	Crossman Greenwood	Herbison Hart Crossman (8)
June 1970–Feb. 1974 Conservative govt	Heath	Barber	Maudling	Joseph	Thatcher	Walker	
Feb. 1974–Mar. 1976 Labour govt	Wilson	Healey	Jenkins	Castle	Prentice Mulley	Crosland	
Mar. 1976–July 1979 Labour govt	Callaghan	Healey	Jenkins Rees	Ennals	Mulley Williams	Shore	
July 1979 Conservative govt	Thatcher	Howe	Whitelaw	Jenkin	Carlisle	Heseltine	
Oct. 1989	Thatcher	Howe	Whitelaw	Fowler	Joseph	Heseltine	
July 1983	Thatcher	Lawson	Brittan	Fowler	Joseph	Jenkin	
Jan. 1984	Thatcher	Lawson	Brittan	Clarke	Joseph	Jenkin	
March 1986	Thatcher	Lawson	Hurd	Clarke	Joseph	Baker	
Oct. 1986	Thatcher	Lawson	Hurd	Clarke	Baker	Ridley	
July 1987	Thatcher	Lawson	Hurd	Moore	Baker	Ridley	
July 1989	Thatcher	Lawson	Hurd	Dept. of Health — Clarke / Dept. of Social Security — Newton	MacGregor	C. Patten	

Ministry	Prime Minister	Chancellor of Exchequer	Home Secretary	Secretary of State for Health	Secretary of State for Education (and Employment) [10]	Secretary of State for the Environment	Secretary of State for Social Security
Feb. 1990	Thatcher	Major	Waddington	Clarke	MacGregor	C. Patten	Newton
Nov. 1990	Major	Lamont	Baker	Waldegrave	Clarke	Heseltine	Newton
May 1992	Major	Lamont	Clarke	Bottomley	J. Patten	Howard	Lilley
August 1993	Major	Clarke	Howard	Bottomley	Dept. for Education J. Patten	Gummer	Lilley
July 1994	Major	Clarke	Howard	Bottomley	Shepherd	Gummer	Lilley
July 1995	Major	Clarke	Howard	Dorrell	Shepherd	Gummer	Lilley
May 1997 Labour govt	Blair	Brown	Straw	Dobson	Blunkett	Prescott	Harman
July 1998	Blair	Brown	Straw	Dobson	Blunkett	Prescott	Darling
Oct. 1999	Blair	Brown	Straw	Milburn	Blunkett	Prescott	Darling

Ministry	Prime Minister		Chancellor of Exchequer	Home Secretary	Secretary of State for Health	Secretary of State for Education and Skills	Secretary of State for the Environment, Food and Rural Affairs	Secretary of State for Work and Pensions
May 2001	Blair		Brown	Blunkett	Milburn	Morris	Beckett	Darling
May 2002	Blair	Office of Deputy Prime Minister takes over local government, regions, sustainable communities and social exclusion Prescott	Brown	Blunkett	Milburn	Morris	Beckett	Darling
Oct. 2002	Blair	Prescott	Brown	Blunkett	Milburn	Clarke	Beckett	Smith
June 2003	Blair	Prescott	Brown	Blunkett	Reid	Clarke	Beckett	Smith
Sept. 2004	Blair	Prescott	Brown	Clarke	Reid	Kelly	Beckett	Johnson
May 2005	Blair	Prescott	Brown	Clarke	Hewitt	Kelly	Beckett	Blunkett
Nov. 2005	Blair	Prescott	Brown	Clarke	Hewitt	Kelly	Beckett	Hutton

Ministry	Prime Minister	Chancellor of Exchequer	Home Secretary	Secretary of State for Health	Secretary of State for Education and Skills	Secretary of State for the Environment	Secretary of State for Community and Local Government	Secretary of State for Work and Pensions
May 2006	Blair	Brown	Reid	Hewitt	Johnson	Miliband	Kelly	Hutton

Notes:

1 Lost responsibility for children's services in 1971 to the Department of Health and Social Security under the Seebohm reorganization.
2 Amalgamated with Social Security in 1968 to form Department of Health and Social Security.
3 Became Department of Education and Science, 1964.
4 Functions performed by Health and a separate Ministry of Town Planning until 1951; combined with Ministry of Transport and other functions to form Department of the Environment, 1971.
5 Separate Pensions and Social Insurance until 1945; then Ministry of Pensions and National Insurance until 1966; then Ministry of Social Security; then amalgamated with Health to form Department of Health and Social Security, 1968; split again in 1989.
6 Pensions.
7 Insurance.
8 Secretary of State for Social Services; combined Health and Social Security, 1968.
9 Departments are of higher status than ministries, having wider responsibilities ('super-ministries'). The politician in charge is a Secretary of State.
10 Employment was added to the Department of Education's responsibility in Gillian Shepherd's time.

Bibliography

Note: sequences of references from the same body (e.g. government departments) are given in chronological order. Where government departments have changed their name (e.g. Department of Education and Science is now Department for Education and Skills; Department of Health and Social Security is now Department for Work and Pensions), all references under the new name fall in the place they would have taken had the name not changed, thus maintaining chronological ordering regardless of strict alphabetical ordering.

Abel-Smith, B. (1958) 'Whose Welfare State?', in N. Mackenzie (ed.) *Conviction*, London: MacGibbon and Kee

Abel-Smith, B. (1964) *The Hospitals 1800 to 1948*, London: Heinemann

Abel-Smith, B. and Townsend, P. (1955) *New Pensions for Old*, London: Fabian Society

Abel-Smith, B. and Townsend, P. (1965) *The Poor and the Poorest*, London: Bell and Sons

Acheson Report (1998) *Independent Inquiry into Inequalities in Health*, London: The Stationery Office

Addison, P. (1975) *The Road to 1945: British Politics and the Second World War*, London: Cape

Adonis, A. and Hames, T. (1994) *A Conservative Revolution? The Thatcher–Reagan Decade in Perspective*, Manchester: Manchester University Press

Agulnik, P. (1999a) *The Proposed State Second Pension and National Insurance*, CASEpaper 24, London: CASE, London School of Economics

Alesina, A. and Glaeser, E. L. (2004) *Fighting Poverty in the US and Europe: A World of Difference*, Oxford: Oxford University Press

Alvarez-Rosete, A., Bevan, G., Mays, N. and Dixon, J. (2005) 'Effect of diverging policy across the NHS' *British Medical Journal*, vol. 331, 22 October, pp. 946–50

Amin, A. (2002) 'Ethnicity and the multi cultural city: living with diversity' *Environment and Planning* A, vol. 34, pp. 959–80

Ashford, D. E. (1986) *The Emergence of the Welfare States*, Oxford: Blackwell

Atkinson, A. B. (1972) 'Inequality and social security', in P. Townsend and N. Bosanquet (eds) *Labour and Inequality*, London: Fabian Society

Audit Commission (1986) *Making a Reality of Community Care*, London: HMSO

Audit Commission (2005) *Early Lessons from Payment by Results*, London: Audit Commission

Bacon, R. and Eltis, W. (1976) *Britain's Economic Problem: Too Few Producers*, London: Macmillan

Baldwin, P. (1990) *The Politics of Social Solidarity*, Cambridge: Cambridge University Press

Baldwin, P. (1994) 'Beveridge in the *Longue Durée*', in J. Hills, J. Ditch and H. Glennerster (eds) *Beveridge and Social Security: an International Retrospective*, Oxford: Clarendon Press

Banks, J., Disney, R., Duncan, A. and Van Reenen, J. (2005) 'The internationalisation of public welfare policy', *Economic Journal*, vol. 115, March, pp. C62–C81

Banks, T. (1979) 'Programme budgeting in the DHSS', in T. Booth (ed.) *Planning for Welfare*, Oxford: Blackwell

Banting, K. G. (1979) *Poverty, Politics and Policy: Britain in the 1960s*, London: Macmillan

Barker, R. (1972) *Education and Politics 1900–1951: a Study of the Labour Party*, Oxford: Oxford University Press

Barna, T. (1945) *Redistribution of Incomes through Public Finance in 1937*, Oxford: Oxford University Press

Barnes, J. and Barr, N. (1988) *Strategies for Higher Education: the Alternative White Paper*, David Hume Paper No. 10, Aberdeen: Aberdeen University Press

Barnett, C. (1986) *The Audit of War: the Illusion and Reality of Britain as a Great Nation*, London: Macmillan

Barnett, C. (1995) *The Last Victory: British Dreams, British Realities 1945–50*, London: Macmillan

Barnett, M. J. (1969) *The Politics of Legislation*, London: Weidenfeld and Nicolson

Barr, N. (2004) *The Economics of the Welfare State*, London: Weidenfeld

Barr, N. and Coulter, F. (1990) 'Social Security: solution or a problem?', in J. Hills (ed.) *The State of Welfare: the Welfare State in Britain since 1974*, Oxford: Clarendon Press

Barr, N. and Crawford, I. (2005) *Financing Higher Education: Answers from the UK*, London: Routledge

Beck, U. (1997) *The Risk Society: Towards a New Modernity*, London: Sage

Beck, U. and Beck-Gernsheim, E. (1995) *The Normal Chaos of Love*, Cambridge: Polity Press

Beland, D. (2005) 'Ideas and social policy: an institutionalist perspective', *Social Policy and Administration*, vol. 39, no. 1, pp. 1–18

Bell, D. and Bowes, A. (2006) *Financial Care Models in Scotland and the UK*, York: Joseph Rowntree Foundation

Berthoud, R. Lakey, J. and McKay, S. (1993) *The Economic Problems of Disabled People*, London: Policy Studies Institute

Beveridge, W. H. (1924) *Insurance for All and Everything*, London: Daily News

Beveridge Report (1942) *Social Insurance and Allied Services*, Cmd 6404, London: HMSO

Beveridge, W. H. (1944) *Full Employment in a Free Society*, London: Allen and Unwin

Beveridge, W. H. (1953) *Power and Influence*, London: Hodder and Stoughton

Bindman, G. and Carrier, J. (1983) 'A multi-racial society', in H. Glennerster (ed.) *The Future of the Welfare State: Remaking Social Policy*, London: Heinemann

Blackaby, F. (ed.) (1979) *De-Industrialisation*, London: Heinemann and the National Institute of Economic and Social Research

Blair, T. (1999) 'Beveridge revisited: a welfare state for the 21st century', in R. Walker (ed.) *Ending Child Poverty: Popular welfare in the 21st century*, Bristol: The Policy Press

Blaug, M. (1984) 'Education vouchers: it all depends on what you mean', in J. Le Grand and R. Robinson (eds) *Privatisation and the Welfare State*, London: Allen and Unwin

Blundell, R., Reed, H., Van Reenen, J. and Shepherd, A. (2003) 'The impact of the New Deal for young People on the labour market: a four year assessment', in R. Dickens, P. Gregg and J. Wadsworth (eds) *The Labour Market under New Labour: The State of Working Britain*, London: Palgrave

Bramley, G. (1997) 'Housing Policy: a case of terminal decline', *Policy and Politics*, vol. 25, no. 4, pp. 382–407

Bridgen, P. and Lowe, R. (1998) *Welfare Policy under the Conservatives 1951–64*, Kew: Public Record Office

Brooke, S. (1996) 'Reassessing a Labour Revisionist', *Twentieth Century British History*, vol. 7, no. 1, pp. 27–37

Brook-Lapping Productions (1999) *Can't Pay Won't Pay*, Channel Four, three-programme documentary, October 1999

Bruegel, I. (1983) 'Women's employment, legislation and the labour market', in J. Lewis (ed.) *Women's Welfare: Women's Rights*, Beckenham: Croom Helm

Burchardt, T. (2000) *Enduring Economic Exclusion: Disabled People, Income and Work*, York: Joseph Rowntree Foundation

Burchardt, T. (2005) 'Selective inclusion: asylum seekers and other marginalised groups', in J. Hills and K. Stewart (eds) *A More Equal Society: New Labour, Poverty, Inequality and Exclusion*, Bristol: Policy Press

Burgess, S., Wilson, D. and Lupton, R. (2005) *Parallel Lives? Ethnic Segregation in Schools and Neighbourhoods*, CASEpaper 101, London: CASE, London School of Economics

Burgess, T. (1986) 'Cambridgeshire's financial management initiative for schools', *Public Money*, 6(1), pp. 21–4

Burghes, L. (1994) *Lone Parenthood and Family Disruption*, Occasional Paper no. 18, London: Family Policy Studies Centre

Burk, K. and Cairncross, A. (1992) *'Goodbye, Great Britain'*, *the 1976 IMF Crisis*, New York: Yale University Press

Butler, D., Adonis, A. and Travers, T. (1994) *Failure in British Government: the Politics of the Poll Tax*, Oxford: Oxford University Press

Butler, J. (1992) *Patients, Policies and Politics*, Milton Keynes: Open University Press

Butler, J. (1994) 'Origins and early development', in R. Robinson and J. Le Grand (eds) *Evaluating the NHS Reforms*, London: King's Fund Institute

Butler, R. A. (1971) *The Art of the Possible*, London: Hamish Hamilton

Butler-Sloss, Lord Justice (1988) *Report of the Inquiry into Child Abuse in Cleveland 1987*, Department of Health and Social Security, Cm. 412, London: HMSO

Cairncross, A. (1992) *The British Economy since 1945*, Oxford: Blackwell

Cairncross, A. (1995) *The British Economy since 1945: Economic Policy and Performance 1945–95*, Oxford: Blackwell

Campbell, N. (1999) *The Decline of Employment among Older People in Britain*, CASEpaper 19, London: CASE, London School of Economics

Carling, A., Duncan, S. and Edwards, R. (eds) (2002) *Analysing Families: Morality and Rationality in Policy and Practice*, London: Routledge

Carrier, J. and Kendall, I. (1998) *Health and the National Health Service*, London: Athlone Press

Cartter, A. M. (1955) *The Redistribution of Income in Post War Britain*, New Haven: Yale University Press

Castle, B. (1980) *The Castle Diaries 1974–76*, London: Weidenfeld and Nicholson

Central Statistical Office (CSO) (1962) *Economic Trends*, no. 109, November, pp. 90–117, London: HMSO

Centre for Contemporary Cultural Studies (1981) *Unpopular Education: Schooling and Social Democracy in England since 1944*, London: Hutchinson

Clark, C. (1938) *National Income and Outlay*, London: Macmillan

Cmd 6404 (1942) *Social Insurance and Allied Services* (Beveridge Report), London: HMSO

Cmd 6502 (1944) *A National Health Service*, London: HMSO

Cmd 6527 (1944) *Employment Policy*, London: HMSO

Cmd 6636 (1945) *Report on the Circumstances that Led to the Boarding Out of Denis and Terence O'Neill at Bank Farm, Minsterley and the Steps taken to Supervise their Welfare* (Monckton Enquiry), London: HMSO

Cmd 6922 (1946) *Report on the Care of Children* (Curtis Report), London: HMSO

Cmd 8996 (1953) *Houses: the Next Step*, Ministry of Housing and Local Government, London: HMSO

Cmd 9333 (1954) *Report of the Committee on the Economic and Financial Problems of Old Age* (Phillips Committee), London: HMSO

Cmd 9663 (1956) *Committee of Enquiry into the Cost of the National Health Service* (Guillebaud Committee), London: HMSO

Cmd 9678 (1956) *Royal Commission on Marriage and Divorce*, London: HMSO

Cmd 9703 (1956) *Technical Education*, Ministry of Education, London: HMSO

Cmd 9725 (1956) *The Economic Implications of Full Employment*, London: HMSO

Cmnd 247 (1957) *Report of the Departmental Committee on Homosexual Offences and Prostitution* (Wolfenden Report), London: HMSO

Cmnd 1191 (1960) *Report of the Committee on Children and Young Persons* (Ingleby Committee), London: HMSO

Cmnd 1246 (1960) *Rent Act Enquiry*, London: HMSO

Cmnd 1432 (1961) *Control of Public Expenditure* (Plowden Committee), London: HMSO

Cmnd 1966 (1963) *Prevention of Neglect of Children*, Edinburgh: HMSO

Cmnd 2154 (1963) *Higher Education* (Robbins Report), London: HMSO

Cmnd 2303 (1964) *Children and Young Persons, Scotland*, Edinburgh: HMSO

Cmnd 2838 (1965) *The Housing Programme 1965–70*, London: HMSO

Cmnd 3006 (1966) *A Plan for Polytechnics and other Colleges: Higher Education in the Further Education System*, London: HMSO

Cmnd 3163 (1966) *Help Towards Home Ownership*, London: HMSO

Cmnd 3602 (1968) *Old Houses Into New Homes*, Ministry of Housing and Local Government, London: HMSO

Cmnd 3703 (1968) *Report of the Committee on Local Authority and Allied Personal Social Services* (Seebohm Committee), London: HMSO

Cmnd 4683 (1971) *Better Services for the Mentally Handicapped*, London: HMSO

Cmnd 5174 (1972) *Education: a Framework for Expansion*, Department of Education and Science, London: HMSO

Cmnd 5579 (1974) *Report of the Committee on the Working of the Abortion Act* (Lane Committee), London: HMSO

Cmnd 5629 (1974) *Report of the Committee on One Parent Families* (Finer Report), London: HMSO

Cmnd 5720 (1974) *Educational Disadvantage and the Educational Needs of Immigrants*, Department of Education and Science, London: HMSO

Cmnd 6453 (1976) *Report of the Enquiry into Local Government Finance* (Layfield Committee), London: HMSO

Cmnd 6845 (1977) *Policy for the Inner Cities?*, London: HMSO

Cmnd 6869 (1977) *Education in Schools*, Department of Education and Science, London: HMSO

Cmnd 7746 (1979) *The Government's Expenditure Plans 1980–81*, London: HMSO

Cmnd 8093 (1980) *The Taxation of Husband and Wife*, HM Treasury, London: HMSO

Cmnd 8427 (1981) *Brixton Disorders 10–12 April 1981*, Report of an Enquiry by the Rt. Hon. Lord Scarman OBE, London: HMSO

Cmnd 9184 (1984) *The Next Ten Years: Public Expenditure and Taxation into the 1990s*, London: HMSO

Cmnd 9469 (1985) *Better Schools*, Department of Education and Science, London: HMSO

Cmnd 9517 (1985) *Reform of Social Security*, Department of Health and Social Security, London: HMSO

Cmnd 9691 (1985) *Reform of Social Security: Programme for Action*, Department of Health and Social Security, London: HMSO

Cm. 412 (1988) *Report of the Inquiry into Child Abuse in Cleveland 1987* (Butler-Sloss Report), Department of Health and Social Security, London: HMSO

Cm. 555 (1989) *Working for Patients*, Department of Health, London: HMSO

Cm. 1264 (1990) *Children Come First*, Department of Social Security, London: HMSO

Cm. 1541 (1991) *Higher Education: a New Framework*, London: HMSO

Cm. 2424 (1993) *Looking to the Future: Mediation and the Ground for Divorce – A Consultation Paper*, London: HMSO

Cm. 2799 (1995) *Looking to the Future: Mediation and the Ground for Divorce – The government's proposals*, London: HMSO

Cm. 3805 (1998) *A New Contract for Welfare*, London: The Stationery Office

Cm. 3807 (1997) *The New NHS: Modern, Dependable*, London: The Stationery Office

Cm. 4045 (1998) *Bringing Britain Together: a National Strategy of neighbourhood renewal*, London: The Stationery Office

Cm. 4179 (1998) *Partnership in Pensions*, London: The Stationery Office

Cm. 4192 (1999) *With Respect to Old Age: Long Term Care – Rights and Responsibilities*, London: The Stationery Office

Cm. 4342 (1999) *Teenage Pregnancy*, Social Exclusion Unit, London: The Stationery Office

Cm. 4405 (1999) *Bridging the Gap: New Opportunities for 16–18 year olds not in Education, Employment or Training*, Social Exclusion Unit, London: The Stationery Office

Cm. 5735 (2003) *The Future of Higher Education*, London: The Stationery Office

Cm. 6677 (2005) *Higher Standards, Better Schools For All: More Choice for Parents and Pupils*, London: The Stationery Office

Cm. 6730 (2005) *A New Deal for Welfare: Empowering People to Work*, London: The Stationery Office

Cm. 6841 (2006) *Security in Retirement: Towards a New Pensions System*, London: The Stationery Office

Cm. 6895 (2006) *A Fresh Start: Child Support Redesign – the Government's Response to Sir David Henshaw*, London: The Stationery Office

Cole, G. D. H. (1957) *The Case for Industrial Partnership*, London: Macmillan

Conservative Party (1951) *Britain Strong and Free*, London: Conservative Central Office

Conservative Party (1987) *The Next Moves Forward*, London: Conservative Central Office

Cox, C. B. and Dyson, A. E. (eds) (1969) *Fight for Education: a Black Paper*, London: Critical Quarterly Society

Crosland, C. A. R. (1956) *The Future of Socialism*, London: Jonathan Cape

Crossman, R. H. S. (1952) *The New Fabian Essays*, London: Fabian Society

Crossman, R. H. S. (1975) *The Diaries of a Cabinet Minister, vol. 1: Minister of Housing 1964–66*, London: Hamish Hamilton, Jonathan Cape

Crossman, R. H. S. (1977) *The Diaries of a Cabinet Minister, vol. 3: Secretary of State for Social Services 1968–70*, London: Hamish Hamilton, Jonathan Cape

Crossman, R. H. S. (1981) *The Backbench Richard Crossman*, London: Hamish Hamilton, Jonathan Cape

Curtis Committee (1946) *Report on the Care of Children*, Cmd 6922, London: HMSO

Cutler, T., Williams, K. and Williams, J. (1986) *Keynes, Beveridge and Beyond*, London: Routledge and Kegan Paul

Daunton, M. J. (1996) 'Payment and Participation: welfare state formation in Britain 1900–51', *Past and Present*, no. 150, pp. 167–216

Daunton, M. J. (2002) *Just Taxes: The Politics of Taxation in Britain*, Cambridge: Cambridge University Press

David, M. and Land, H. (1983) 'Sex and social policy', in H. Glennerster (ed.) *The Future of the Welfare State: Remaking Social Policy*, London: Heinemann

Davies, G. and Piachaud, D. (1983) 'Social policy and the economy', in H. Glennerster (ed.) *The Future of the Welfare State: Remaking Social Policy*, London: Heinemann

Davis, G., Cretney, S. and Collins, S. (1994) *Simple Quarrels*, Oxford: Oxford University Press

Davis, J. (2001) 'Rents and race in 1960s London: New Left on Rachmanism', *Twentieth Century British History*, vol. 12, no. 1, pp. 69–92

Deacon, A. (2002) *Perspectives on Welfare: Ideas, Ideologies and Policy Debates*, Buckingham: Open University Press

Deakin, N. (1994) *The Politics of Welfare: Continuities and Change*, London: Harvester

Dearing Committee (1997) *Higher Education in the Learning Society*, London: HMSO

Department of Education and Science (1967) *Children and their Primary Schools* (Plowden Committee), London: HMSO

Department of Education and Science (1968) *First Report of the Public Schools Commission*, London: HMSO

Department of Education and Science (1970) *Second Report of the Public Schools Commission*, London: HMSO

Department of Education and Science (1972) *Education: a Framework for Expansion*, Cmnd 5174, London: HMSO

Department of Education and Science (1974) *Educational Disadvantage and the Educational Needs of Immigrants*, Cmnd 5720, London: HMSO

Department of Education and Science (1977) *Education in Schools*, Cmnd 6069, London: HMSO

Department of Education and Science (1985) *Better Schools*, Cmnd 9469, London: HMSO

Department for Education and Skills (2005a) *National Curriculum Assessments at Key Stage 2 and Key Stage 1 to Key Stage 2 Value Added Measures in England, 203/4* (Final), SFR 22/2005

Department for Education and Skills (2005b) *National Curriculum Assessment of 11 year olds in England 1997–2005 Pupils Achieving Level 4 in Combinations of Tests*, SFR 47/2005

Department of Health (1989a) *An Introduction to the Children Act 1989*, London: HMSO

Department of Health (1989b) *Working for Patients*, Cm. 555, London: HMSO

Department of Health (1998) *Independent Inquiry into Inequalities in Health: Report*, London: The Stationery Office

Department of Health (2000) *The NHS Plan – A Plan for Investment, a Plan for Reform*, London: The Stationery Office

Department of Health (2003) *Report of an Inquiry by Lord Laming*, London: The Stationery Office

Department of Health (2004) *The NHS Improvement Plan: Putting People at the Heart of Public Services*, London: The Stationery Office

Department of Health (2005a) *Tackling Health Inequalities: Status Report on the Programme of Action*, London: Department of Health

Department of Health (2005b) *Independence, Well-being and Choice*, London: Department of Health

Department of Health and Social Security (DHSS) (1970) *The Future Structure of the National Health Service* (2nd Green Paper), London: HMSO

Department of Health and Social Security (DHSS) (1978) *Social Assistance: a Review of the Supplementary Benefits Scheme in Great Britain*, London: HMSO

Department of Health and Social Security (DHSS) (1980) *Inequality in Health: Report of a Research Working Group*, London: Department of Health and Social Security

Department of Health and Social Security (DHSS) (1985a) *Reform of Social Security*, Cmnd 9517, London: HMSO

Department of Health and Social Security (DHSS) (1985b) *Reform of Social Security: Programme for Action*, Cmnd 9691, London: HMSO

Department of Social Security (1990) *Children Come First*, Cm. 1264, London: HMSO

Department of Social Security (1993a) *Households Below Average Income: a Statistical Analysis 1979–1990/91*, London: HMSO

Department of Social Security (1993b) *The Growth of Social Security*, London: HMSO

Department for Work and Pensions (2003) *Measuring Child Poverty*, London: Department for Work and Pensions

Digby, A. (1989) *British Welfare Policy: Workhouse to Welfare*, London: Faber

Dilnot, A. and Webb, S. (1988) 'The 1988 Social Security reforms', *Fiscal Studies*, 9(3), pp. 26–53

Dobash, R. and Dobash, R. (1992) *Women, Violence and Social Change*, London: Routledge

Dobash, R. and Dobash, R. (2000) 'Violence Against Women in the Family', in S. N. Katz, J. Eekelaar and M. Maclean (eds) *Cross Currents: Family Law and Policy in the US and England*, Oxford: Oxford University Press

Donnison, D. V. (1960) *Housing Policy since the Second World War*, Occasional Papers in Social Administration, Welwyn: Codicote Press

Dunleavy, P. (1981) *The Politics of Mass Housing in Britain 1945–75: a Study of Corporate Power, and Professional Influence in the Welfare State*, Oxford: Clarendon Press

Dunleavy, P. (1991) *Democracy, Bureaucracy and Public Choice*, Hemel Hempstead: Harvester

Durbin, E. F. M. (1949) *Problems of Economic Planning*, London: Routledge and Kegan Paul

Durbin, E. (1985) *New Jerusalems: the Labour Party and the Economics of Democratic Socialism*, London: Routledge and Kegan Paul

Eckstein, H. (1958) *The English Health Service*, Cambridge, Mass.: Harvard University Press

Edwards, J. and Batley, R. (1978) *The Politics of Positive Discrimination: an Evaluation of the Urban Programme 1967–77*, London: Tavistock

Egerton, M. and Halsey, A. H. (1993) 'Trends by social class and gender in access to higher education', *Oxford Review of Higher Education*, 19(2)

Ellison, N. (1988) 'The idea of equality in the British Labour Party 1931–64', unpublished PhD thesis, University of London

Ellison, N. (1994) *Egalitarian Thought and Labour Politics: Retreating Visions*, London: Routledge

Evandrou, M. and Falkingham, J. (1998) 'The Personal Social Services', *The State of Welfare: The Economics of Social Spending*, Oxford: Oxford University Press

Evans, M. (1998) 'Social Security: Dismantling the Pyramids?', in H. Glennerster and J. Hills (eds) *The State of Welfare: The Economics of Social Spending*, Oxford: Oxford University Press

Evans, M. and Glennerster, H. (1993) 'Squaring the circle? The inconsistencies and constraints of Beveridge's plan', STICERD Welfare State Programme Discussion Paper WSP/86, London: London School of Economics

Evans, M., Piachaud, D. and Sutherland, H. (1994) 'Designed for the poor – poorer by design? The effects of the 1986 Social Security Act on family incomes', STICERD Welfare State Programme Discussion Paper WSP/105, London: London School of Economics

Faggio, G. and Nickell, S. (2003) 'The rise in inactivity among adult men', in R. Dickens, P. Gregg and J. Wadsworth (eds) *The New Labour Market under New Labour: The State of Working Britain*, London: Palgrave

Feinstein, L. (2000) 'Inequality in the early cognitive development of British children in the 1970 cohort', *Economica*, vol. 70, no. 277, pp. 73–97

Field, F. (1982) *Poverty and Politics: the Inside Story of the Child Poverty Action Group's Campaigns in the 1970s*, London: Heinemann

Field, F. (1995) *Making Welfare Work*, London: Institute for Community Studies

Field, F. (1996) *How to Pay for the Future: Building a Stakeholders' Welfare*, London: Institute for Community Studies

Field, F. and Piachaud, D. (1971) 'The poverty trap', *New Statesman*, 3 December 1971

Finer Committee (1974) *Report of the Committee on One Parent Families*, Cmnd 5629, London: HMSO

Fleming Committee (1944) *The Public Schools and the General Education System*, London: HMSO

Flora, P. and Heidenheimer, A. (eds) (1981) *The Developments of Welfare States in Europe and America*, London and New Brunswick, NJ: Transaction Books

Floud, J. and Halsey, A. H. (1957) 'Intelligence tests, social class, and selection for secondary schools', *British Journal of Sociology*, 8, pp. 33–9

Foot, M. (1975) *Aneurin Bevin 1945–1960*, St Alban's: Paladin

Friedman, M. (1962) *Capitalism and Freedom*, Chicago: University of Chicago Press

Frost, N. and Stein, M. (1990) 'The politics of the Children Act', *Childright*, 68

Galbraith, J. K. (1958) *The Affluent Society*, London: Hamish Hamilton

Gamble, A. and Walton, P. (1976) *Capitalism in Crisis Inflation and the State*, London: Macmillan

Gardiner, K. (1993) 'A survey of income inequality over the last twenty years – How does the UK compare?', STICERD Welfare State Programme Discussion Paper WSP/100, London: London School of Economics

Gibson, J. (1990) *The Politics and Economics of the Poll Tax: Mrs Thatcher's Downfall*, Warley: EMAS

Giddens, A. (1992) *The Transformation of Intimacy: Sexuality, Love and Eroticism in Modern Societies*, Cambridge: Polity Press

Giddens, A. (1998) *The Third Way: The Renewal of Social Democracy*, Cambridge: Polity Press

Gilmour, I. (1992) *Dancing with Dogma: Britain under Thatcherism*, Hemel Hempstead: Simon and Schuster

Gilmour, I. and Garnett, M. (1998) *Whatever happened to the Tories: The Conservatives since 1945*, London: The Fourth Estate

Giles, C. and Johnson, P. (1994) *Taxes Down, Taxes Up*, London: Institute of Fiscal Studies Commentary no. 41

Glennerster, H. (1962) *National Assistance: Service or Charity?* London: Fabian Society

Glennerster, H. (1972) 'Education and inequality', in P. Townsend and N. Bosanquet (eds) *Labour and Inequality*, London: Fabian Society

Glennerster, H. (1975) *Social Service Budgets and Social Policy: British and American Experience*, London: Allen and Unwin

Glennerster, H. (1976) 'In praise of public expenditure', *New Statesman*, 91(2345), pp. 252–4

Glennerster, H. (1997) *Paying for Welfare: Towards 2000*, Hemel Hempstead: Harvester

Glennerster, H. (2000) *British Social Policy since 1945*, 2nd ed, Oxford: Blackwell

Glennerster, H. (2002) 'United Kingdom education 1997–2001', *Oxford Review of Economic Policy*, vol. 18, no. 2, pp. 120–36

Glennerster, H. (2004) 'Mrs Thatcher's legacy: Getting it in perspective', in N. Ellison, L. Bauld and M. Powell (eds) *Social Policy Review 16*, Bristol: Policy Press

Glennerster, H. (2006) *The Redistributive Impact of Taxes and Social Policies in the UK 1937–2005*, CASEpaper no. 113, London: CASE, London School of Economics

Glennerster, H. and Hills, J. (eds) (1998) *The State of Welfare: The Economics of Social Spending*, Oxford: Oxford University Press

Glennerster, H. with Korman, N. and Marsden-Wilson, F. (1983) *Planning for Priority Groups*, Oxford: Blackwell

Glennerster, H. and Low, W. (1990) 'Education and the Welfare State: Does it add up?', in J. Hills (ed.) *The State of Welfare: the Welfare State in Britain from 1974*, Oxford: Clarendon Press

Glennerster, H. and Pryke, R. (1964) *The Public Schools*, London: Fabian Society

Glennerster, H. and Turner, T. (1993) *Estate Based Housing Management: an Evaluation*, London: HMSO

Glennerster, H. and Wilson, G. (1970) *Paying for Private Schools*, London: Allen Lane

Glennerster, H., Matsaganis, M. and Owens, P. (1994) *Implementing Fundholding*, Milton Keynes: Open University Press

Glennerster, H., Power, A. and Travers, T. (1991) 'A new era for social policy: a new Enlightenment or a new Leviathan?', *Journal of Social Policy*, 20(3), pp. 389–414

Glennerster, H., Hills, J., Piachaud, D. and Webb, J. (2004) *One Hundred Years of Poverty and Policy*, York: Joseph Rowntree Foundation

Goodin, R. and Le Grand, J. (1987) *Not Only the Poor: the Middle Classes and the Welfare State*, London: Allen and Unwin

Goodman, A. and Webb, S. (1994) *For Richer for Poorer: the Changing Distribution of Income in the United Kingdom 1961–91*, London: Institute of Fiscal Studies

Gorsky, M., Mohan, J. and Powell, M. (2002) 'The financial health of voluntary hospitals in interwar Britain', *Economic History Review*, vol. LV, no. 3, pp. 533–57

Gosden, P. H. J. H. (1976) *Education in the Second World War*, London: Methuen

Gosling, A., Machin, S. and Meghir, C. (1994) *What Has Happened to Wages?*, London: Institute of Fiscal Studies

Gough, I. (1979) *The Political Economy of the Welfare State*, London: Macmillan

Green, D. G. (1993) *Reinventing Civil Society: the Rediscovery of Welfare without Politics*, London: Institute of Economic Affairs

Green, A. and Steedman, H. (1993) *Education Provision, Educational Attainment and the Needs of Industry: a Review of Research for Germany, France, Japan, the USA and Britain*, London: National Institute for Economic and Social Research

Greer, S. L. (2004) *Territorial Politics and Health Policy: UK Health Policy in Comparative Perspective*, Manchester: Manchester University Press

Gregg, P. and Harkness, S. (2003) 'Welfare reform and the employment of lone parents', in R. Dickens, P. Gregg and J. Wadsworth (eds) *The New Labour Market under New Labour: The State of Working Britain*, London: Palgrave

Gretton, J. and Jackson, M. (1976) *William Tyndale: Collapse of a School or a System?*, London: Allen and Unwin

Griffiths Report (1983) *Recommendations on the Effective Use of Manpower and Related Resources*, London: DHSS

Griffiths Report (1988) *Community Care Agenda for Action*, London: HMSO

Hall, P. (1976) *Reforming the Welfare: the Politics of Change in the Personal Social Services*, London: Heinemann

Gundlach, E., Woessman, L. and Gmelin, J. (2001) 'The Decline of Schooling Productivity in OECD Countries', *Economic Journal*, 11 (May), pp. C135–C147

Hall, P. (1993) 'Policy paradigms, social learning and the state: the case of economic policy-making in Britain', *Comparative Politics*, vol. 25, no. 3, pp. 275–96

Hall, P. and Taylor, R. C. R. (1996) 'Political science and the three institutionalisms', *Political Studies*, vol. 44, pp. 936–57

Hall, P., Land, H., Parker, R. and Webb, A. (1975) *Change, Choice and Conflict in Social Policy*, London: Heinemann

Halsey, A. H. (1991) 'Failing education?', in *British Social Attitudes: the 8th Report*, Aldershot: Dartmouth Publishing

Halsey, A. H., Heath, A. F. and Ridge, J. (1980) *Origins and Destinations*, Oxford: Clarendon Press

Hampshire, J. and Lewis, J. (2004) ' "The Ravages of Permissiveness": sex education and the permissive society', *Twentieth Century British History*, vol. 15, no. 3, pp. 290–312

Harris, J. (1975) 'Social planning in war-time: some aspects of the Beveridge Report', in J. M. Winter (ed.) *War and Economic Development*, Cambridge: Cambridge University Press

Harris, J. (1977) *William Beveridge: a Biography*, Oxford: Oxford University Press

Harris, J. (1986) 'Political ideas and the debate on state welfare, 1940–5', in H. L. S. Smith, *British Society in the Second World War*, Manchester: Manchester University Press

Harris, J. (1990) 'Enterprise and Welfare States: a comparative perspective', *Transactions of the Royal Historical Society*, 40

Harris, J. (1992) 'Political thought and the Welfare State 1870–1940: an intellectual framework for British social policy', *Past and Present*, 135, pp. 116–41

Harris, J. (1993) *Private Lives, Public Spirit: a Social History of Britain 1870–1914*, Oxford: Oxford University Press

Harris, J. (1994) 'Contract and citizenship in social welfare 1934–48', paper given at the conference, Comparing Social Welfare Systems in Europe, Oxford, May 1994. Paris: MIRE

Harris, J. (1997) *William Beveridge: a Biography*, 2nd edn, Oxford: Oxford University Press

Harris, J. (1999) 'Ruskin and Social Reform', in D. Birch (ed.) *Ruskin and the Dawn of the Modern*, Oxford: Oxford University Press

Harris, J. (2006) 'Beveridge and pensions', in H. Pemberton, P. Thane and N. Whiteside (eds) *The Past, Present and Future of British Pensions*, Oxford: Oxford University Press

Harrison, A. J. (1989) *The Control of Public Expenditure*, Oxford: Transaction Books, Policy Journals

Hayek, F. A. (1944) *The Road to Serfdom*, London: Routledge and Kegan Paul

Heclo, H. (1974) *Modern Social Politics in Britain and Sweden: From Relief to Income Maintenance*, New Haven and London: Yale University Press

Heclo, H. and Wildavsky, A. (1981) *The Private Government of Public Money*, London: Macmillan

Hennessy, P. (1992) *Never Again: Britain 1945–51*, London: Cape

Higgins, J. (1978) *The Poverty Business*, Oxford: Blackwell

Hill, M. (1990) *Social Security Policy in Britain*, Aldershot: Edward Elgar

Hills, J. (1988) *Changing Tax*, London: Child Poverty Action Group

Hills, J. (ed.) (1990) *The State of Welfare: the Welfare State in Britain from 1974*, Oxford: Clarendon Press

Hills, J. (1993) *The Future of Welfare: a Guide to the Debate*, York: Joseph Rowntree Foundation

Hills, J. (ed.) (1996) *New Inequalities: The Changing Distribution of Income in the United Kingdom*, Cambridge: Cambridge University Press

Hills, J. (2004) *Inequality and the State*, Oxford: Oxford University Press

Hills, J. and Mullings, B. (1990) 'Housing: a Decent Home for all at a Price within their Means?', in J. Hills (ed.) *The State of Welfare: the Welfare State in Britain from 1974*, Oxford: Clarendon Press

Hills, J. and Stewart, K. (2005) *A More Equal Society? New Labour, Poverty, Inequality and Exclusion*, Bristol: Policy Press

Hills, J., Ditch, J. and Glennerster, H. (eds) (1994) *Beveridge and Social Security: an International Retrospective*, Oxford: Oxford University Press

Hills, J., Smithies, R. and McKnight, A. (2006) *Tracking Income: How Working Families' Incomes vary through the Year*, CASEreport 32, London: CASE, London School of Economics

Hinchliffe Committee (1959) *Report of a Committee on the Costs of Prescribing*, London: HMSO

Hirschman, A. O. (1970) *Exit, Voice and Loyalty: Responses to Decline in Firms, Organisations and States*, Cambridge, Mass.: Harvard University Press

Holmans, A. E. (1987) *Housing Policy in Britain*, Beckenham: Croom Helm

Home Office (1998) *Supporting Families*, London: The Stationery Office

Honnigsbaum, F. (1979) *The Division of Medicine in British Medicine: a History of the Separation of General Practice from Hospital Care 1911–68*, London: Kogan Page

Honnigsbaum, F. (1989) *Health, Happiness and Security: the Creation of the National Health Service*, London: Kogan Page

House of Commons *Debates 1947/8*, vol. 444, column 1609

House of Commons (1996/7) *Financial Statement and Budget Report 1997/8*, HC 90, London: The Stationery Office

House of Commons Committee of Public Accounts (2005/6) *Inland Revenue: Tax Credits and Deleted Tax Cases*, HC 412, Fifth Report of Session 2005/6, London: House of Commons

House of Commons Education and Skills Committee (2005/6) *The Schools White Paper: Higher Standards, Better Schools for All*, HC 633-I, First Report of Session 2005/6, London: House of Commons

House of Commons Home Affairs Committee (1980/1) *Racial Disadvantage*, HC 424-I, Fifth Report of Session 1980/1, London: HMSO

House of Commons Social Services Committee (1984/5) *Community Care with Special Reference to Adult Mentally Ill and Mentally Handicapped People*, HC 13-I, Second Report of Session 1984/5, London: HMSO

House of Lords *Debates 1995/6*, vol. 567, columns 701 and 733

Howe, G. (1961) 'Reform of the Social Services', *Principles in Practice*, London: Conservative Political Centre

Illsley, R., Le Grand, J. and Mullings, C. (1991) 'Regional inequalities in mortality', STICERD Welfare State Programme Discussion Paper WSP/57, London: London School of Economics

Johnson, N. (1987) *The Welfare State in Transition: the Theory and Practice of Welfare Pluralism*, Brighton: Wheatsheaf Books

Johnson, N. (1990) *Reconstructing the Welfare State: a Decade of Change*, Hemel Hempstead: Harvester Wheatsheaf

Jones, F. (2005) 'The effects of taxes and benefits on household income, 2003/4', *Economic Trends*, vol. 620, pp. 15–61, <http://www.statistics.gov.uk>

Jones, H. O. W. (1992) 'The Conservative Party and the Welfare State 1942–1955', unpublished PhD thesis, University of London

Jones, H. and Kandiah, K. (1996) *The Myth of the Consensus: New Views on British History*, London: Macmillan

Jones, K. (1994) *An Economist among Mandarins: a Biography of Robert Hall (1901–1988)*, Cambridge: Cambridge University Press

Joseph Rowntree Foundation (1995) *Inquiry into Income and Wealth* (Chairman Sir Peter Barclay), York: Jospeh Rowntree Foundation

Katz, S. N., Eekelaar, J. and Maclean, M. (eds) (2000) *Cross Currents: Family Law and Policy in US and England*, Oxford: Oxford University Press

Kavanagh, D. (2005) 'The Blair Premiership', in A. Seldon and D. Kavanagh (eds) *The Blair Effect 2001–5*, Cambridge: Cambridge University Press

Kavanagh, D. and Morris, P. (1989) *Consensus Politics from Attlee to Thatcher*, Oxford: Blackwell

Kavanagh, D. and Seldon, A. (eds) (1994) *The Major Effect*, London: Macmillan

Kennedy, H. (1992) *Eve Was Framed: Women and British Justice*, London: Chatto and Windus

Keynes, J. M. (1936) *The General Theory of Employment, Interest and Money*, London: Macmillan

Kiernan, K. (1998) 'The changing demography of lone motherhood', in K. Kiernan, H. Land and J. Lewis (eds) *Lone Motherhood in the Twentieth Century*, Oxford: Oxford University Press

Kiernan, K., Land, H. and Lewis, J. (1998) *Lone Motherhood in Twentieth Century Britain*, Oxford: Oxford University Press

Kiernan, K. and Wicks, M. (1990) *Family Change and Future Policy*, York: Joseph Rowntree Memorial Trust

King, D. (1990) 'Accountability and equity in British local finance: the poll tax', in R. J. Bennett (ed.) *Decentralisation, Local Governments and Markets: Towards a Post-Welfare Agenda*, Oxford: Clarendon Press

King, D. and Nash, V. (2001) 'Continuity of ideas and the Politics of Higher Education in Britain from Robbins to Dearing', *Twentieth Century British History*, vol. 12, no. 1, pp. 185–207.

King's Fund (2006) *Securing Good Care for Older People*, London: King's Fund

King's Fund Institute (1988) *Health Finance: Assessing the Options*, London: King's Fund Institute

Klein, R. (1989) *The Politics of the National Health Service*, 2nd edn, London: Longman

Klein, R. (1995) *The New Politics of the NHS*, London: Longman

Kleinman, M. (1999) 'Housing Policy: Does it have a future? A reply', *Policy and Politics*, vol. 27, no. 2, pp. 229–30

Kullmann, M. (1960) 'Notting Hill hustings', *New Left Review*, 1, pp. 19–21

Labour Party (1957) *National Superannuation*, London: Labour Party

Labour Party (1959) *The Tory Pensions Swindle*, London: Labour Party

Labour Party (1961) *Signposts for the Sixties*, London: Labour Party

Labour Party (1963a) *Thirteen Wasted Years*, London: Labour Party

Labour Party (1963b) *Years of Crisis*, London: Labour Party

Labour Party (2005) *Election Manifesto*, London: Labour Party

Labour Research Department (1994) *Maternity Rights: a Guide to the New Law*, London: Labour Research Department

Lambert, R. (1964) *Nutrition in Britain, 1950–60*, Welwyn: Codicote Press

Land, H. (1983) 'Who still cares for the family? Recent developments in income maintenance, taxation and family law', in J. Lewis (ed.) *Women's Welfare/Women's Rights*, Beckenham: Croom Helm

Land, H. (1994) 'The demise of the male breadwinner – in practice but not in theory: a challenge for social security systems', in S. Baldwin and J. Falkingham (eds) *Social Security and Social Change: New Challenges to the Beveridge Model*, Hemel Hempstead: Harvester Wheatsheaf

Land, H. (2004) 'Privatisation, privatisation, privatisation: the British welfare state since 1979', in N. Ellison, L. Bauld and M. Powell (eds) *Social Policy Review* 16, Bristol: Policy Press

Lane Committee (1974) *Report of the Committee on the Working of the Abortion Act*, Cmnd 5579, London: HMSO

Law Commission (1966) *Report on the Reform of the Grounds of Divorce: the Field of Choice*, LC no. 6, London: HMSO

Law Commission (1988) *Facing the Future: a discussion paper on the grounds for divorce*, LC no. 170, HC 479, London: HMSO

Lawson, N. (1993) *The View from No. 11: Memoirs of a Tory Radical*, London: Corgi

Layard, R. (1997a) *What Labour Can Do*, London: Warner Books

Layard, R. (1997b) 'Preventing long term unemployment: an economic analysis', in D. J. Snower and G. de la Dehasa (eds) *Unemployment Policy: Government Options for the Labour Market*, Cambridge: Cambridge University Press

Le Grand, J. (1999) 'Competition, Co-operation or Control? Tales from the British National Health Service', *Health Affairs*, May/June 1999, vol. 18, no. 3, pp. 27–39

Le Grand, J. (2003) *Motivation, Agency, and Public Policy: Of Knights and Knaves, Pawns and Queens*, Oxford: Oxford University Press

Lewis, J. (1980) *The Politics of Motherhood: Child and Maternal Welfare in England 1900–1939*, London: Croom Helm

Lewis, J. (1984) *Women in England 1870–1950: Sexual Divisions and Social Change*, Brighton: Wheatsheaf

Lewis, J. (1992a) *Women in Britain since 1945*, Oxford: Blackwell

Lewis, J. (1992b) 'Gender and the Development of Welfare Regimes', *Journal of European Social Policy*, vol. 3, pp. 159–73.

Lewis, J. (1994) *The Problem of Lone Mother Families in 20th Century Britain*, STICERD Welfare State Programme Discussion Paper WSP 114, London: London School of Economics

Lewis, J. (1998) 'The Debate about the Law Affecting Marriage and Divorce in Twentieth Century Britain', in K. Kiernan, H. Land and J. Lewis, *Lone Motherhood in Twentieth Century Britain*, Oxford: Oxford University Press

Lewis, J. (2000) 'Family Policy in the Post-War Period', in S. Katz, J. Eekaar and M. Maclean (eds) *Cross Currents: Family Law and Policy in the US and England*, Oxford: Oxford University Press

Lewis, J. (2002) 'Individualisation, assumptions about the existence of an adult worker model and the shift towards contractualism', in A. Carling, S. Duncan and R. Edwards (eds) *Analysing Families*, London: Routledge

Lewis, J. (2005) 'The changing context for the obligation to care and to earn', in M. Maclean (ed.) *Family Law and Family Values*, Oxford: Hart Publishing

Lewis, J. and Glennerster, H. (1996) *Implementing the New Community Care*, Milton Keynes: Open University Press

Lewis, J. and Piachaud, D. (1987) 'Women and poverty in the twentieth century', in C. Glendinning and J. Millar (eds) *Women and Poverty in Britain*, Brighton: Wheatsheaf

Lindert, P. (2004) *Growing Public: Social Spending and Economic Growth since the Eighteenth Century*, Cambridge: Cambridge University Press

Lipsey, D. and Leonard, D. (1981) *The Socialist Agenda: Crosland's Legacy*, London: Jonathan Cape

Lodemel, I. and Trickey, H. (2000) *'An Offer you Cannot Refuse': Workfare in an International Perspective*, Bristol: Policy Press

Lowe, R. (1989) 'Resignation at the Treasury: the Social Services Committee and the failure to reform the Welfare State 1955–57', *Journal of Social Policy*, 18(4), pp. 505–26

Lowe, R. (1990) 'The Second World War, consensus and the foundations of the Welfare State', *Twentieth Century British History*, 1(2), pp. 152–82

Lowe, R. (1993) *The Welfare State in Britain since 1945*, London: Macmillan

Lowe, R. (1994) 'The rejection of Beveridge in Britain', in J. Hills, J. Ditch and H. Glennerster, *Beveridge and Social Security: an International Retrospective*, Oxford: Oxford University Press.

Lowe, R. (1997a) 'Milestone or Millstone: The 1959–61 Plowden Committee and its Impact on British Welfare Policy', *Historical Journal*, vol. 40, no. 2, pp. 463–91

Lowe, R. (1997b) 'The Core Executive, Modernisation and the Creation of PESC 1960–64', *Public Administration*, vol. 75, Winter, pp. 601–15

Lowe, R. (1999) *The Welfare State in Britain since 1945*, 2nd edn, London: Macmillan

Lowe, R. (2005) *The Welfare State in Britain since 1945*, 3rd edn, London: Palgrave

Lupton, R. (2003) *Poverty Street: The Dynamics of Neighbourhood Decline and Renewal*, Bristol: Policy Press

Lupton, R. and Power, A. (2005) 'Disadvantaged by where you live? New Labour and neighbourhood renewal', in J. Hills and K. Stewart (eds) *A More Equal Society? New Labour, Poverty, Inequality and Exclusion*, Bristol: Policy Press

McCann, K. (1985) 'Battered women and the law: the limits of the legislation', in J. Brophy and C. Smart (eds) *Women In Law*, London: Routledge and Kegan Paul

McCarthy, M. (1986) *Campaigning for the Poor: CPAG and the Politics of Welfare*, Beckenham: Croom Helm

Machin, S. and McNally, S. (2005) 'Gender and student achievement in English schools', *Oxford Review of Economic Policy*, vol. 21, no. 3, pp. 357–72

Machin, S. and Waldfogel, J. (1994) 'The decline of the male breadwinner', STICERD Welfare State Programme Discussion Paper WSP/103, London: London School of Economics

McKeown, T. (1979) *The Role of Medicine*, Oxford: Blackwell

McKnight, A. (2005) 'Employment: tackling poverty through "work for those who can"', in J. Hills and K. Stewart (eds) *A More Equal Society? New Labour, Poverty, Inequality and Exclusion*, Bristol: Policy Press

McLean, I. (2005) 'The National Question', in A. Seldon and D. Kavanagh (eds) *The Blair Effect 2001–5*, Cambridge: Cambridge University Press

McLean, I. and McMillan, A. (2003) 'The distribution of public expenditure across the UK regions', *Fiscal Studies*, vol. 24, no. 1, pp. 45–71

Maclean, M. (2002) 'The Green Paper *Supporting Families*', in A. Carling, S. Duncan and R. Edwards (eds) *Analysing Families: Morality and Rationality in Policy and Practice*, London: Routledge

Maclean, M. (ed.) (2005) *Family Law and Family Values*, London: Hart

Macleod, I. and Powell, E. (1952) *The Social Services Needs and Means*, London: Conservative Political Centre

Macnicol, J. (1980) *The Movement for Family Allowances 1918–45*, London: Heinemann

Macnicol, J. (1998) *The Politics of Retirement in Britain 1878–1948*, Cambridge: Cambridge University Press

McRae, S. (1993) *Cohabiting Mothers: Changing marriage and motherhood*, London: Policy Studies Institute

Malpass, P. (1999) 'Housing policy – does it have a future?', *Policy and Politics*, vol. 27, no. 2, pp. 217–28

Marshall, T. (1950) *Citizenship and Social Class*, Cambridge: Cambridge University Press

Marshall, T. (1963) *Sociology at the Crossroads*, London: Heinemann

Marsland, D. (2004) 'Social policy since 1979: a view from the right', in N. Ellison, L. Bauld and M. Powell (eds) *Social Policy Review* 16, Bristol: Policy Press

Martin, J. P. and Evans, D. (1984) *Hospitals in Trouble*, Oxford: Blackwell

Marwick, A. (1990) *British Society since 1945*, Harmondsworth: Penguin Books

Mason, M. A. (1999) *The Custody Wars*, Basic Books: New York

Martin, J. P. (1984) *Hospitals in Trouble*, Oxford: Blackwell

Metcalf, D. (1999) 'The British National Minimum Wage', *British Journal of Industrial Relations*, vol. 37, no. 2, pp. 171–201

Miliband, R. (1961) *Parliamentary Socialism*, London: Allen and Unwin

Miliband, R. (1969) *The State in Capitalist Society*, London: Weidenfeld and Nicolson

Millar, J. (1989) *Poverty and the Lone Parent Family: the Challenge to Social Policy*, Aldershot: Avebury

Ministry of Education (1945) *The Nation's Schools: their Plan and Purpose*, London: HMSO

Ministry of Education (1954) *Early Leaving*, Report of the Central Advisory Council for Education, London: HMSO

Ministry of Education (1956) *Technical Education*, Cmd 9703, London: HMSO

Ministry of Education (1959) *15–18*, Report of the Central Advisory Council for Education (Crowther Report), London: HMSO

Ministry of Education (1963) *Half Our Future*, Report of the Central Advisory Council for Education (Newsom Report), London: HMSO

Ministry of Housing and Local Government (1953) *Houses: the Next Step*, Cmd 8996, London: HMSO

Ministry of Housing and Local Government (1968) *Old Houses into New Homes*, Cmnd 3602, London: HMSO

Monckton Enquiry (1945) *Report on the Circumstances that Led to the Boarding Out of Denis and Terence O'Neill at Bank Farm, Minsterley and the Steps taken to Supervise their Welfare*, London: HMSO

Morgan, K. O. (1990) *The People's Peace: British History 1945–1990*, Oxford: Oxford University Press

Morgan, P. (1995) *Farewell to the Family: Public Policy and Family Breakdown in Britain and the USA*, Choice in Welfare Series no. 21, London: Institute of Economic Affairs

Murray, C. (1984) *Losing Ground: American Social Policy 1950–1980*, New York: Basic Books

Narendranathan, W., Nickell, S. and Stern, J. (1983) 'Unemployment benefits revisited', Centre for Labour Economics Discussion Paper no. 153, London: London School of Economics

National Assembly for Wales (2005) *Childcare is for Children*, Cardiff: Department for Education and Training

National Commission on Education (1993) *Learning to Succeed: a Radical Look at Education Today and a Strategy for the Future*, London: Heinemann

Nevitt, A. A. (1966) *Housing Taxation and Subsidies*, London: Nelson

Newsom Report (1963) *Half our Future*, London: HMSO

Nickell, S., Nunziata, L. and Ochel, W. (2005) 'Unemployment in the OECD since the 1960s. What do we know?', *Economic Journal*, vol. 115, January, pp. 1–27

Nickell, S. and Quintini, G. (2002) 'Recent performance of the UK labour market', *Oxford Review of Economic Policy*, vol. 18, no. 2, pp. 202–20

Nuttall, J. (2004) 'Tony Crosland and the many falls and rises of British Social Democracy', *Contemporary British History*, vol. 18, no. 4, pp. 52–79

O'Connor, J. (1973) *The Fiscal Crisis of the State*, New York: St Martin's Press

Office of the Deputy Prime Minister (ODPM) (2003) *Sustainable Communities: Building for the Future*, London: Office of the Deputy Prime Minister

O'Hara, G. (2004) ' "We are faced everywhere with a growing population": demographic change and the British state, 1955–64', *Twentieth Century British History*, vol. 15, no. 3, pp. 243–66

O'Higgins, M. (1983) 'Rolling back the Welfare State: the rhetoric and the reality of public expenditure and social policy under the Conservative government', in C. Jones and J. Stevenson (eds) *The Year Book of Social Policy in Britain 1982*, London: Routledge and Kegan Paul

Office for National Statistics (1999) 'The effects of taxes and benefits on household income 1997–8', *Economic Trends*, April 1999, pp. 27–63

One Nation Group (1950) *One Nation*, London: Conservative Political Centre

One Nation Group (1959) *The Responsible Society*, London: The Conservative Political Centre

Organisation for Economic Cooperation and Development (OECD) (2001) *Knowledge and Skills for Life: First Results from PISA 2000*, Paris: Organisation for Economic Cooperation and Development

Page, R. and Deakin, N. (1993) *The Costs of Welfare*, Aldershot: Avebury

Parker, S. (1990) *Informal Marriage, Cohabitation and the Law 1750–1989*, London: Macmillan

Paskell, C. and Power, A. (2005) *'The Future's Changed': Local Impacts of Housing, Environment and Regeneration Policy since 1997*, CASEreport 29, London: CASE, London School of Economics

Peacock, A. T. (1954) *Income Distribution and Social Policy*, London: Cape

Pemberton, H., Thane, P. and Whiteside, N. (2006) *Why has it all Gone Wrong? The Past, Present and Future of British Pensions*, Oxford: Oxford University Press

Pensions Commission (2004) *Pensions: Challenges and Choices. The First Report of the Pensions Commission*, London: The Stationery Office

Pensions Commission (2005) *A New Pensions Settlement for the Twenty-First Century. The Second Report of the Pensions Commission*, London: The Stationery Office

Phillips, C. (2005) 'Ethnic inequalities under New Labour: progress or entrenchment?', in J. Hills and K. Stewart (eds) *A More Equal Society: New Labour, Poverty, Inequality and Exclusion*, Bristol: Policy Press

Phillips Committee (1954) *Report of the Committee on the Economic and Financial Problems of Old Age*, Cmd 9333, London: HMSO

Piachaud, D. (1999) 'Progress on Poverty: Will Blair deliver on eliminating child poverty?', *New Economy*, vol. 6, no. 3, pp. 154–60

Pierson, P. (1994) *Dismantling the Welfare State? Regan, Thatcher, and the Politics of Retrenchment*, Cambridge: Cambridge University Press

Pierson, P. (1996) 'The new politics of the welfare state', *World Politics*, vol. 48, pp. 143–79

Pimlott, B. (1989) 'Is post-war consensus a myth?', *Contemporary Record*, 2(6), pp. 12–14

Pimlott, B. (1992) *Harold Wilson*, London: HarperCollins

Pinder, J. (1981) *Fifty Years of Political and Economic Planning*, London: Heinemann

Plowden Committee (1967) *Children and their Primary Schools*, London: HMSO

Potts, M., Diggory, P. and Peel, J. (1977) *Abortion*, Cambridge: Cambridge University Press

Powell, M. (ed.) (2002) *Evaluating New Labour's Welfare Reforms*, Bristol: Policy Press

Power, A. (1988) *Property Before People: the Management of Twentieth-Century Council Housing*, London: Allen and Unwin

Power, A. (1993) *Hovels to High Rise: State Housing in Europe since 1850*, London: Routledge

Rake, K., Falkingham, J. and Evans, M. (1999) *Tightropes and tripwires: New Labour's Proposals and Means-testing in Old Age*, CASEpaper 23, London: Centre For Analysis of Social Exclusion, London School of Economics

Ramsden, J. (1980) *The Making of Conservative Party Policy: The Conservative Research Department since 1929*, London: Longman

Read, M. D. and Marsh, D. (1997) 'The Family Law Bill; Conservative Party Splits and Labour Cohesion', *Parliamentary Affairs*, April, 50(2), pp. 263–79

Rigg, J. (2005) *Labour Market Disadvantage amongst Disabled People: A Longitudinal Perspective*, CASEpaper no. 103, London: CASE, London School of Economics

Rivett, G. (1998) *Cradle to Grave: Fifty years of the NHS*, London: King's Fund

Robb, B. (1967) *Sans Everything: a Case to Answer*, London: Nelson

Robbins Committee (1963) *Higher Education*, Cmnd 2154, London: HMSO

Roberts, S. (1993) 'Mediation and the Family Justice System', *Family Mediation*, vol. 3, no. 1, pp. 5–7

Robinson, E. E. (1968) *The New Polytechnics*, London: Cornmarket Press

Robinson, J. and Banks, P. (2005) *The Business of Caring: The King's Fund Inquiry into Care Services for Older People in London*, London: King's Fund

Robinson, R. and Le Grand, J. (1994) *Evaluating the NHS Reforms*, London: King's Fund

Rogers, R. (2005) *Towards a Strong Urban Renaissance*, <http://www.urbantaskforce.org>

Rose, E. J. B. (ed.) (1969) *Colour and Citizenship*, Oxford: Oxford University Press

Rose, H. (1981) 'Rereading Titmuss: the Sexual Division of Welfare', *Journal of Social Policy*, 10(4), pp. 477–502

Rose, H. (1985) 'Women's refuges: creating new forms of welfare?', in C. Ungerson (ed.) *Women and Social Policy: a Reader*, London: Macmillan

Rowntree, B. S. (1941) *Poverty and Progress: a Second Social Survey*, London: Longman Green

Rowntree, B. S. and Lavers, R. G. (1951) *Poverty and the Welfare State*, London: Longman Green

Scarman, Rt Hon. Lord (1981) *Brixton Disorders 10–12 April 1981* (Scarman Report), Cmnd 8427, London: HMSO

Scotland Office (1998) *Meeting the Child Care Challenge: A Child Care Strategy for Scotland*, London: Stationery Office

Secretary of State for Scotland (1997) *Designed to Care*, Edinburgh: The Stationery Office

Sefton, T. and Sutherland, H. (2005) 'Inequality and poverty under New Labour', in J. Hills and K. Stewart (eds) *A More Equal Society? New Labour, Poverty, Inequality and Exclusion*, Bristol: Policy Press

Sefton, T. (2005) 'Give and take: public attitudes to redistribution', in A. Park, J. Curtis, K. Thomson, C. Bromley, M. Phillips and M. Johnson (eds) *British Social Attitudes: the 22nd Report. Two Terms of New Labour: The Public's Reaction*, London: Sage

Seldon, A. (1981) *Churchill's Indian Summer*, London: Hodder and Stoughton

Seldon, A. (1986) *The Riddle of the Voucher*, London: Institute of Economic Affairs

Seldon, A. and Kavanagh, D. (eds) (2005) *The Blair Effect 2001–5*, Cambridge: Cambridge University Press

Shapely, P., Tanner, D. and Walling, A. (2004) 'Civic culture and housing policy in Manchester 1945–79', *Twentieth Century British History*, vol. 15, no. 4, pp. 410–34

Simms, M. (1985) 'Legal abortion in Great Britain', in H. Homans (ed.) *The Sexual Politics of Reproduction*, Aldershot: Gower

Smart, C. (1984) *The Ties that Bind: Law, Marriage and the Reproduction of Patriarchal Relations*, London: Routledge and Kegan Paul

Smart, C. (1997) 'Wishful Thinking and Harmful Tinkering? Sociological Reflections on Family Policy', *Journal of Social Policy*, vol. 26, pt. 3, pp. 301–21

Smart, C. and Neale, B. (1997) 'Good Enough Morality? Divorce and Post Modernity', *Critical Social Policy*, vol. 17, no. 4, pp. 3–27

Snower, D. J. (1993) 'The future of the Welfare State', *The Economic Journal*, 103, pp. 700–17

Social Justice Commission (1994) *Social Justice: Strategies for National Renewal*, London: Institute for Public Policy Research

Stewart, K. (2005) 'Towards an equal start? Addressing childhood poverty and deprivation', in J. Hills and K. Stewart (eds) *A More Equal Society? New Labour, Poverty, Inequality and Exclusion*, Bristol: Policy Press

Tawney, R. H. (1924) *Secondary Education for All: a Policy for Labour*, London: Labour Party

Tawney, R. H. (1964) [1931] *Equality*, with an introduction by R. M. T. Titmuss, London: Allen and Unwin

Taylor-Gooby, P. (ed.) (2004) *New Risks, New Welfare: The Transformation of the European Welfare State*, Oxford: Oxford University Press

Taylor-Gooby, P. (2005) 'Is the future American? Or can Left politics preserve European Welfare States from erosion through growing "racial" diversity?', *Journal of Social Policy*, vol. 34, pt. 4, pp. 661–72

Taylor-Gooby, P. and Hastie, C. (2002) 'Support for state spending: has New Labour got it right?', in A. Park, J. Curtis, K. Thompson, L. Jarvis and C. Bromley (eds) *British Social Attitudes: 19th Report*, London: Sage, pp. 75–96

Thain, C. and Wright, M. (1990) 'Coping with difficulty: the Treasury and public expenditure 1976–89', *Policy and Politics*, 18(1), pp. 1–15

Thain, C. and Wright, M. (1995) *The Treasury and Whitehall: The Planning and Control of Public Expenditure 1976–1993*, Oxford: Oxford University Press

Thane, P. (2000) *Old Age in English History: Past Experiences, Present Issues*, Oxford: Oxford University Press

Thane, P. (2005) 'Michael Young and welfare', *Contemporary British History*, vol. 19, no. 3, pp. 293–9

Thane, P. (2006) 'The "Scandal" of women's pensions: How did it come about?', in H. Pemberton, P. Thane and N. Whiteside (eds) *The Past, Present and Future of British Pensions*, Oxford: Oxford University Press

Thatcher, M. (1979) *Let Them Grow Tall*, London: Conservative Party Centre

Thatcher, M. (1993) *The Downing Street Years*, London: HarperCollins

Thompson, F. M. L. (1990) *The Cambridge Social History of Britain 1750–1950*, vol. 3, Cambridge: Cambridge University Press

Timmins, N. (1995) *The Five Giants: A Biography of the Welfare State*, London: HarperCollins

Titmuss, R. M. T. (1950) *The Problems of Social Policy*, London: HMSO

Titmuss, R. M. T. (1958) *Essays on the Welfare State*, London: Allen and Unwin

Titmuss, R. M. T. (1963) *The Irresponsible Society*, London: Fabian Society (also published in his *Essays on the Welfare State*, 2nd edn).

Titmuss, R. M. T. (1972) *The Gift Relationship*, London: Allen and Unwin

Tomlinson, J. (1998) 'Why so Austere? The British Welfare State of the 1940s', *Journal of Social Policy*, vol. 27, pt. 1, pp. 63–77

Tomlinson, J. (2004) *The Labour Governments 1964–70*, vol. 3: *Economic Policy*, Manchester: Manchester University Press

Townsend, P. (1954a) 'Measuring poverty', *British Journal of Sociology*, 5, pp. 130–7

Townsend, P. (1954b) 'Poverty ten years after Beveridge', *Planning*, 19

Townsend, P. (1957) *The Family Life of Old People*, Harmondsworth: Penguin Books

Townsend, P. (1970) *The Concept of Poverty*, London: Heinemann

Townsend, P. and Davidson, N. (eds) (1982) *Inequalities in Health: The Black Report*, Harmondsworth: Penguin Books

Treasury, HM (1980) *The Taxation of Husband and Wife*, Cmnd 8093, London: HMSO

Treasury, HM (1984) *The Next Ten Years: Public Expenditure and Taxation into the 1990s*, Cmnd 9184, London: HMSO

Treasury, HM (2002) *Securing our Future Health: Taking the Long Term View Final Report*, London: HM Treasury

Treasury, HM (2004) *Choice for Parents, the Best Start for Children: a Ten Year Strategy for Child Care*, London: HM Treasury

Treasury, HM (2005) *Public Expenditure Analysis 2005*, London: HM Treasury

Tymms, P. (2004) 'Are standards rising in English primary schools?', *British Educational Research Journal*, vol. 30, no. 4, pp. 477–94

Urban Task Force (1999) *Towards an Urban Renaissance: Final Report of the Urban Task Force*, London: The Stationery Office

Veit-Wilson, J. (1994) 'Condemned to deprivation', in J. Hills, J. Ditch and H. Glennerster (eds) *Beveridge and Social Security: an International Retrospective*, Oxford: Oxford University Press

Waldfogel, J. (1998) *Early Childhood Interventions and Outcomes*, CASEpaper 21, London: CASE, London School of Economics

Walker, A. (1982) *The Poverty of Taxation*, London: Child Poverty Action Group

Walker, J. (1996) 'Is there a future for lawyers in divorce?', *International Journal of Law Policy and the Family*, vol. 10, no. 1, pp. 52–73

Weale, A., Bradshaw, J., Maynard, A. and Piachaud, D. (1984) *Lone Mothers, Paid Work and Social Security*, Occasional Papers on Social Administration no. 77, London: Bedford Square Press

Webb, S. and B. (1920) [1897] *Industrial Democracy*, 2nd edn, London: Longmans

Webster, C. (1988) *The Health Services since the War*, vol. 1, London: HMSO

Webster, C. (1990) 'Conflict and consensus: explaining the British Health Service', *Twentieth Century British History*, 1(2), pp. 115–51

Webster, C. (1996) *The Health Service Since the War*, vol. 2: *Government and Health Care. The British National Health Service 1958–79*, London: HMSO

Weeks, J. (1990) *Coming Out*, London: Quartet

Whiteley, P. (1981) 'Public opinion and the demand for social welfare in Britain', *Journal of Social Policy*, 10(4), pp. 435–75

Whiteside, N. (1996) 'Creating the Welfare State in Britain 1945–60', *Journal of Social Policy*, vol. 25, pt. 1, pp. 83–103

Wistow, G., Knapp, M., Hardy, B. and Allen, C. (1994) *Social Care in a Mixed Economy*, Milton Keynes: Open University Press

Wolfenden Report (1957) *Report of the Departmental Committee on Homosexual Offences and Prostitution*, Cmd 247, London: HMSO

Wootton, B. (1943) 'Before and after Beveridge', *Political Quarterly*, 14(4), pp. 357–63

Wright, M. (ed.) (1980) *Public Spending Decisions: Growth and Restraint in the 1970s*, London: Allen and Unwin

Index